Holt Spanish 1A

Lesson Planner
with Differentiated Instruction

HOLT, RINEHART AND WINSTON

A Harcourt Education Company

Orlando • **Austin** • New York • San Diego • Toronto • London

Contributing Writers:

Jodee Costello

Printed in the United States of America

ISBN 0-03-074388-5

2 3 4 5 6   073   06 05

Table of Contents

▲ = Advanced Learners   ◆ = Slower Pace Learners   ● = Special Learning Needs   ■ = Heritage Speakers

To the Teacher

You will find that the *¡Exprésate! Lesson Planner* facilitates the planning, execution, and documentation of your classroom work.

For more help in organizing your lessons, use the *One-Stop Planner* CD-ROM. For each chapter, this computer-ready version of the *Lesson Planner* includes: editable lesson plans with direct links to teaching resources, printable worksheets from resource books, direct launches to the HRW Internet activities, video and audio segments, the *Test Generator,* and clip art for vocabulary items.

Standards for Foreign Language Learning

At the top of each page of the lesson plan is a box showing the correlations of the *Student Edition* and the *Teacher's Edition* to the Standards for Foreign Language Learning. In addition, the chart on page xiv provides a summary of the five major goals and the standards within each goal, so that you can more easily understand the correlation within each section of the *Lesson Planner.*

Calendario de tareas cotidianas

On page xii you will find a homework calendar (**Calendario de tareas cotidianas**) that you can copy and distribute to your class so that you and your students can keep track of their assignments each week.

Chapter-Specific Lesson Plans

Each daily or block lesson plan consists of timed suggestions for core instruction (regular lesson plans total 50 minutes, block lesson plans total 90 minutes each), Optional Resources (also timed) that can be integrated into the lesson plan, and correlations to the Standards for Foreign Language Learning. There are 16 50-minute lesson plans and eight 90-minute lesson plans per chapter.

Differentiated Instruction

Within each chapter's lesson plans are suggestions for differentiating instruction.
- ▲ Advanced Learners
- ◆ Slower Pace Learners
- ● Students with Special Learning Needs
- ■ Heritage Speakers

Geocultura

Suggestions for presenting and teaching **Geocultura** are on page xv.

Substitute Teacher Lesson Plans

These lesson plans have been designed with the goal of making class time productive on the days when a substitute teacher conducts class. They provide instructive activities that can be administered by a substitute who does not speak Spanish. Each chapter has several days' worth of suggestions for activities.

▲ = Advanced Learners   ◆ = Slower Pace Learners   ● = Special Learning Needs   ■ = Heritage Speakers

(**iv**)

Differentiated Instruction Strategies and Tips

Mayanne Wright

In today's classroom no two students are exactly alike. Students vary in their readiness to learn, the ways in which they learn, and their interests. In order to meet each student's learning needs, many teachers are turning to differentiated instruction in order to teach all students in an effective and equitable manner. Advanced, on-level, and struggling students, as well as students with special academic, behavioral, or language needs can all be taught in the same classroom when instruction is differentiated.

Instruction may be differentiated by varying one of three components in a lesson: content, process, or product. Teachers differentiate by varying either what students learn, or the activities they use to comprehend and practice what they learn, or how they express what they've learned. They decide how to differentiate instruction based on students' readiness, on their interests, and on their learning profiles or preferred styles and modes of learning.

There are four steps to follow when planning a differentiated lesson using *¡Exprésate!* First, determine what the essential knowledge is that all students must learn. Review the learning objectives listed in the *Teacher's Edition* and at the top of each page of this *Lesson Planner* to help you make this determination. Second, decide if and when grouping might be appropriate during different phases of the learning process based on students' readiness, interests, and learning profiles. Consider how to group students and what each group will do differently. The *Student Edition* has many activities that are already marked for pairs and groups. You may decide to have students do these as marked, and you may also choose for students to do individual activities in pairs or groups. The *Teacher's Edition* also offers suggestions for adapting activities. Third, choose what part of the lesson to vary: content, process, or product. Do not vary everything in one lesson; instead, focus on one area, based on students' needs. For suggestions regarding ways to differentiate your lessons, begin with the wrap in the *Teacher's Edition*. There you will find suggestions for varying presentations, activities, products, and assessments according to students' different learning styles, preferred modes of learning, and interests. Also, see the coded lesson plans in this *Lesson Planner* and the teaching strategies outlined in this essay. Finally, determine how you will evaluate students' needs and progress, and what the final assessment will be. To evaluate student progress, there are culminating activities featured in each chapter of the *Student Edition* and *Teacher's Edition*, as well as in the *Interactive Tutor* and various ancillaries. See the coded lesson plans in this *Lesson Planner* for ideas. To assess what students have learned when instruction has been completed, *¡Exprésate!* offers several options. You may choose to use the tests or one of the alternative assessments in the *Assessment Program*, or create your own test using the *Test Generator*.

As you work through the four steps above, you may wish to consider using one of the instructional strategies that follow. Each strategy is designed to address the special needs of advanced, on-level, and struggling learners as well as native speakers. They will provide you with concrete tools for varying the content, process, or product in each of the following areas of foreign language learning: vocabulary, grammar, listening, speaking, reading, writing, culture, and assessment.

Vocabulary

Using Multiple Resources

One of the most effective ways to vary the content of a lesson is to use **multiple resources.** Using a variety of resources to teach essential vocabulary allows teachers to meet the needs of students with different learning profiles and varied readiness to learn. Teachers may use the *Student Edition*, which presents vocabulary visually and verbally; the *Teacher's Edition*, which

▲ = Advanced Learners   ◆ = Slower Pace Learners   ● = Special Learning Needs   ■ = Heritage Speakers

provides suggestions for presenting vocabulary using a variety of instructional techniques; the *Teaching Transparencies* and accompanying teaching suggestions; the *Interactive Tutor*; and the **Novela en video** in the *Video/DVD Program*, which presents vocabulary in context. Each resource lends itself to different intelligences, learning styles, and paces. Each also provides for different grouping possibilities, from whole class to individual instruction, and multiple entry points to learning, from the very concrete to the more complex. For example, the **Novela en video** might be more appropriate for native speakers and advanced learners, since the vocabulary is presented in a more complex manner, while the teaching suggestions in the *Teacher's Edition* and for the *Teaching Transparencies* might better address the needs of struggling and on-level learners.

Jigsaw

Jigsaw is a cooperative learning strategy. The teacher divides students into heterogeneous base groups and gives them a vocabulary assignment consisting of several components. For example, in order to review a particular chapter's vocabulary, the teacher might have students complete selected activities from the *Student Edition*, *Teacher's Edition*, *Teaching Transparencies Binder*, **Cuaderno de vocabulario y gramática**, **Cuaderno de actividades**, or the *Interactive Tutor*. Members of the base groups divide the assignment among themselves. Each member takes responsibility for teaching or leading students through one or more of the activities from the list. Members then work individually to decide how they will teach their activities to fellow group members. Finally, students return to their base groups to teach their material. Jigsaw activities differentiate by allowing students to use their preferred learning styles, set their own pace, and choose the level of difficulty for a particular task. Thus, this type of activity is ideal for students at all levels of learning. See the Cooperative Learning activities in the wrap of the *Teacher's Edition* for jigsaw ideas or create your own using the resources listed above.

Grammar

Stations

To practice a grammar concept, the teacher might create **stations** at different locations in the classroom, where students work on various tasks simultaneously. Each station has materials that practice the chosen grammar concept at a different level of difficulty. For example, the first station might provide reteaching and guided practice. At this station the teacher provides instruction, then guides student practice using resources such as the *Interactive Tutor*. The second station might provide simple independent practice using selected core activities from the *Student Edition*, **Juegos interactivos**, **Cuaderno de actividades**, or **Cuaderno de vocabulario y gramática**. The third station might provide more complex independent practice, using the same resources as the second station. The fourth and fifth stations might have students using the grammar concept in communicative contexts such as those featured in the culminating activities of the *Student Edition*, **Cuaderno de actividades**, **Cuaderno para hispanohablantes**, or *Activities for Communication*. Some students will need to go to several stations, while others will not. For example, struggling students might go to the first three stations, on-level students might go to the second, third, and fourth stations; advanced students might go to the third, fourth, and fifth stations; and native speakers might go only to the fourth and fifth stations. Students will also spend different amounts of time at each station, according to their needs.

Tiered Activities

Tiered activities allow all students to focus on the same essential knowledge and skills, but at different levels of complexity, abstractness, and open-endedness. By assigning tiered grammar activities, teachers ensure challenge and success for all learners. To create a tiered activity to practice a grammatical concept, follow these steps:

▲ = Advanced Learners   ◆ = Slower Pace Learners   ● = Special Learning Needs   ■ = Heritage Speakers

- Select the concept to be practiced.
- Assess students' readiness, interests, and learning profiles.
- Choose an activity from the *Student Edition*.
- Assess the complexity and level of the activity.
- Adapt the activity to different student levels by choosing an alternative activity from the *Teacher's Edition*, or from one of the following: *Interactive Tutor*, *Juegos interactivos*, *Activities for Communication*, *Cuaderno de actividades*, or *Cuaderno de actividades*.
- Match the original and adapted activities to the appropriate students. Assign the most concrete and close-ended version of the activity to struggling learners and the most complex and open-ended version to advanced learners. On-level learners do the activity that falls somewhere in-between.

Listening

Using Multiple Resources

Students vary greatly in their ability to listen, due to different learning styles and the degree to which they are comfortable with the language and learning contexts. An excellent way to address students' differing needs is to vary the lesson content by using **multiple resources.** For struggling and on-level students, teachers may choose from listening activities in the *Student Edition*; **ExpresaVisión** and **GramaVisión**; the suggestions in the *Teacher's Edition*; or the suggested activities accompanying the *Teaching Transparencies*. All levels of students may practice their listening skills through the pair and group work activities in the *Student Edition*, *Teacher's Edition*, or *Activities for Communication*. The *Interactive Tutor* is also appropriate for all levels of students, particularly struggling learners, since it provides a great deal of repetition. By choosing a variety of resources, teachers provide listening practice at an appropriate level for each student while addressing students' different learning styles and preferences.

Vary The Task

Teachers can also **vary the listening task** to meet students' level of readiness. There are two ways to vary a listening task. One way is to vary the complexity of what students listen for. For example, struggling students may listen for the main idea in a story, on-level students listen for the main idea and a few significant details, and advanced students listen for more specific detailed information. The second way to adapt a listening task is to vary how students demonstrate what they comprehend. Struggling students may demonstrate comprehension by listing items, on-level students by summarizing the text, and advanced students by interpreting what they heard. See the *Teacher's Edition* for more ideas about varying listening tasks.

Speaking

Tiered Assignments

Tiered assignments allow students to express essential knowledge and skills at different levels of complexity, abstractness, and open-endedness. To create a tiered speaking assignment, take the following steps:

- Choose a function or set of functions to be demonstrated.
- Assess students' readiness, interests, and learning profiles.
- Choose a speaking activity from the *Student Edition*, *Teacher's Edition*, *Activities for Communication*, or Picture Sequences, Portfolio, Suggestions, or Performance Assessment in the *Assessment Program*.
- Determine where on a continuum of difficulty the activity falls. Is it closed—, or open-ended? Is there just one task to complete or several? Is the assignment highly or loosely structured?

▲ = Advanced Learners   ◆ = Slower Pace Learners   ● = Special Learning Needs   ■ = Heritage Speakers

- Adapt the assignment or choose alternate assignments from one of the resources previously mentioned. Give advanced students multi-faceted, open-ended, more complex assignments; assign simpler and more closed-ended assignments to struggling students; and have on-level students complete assignments that fall somewhere in between.

Learning Scenarios

Learning scenarios give teachers a framework for organizing instruction, and provide students with the opportunity to carry out communicative functions in culturally authentic situations. Students can adapt the scenarios to reflect their personal interests, preferred learning styles, and level of learning. To develop a scenario, decide what type of situation students should be able to handle when they complete a chapter. For ideas, see the culminating activities in the *Student Edition*; projects or role-plays from the *Teacher's Edition*; activities in *Activities for Communication*; and suggestions in the *Assessment Program*. Next, teach the functions, grammar, vocabulary, culture, and life skills students need in order to carry out the scenario. Use the *Student Edition* as a guide, but add to or subtract content based on your students' needs. For example, you may need to focus on some components of the chapter more than on others, or review skills and information from previous chapters. Finally, create a checklist of activities that students need to complete to prepare them for the scenario. After students complete the checklist, divide them into heterogeneous groups to carry out the scenario.

Reading

Varied Graphic Organizers

A **graphic organizer** is a visual framework that helps students make connections between concepts. They may be used before, during, and after reading to aid students in comprehension. Some common graphic organizers are Venn diagrams, which help to compare and contrast information; time lines or flow charts, which help with sequencing events; and multiple causes-or-effects maps, which help to identify cause-and-effect relationships. By using different graphic organizers for a particular reading, teachers can adjust the reading objectives or tasks to match students' readiness, as well as address a variety of learning styles. For example, a time line to sequence events in a story may be appropriate for struggling learners, while a multiple causes-and-effects map may be more appropriate for on-level students. See the *Reading Strategies and Skills Handbook* for a variety of graphic organizers to use with *Student Edition* readings and the *¡Lee conmigo!* readers.

Choice Boards

A **choice board** is a menu of activities set up like a Bingo card. Each column on the board reflects a different level of learning, and each activity in a given column calls for the use of a different learning style. The teacher directs students to a particular column on the board from which they choose an activity. By asking students to select an activity from a particular row, the teacher addresses students' learning needs while at the same time allowing students to make choices based on their preferred learning styles and interests. For activities to include on a choice board, see the *Student Edition, Teacher's Edition,* **Cuaderno de actividades**, **Cuaderno para hispanohablantes, ¡Lee conmigo!,** and *Reading Strategies and Skills Handbook*. You may also wish to use the following sample choice board as a model. The first column's activities are directed toward struggling learners, the second column toward on-level learners, and the third column toward advanced learners.

▲ = Advanced Learners   ◆ = Slower Pace Learners   ● = Special Learning Needs   ■ = Heritage Speakers

Sample Choice Board For A Story

Column 1	Column 2	Column 3
Act out the story and perform it for a small group or the class.	Create a Venn diagram comparing and contrasting two characters in the story.	Create a treasure chest of symbols that represent each of the characters, the main events of the story, and the theme(s) of the story. Present your treasure chest to the class.
Create a timeline of key events in the story.	Retell the story from the perspective of another character.	Write an essay that compares and contrasts your qualities and faults, or those of one character, with those of another character.
Make four illustrations to accompany the story.	Create a collage that expresses the personality of one of the characters.	Interview students about their reactions to the story, graph their answers, and write a summary of the results.

Writing

R.A.F.T.

R.A.F.T. is an instructional strategy that allows students to pick the **Role** of the writer, the **Audience**, the **Format**, and/or the **Topic** of a writing assignment. By allowing students to choose one or more of these components, teachers can address students' different interests and learning styles. Such choices make this strategy appropriate for students at all levels of learning and for native speakers. To create a R.A.F.T. assignment, teachers may choose from among the writing activities in the *Student Edition*, *Teacher's Edition*, and the ***Cuaderno de actividades***, as well as the portfolio suggestions in the *Assessment Program*. Although many of these activities provide general guidelines for the role of the writer, audience, format, and topic, teachers may invite students to narrow their focus within each of these components, or they may adapt the activities by allowing students to change one of the R.A.F.T. components. For example, a writing activity might ask students to write a letter to an exchange student describing their family members and typical family activities. In a R.A.F.T. assignment, students may be asked to narrow their focus by deciding exactly who the exchange student is (audience), who their family members are, and what activities they will talk about (topic). Or, teachers may suggest that students change the format of the assignment, creating a family album, scrapbook, journal entry, song, or poem instead of writing a letter.

Cubing

Cubing is a strategy that allows students to think about a topic, idea, or task from different angles. Each facet of a cube features a writing prompt that describes the task to be completed. Cubes can differentiate instruction by having prompts that practice the same skills, but call for different learning styles. For example, one cube will have six different prompts, each one calling for a different learning style. Three possible prompts on one cube might be:

- Create a timeline of the activities you did last week (for mathematical/logical learners).
- Write a paragraph describing what you did last week (for verbal learners).
- Create a cartoon strip about what you did last week (for visual learners).

Students then choose the prompt they prefer. Another way cubes can differentiate instruction is by having prompts at different levels of difficulty. For example, the teacher might create four different cubes for an assignment, one for struggling learners, one for on-level learners,

▲ = Advanced Learners   ◆ = Slower Pace Learners   ● = Special Learning Needs   ■ = Heritage Speakers

one for advanced learners, and one for native speakers. Students would then choose an activity from the cube that best matches their level of learning. Teachers may choose from among the writing activities in the *Student Edition*, *Teacher's Edition*, *Interactive Tutor*, and **Cuaderno para hispanohablantes** or from among the portfolio and performance assessment suggestions in the *Assessment Program* to feature on a cube. These activities can be used as written, or the teacher can adapt one or more of them to meet their students' needs.

Culture

Learning Centers

A **learning center** is a location in a classroom where students use activities and materials to learn about, reinforce, or expand on a particular topic. Students explore a different topic at each center. Because centers feature a variety of materials and activities, they can easily be designed to meet the needs of students' multiple intelligences, different learning styles, and varying degrees of readiness. To use centers for teaching culture, first decide on the topic to be taught at each center. For example, centers for the following topics might be created to study Puerto Rican culture: music, festivals, sports, food, and traditions. Next, select materials and activities that explore each topic. Each center should have activities that reflect the different levels of learning in the classroom. For example, at the center on music, struggling learners might write their impressions of a music selection that they listen to while on-level learners might compare the selection to other types of music they've heard. Some resources to use in centers are the presentations and activities in the *Student Edition*; the notes, suggestions, and projects in the wrap of the *Teacher's Edition* as well as the projects and activities featured in the interleaf pages; the *Video/DVD Program* and accompanying activity masters in the *Video Guide*; the *Interactive Tutor*; and, the activities in the **Cuaderno para hispanohablantes** and **Cuaderno de actividades**. You may also choose to use resources from your community or that you've collected. Once you've selected appropriate materials and activities, create a checklist of activities for each learning level for each center. Finally, assign or let students choose a center. Give each student the checklist that is appropriate for him/her. You may wish to have students complete the tasks at every center or at only one or two of the centers according to their individual interests.

Interest-Based Mini-Lessons

After having taught the essential culture for a particular chapter, you may wish to provide an opportunity for students to further explore a topic or learn about something totally different. One way to provide such an opportunity is to create **interest-based mini lessons** for your students to complete. By allowing students to choose what they would like to study and how to demonstrate what they have learned, you can address the needs of different learning profiles. For expanding on a cultural topic already covered in the *Student Edition*, you may suggest that students choose from among the activities in **Cuaderno para hispanohablantes**, **Cuaderno de actividades**, *Video Guide*, *Interactive Tutor*, or in the wrap of the *Teacher's Edition*. For ideas regarding other topics for students to explore, see the wrap and the Projects and Traditions interleaf pages of the *Teacher's Edition*.

Assessment

Alternative Assessments

One of the best ways to assess whether every student has mastered essential knowledge and skills is to offer **alternative assessments**. By choosing the appropriate assessment tool based on students' learning profile and readiness, you can better determine what students have actually learned. First, determine the essential knowledge and skills all students should have learned. Next, decide whether the assessment should be objective or performance-based, or a combination of the two. Then decide on the assessment mode based on students' learning profiles. Which would be more appropriate: a pencil-and-paper test, a test taken on a computer, a product, or a performance? Finally, adapt the assessment instrument to match the level of students' learning by altering testing

▲ = Advanced Learners ◆ = Slower Pace Learners ● = Special Learning Needs ■ = Heritage Speakers

items, simplifying directions, reducing the number of tasks, or varying the rubric for evaluating a product or performance. The following assessment options will allow you to address a variety of learning profiles and may be adapted to students' level of learning: Grammar and Vocabulary quizzes, *Aplicación, Lectura, Escritura,* and *Geocultura* quizzes, *Assessment Program,* and *Test Generator.*

Choice Board

An assessment **choice board** is a menu of tests, performances, and products from which students choose to demonstrate that they have learned a particular set of concepts or skills. Assessment choice boards allow you to better address the needs of your students when evaluating what they have learned. They are set up like Bingo cards with three columns and three rows. Each column on the board reflects a different type of assessment while each activity in a column calls for the use of a different learning style. To address different levels of learning, there may be different choice boards for different students. Students choose one activity from each column of the choice board given to them to demonstrate mastery of essential knowledge and skills. For options to include in the test column, see *Assessment Program* or *Test Generator.* For product options, see the project suggestions in the wrap and interleaf pages of the *Teacher's Edition* and the portfolio suggestions in the *Assessment Program.* For performance options, see the portfolio and performance suggestions in the *Assessment Program.*

Sample Assessment Choice Board
(based on Chapter 5, Level 1 ¡Exprésate!)

Test Options Column	Product Options Column	Performance Options Column
Chapter 5 Test, *Assessment Program, Test Generator*	Written Portfolio Suggestion for Chapter 5, *Assessment Program*	Oral Portfolio Suggestion for Chapter 5, *Assessment Program*
Chapter 5, *Grammar and Vocabulary Quizzes*	Project: **Árbol genealógico,** *Teacher's Edition*	Performance Assessment for Chapter 5, *Assessment Program*

Differentiated Instruction Bibliography

The following references are a starting point for the teacher interested in learning more about the topic of differentiated instruction.

Gardner, H. *Multiple Intelligences: The Theory in Practice.* New York: Basic Books, 1993.

Tomlinson, C., and Eidson, C. *Design for Differentiation: Curriculum for the Differentiated Classroom, Grades 5–9.* Alexandria, VA: Association for Supervision and Curriculum Development (in press).

Tomlinson, C. *The Differentiated Classroom: Responding to the Needs of All Learners.* Alexandria, VA: Association for Supervision and Curriculum Development, 1999.

Tomlinson, C. *How to Differentiate Instruction in Mixed-Ability Classrooms,* 2/e. Alexandria, VA: Association for Supervision and Curriculum Development, 2001.

Tomlinson, C., and Allan, S. *Leadership for Differentiating Schools and Classrooms.* Alexandria, VA: Association for Supervision and Curriculum Development, 2000.

Udall, A., and Daniels, J. *Creating the Thoughtful Classroom: Strategies to Promote Student Thinking.* Tucson, AZ: Zephyr Press, 1991.

Winebrenner, S. *Teaching Gifted Kids in the Regular Classroom.* Minneapolis, MN: Free Spirit, 1992.

Winebrenner, S. *Teaching Kids with Learning Difficulties in the Regular Classroom.* Minneapolis, MN: Free Spirit, 1996.

▲ = Advanced Learners   ◆ = Slower Pace Learners   ● = Special Learning Needs   ■ = Heritage Speakers

Calendario de tareas cotidianas

Fechas: del **lunes** _____ al **viernes** _____

Día	Tareas
lunes, el ▭ _____ _____ _____	_Textbook:_ _____ **_Cuaderno de actividades:_** _____ **_Cuaderno de vocabulario y gramática:_** _____ _Interactive Tutor:_ _____ _Other:_ _____
martes, el ▭ _____ _____ _____	_Textbook:_ _____ **_Cuaderno de actividades:_** _____ **_Cuaderno de vocabulario y gramática:_** _____ _Interactive Tutor:_ _____ _Other:_ _____
miércoles, el ▭ _____ _____ _____	_Textbook:_ _____ **_Cuaderno de actividades:_** _____ **_Cuaderno de vocabulario y gramática:_** _____ _Interactive Tutor:_ _____ _Other:_ _____
jueves, el ▭ _____ _____ _____	_Textbook:_ _____ **_Cuaderno de actividades:_** _____ **_Cuaderno de vocabulario y gramática:_** _____ _Interactive Tutor:_ _____ _Other:_ _____
viernes, el ▭ _____ _____ _____	_Textbook:_ _____ **_Cuaderno de actividades:_** _____ **_Cuaderno de vocabulario y gramática:_** _____ _Interactive Tutor:_ _____ _Other:_ _____

▲ = Advanced Learners   ◆ = Slower Pace Learners   ● = Special Learning Needs   ■ = Heritage Speakers

Holt Spanish 1A

Lesson Planner

STUDENT PROGRESS REPORT

Name _____ Class _____ Date _____

From _____ To _____

	1 Very poor	2 Poor	3 Average	4 Good	5 Excellent	Comments
Reading						
Speaking						
Writing						
Quizzes/Tests						
Completion of assignments						
Class participation						

Overall effort and involvement in language learning

_____

_____

_____

Teacher signature   Parent or guardian signature

_____   _____

▲ = Advanced Learners   ◆ = Slower Pace Learners   ● = Special Learning Needs   ■ = Heritage Speakers

Holt Spanish 1A   Lesson Planner

STANDARDS FOR FOREIGN LANGUAGE LEARNING

Communication Communicate in Languages Other Than English	**Standard 1.1**	Students engage in conversations, provide and obtain information, express feelings and emotions, and exchange opinions.
	Standard 1.2	Students understand and interpret written and spoken language on a variety of topics.
	Standard 1.3	Students present information, concepts, and ideas to an audience of listeners or readers on a variety of topics.
Cultures Gain Knowledge and Understanding of Other Cultures	**Standard 2.1**	Students demonstrate an understanding of the relationship between the practices and perspectives of the culture studied.
	Standard 2.2	Students demonstrate an understanding of the relationship between the products and perspectives of the culture studied.
Connections Connect with Other Disciplines and Acquire Information	**Standard 3.1**	Students reinforce and further their knowledge of other disciplines through the foreign language.
	Standard 3.2	Students acquire information and recognize the distinctive viewpoints that are only available through the foreign language and its cultures.
Comparisons Develop Insight into the Nature of Language and Culture	**Standard 4.1**	Students demonstrate understanding of the nature of language through comparisons of the language studied and their own.
	Standard 4.2	Students demonstrate understanding of the concept of culture through comparisons of the cultures studied and their own.
Communities Participate in Multilingual Communities at Home and Around the World	**Standard 5.1**	Students use the language both within and beyond the school setting.
	Standard 5.2	Students show evidence of becoming life-long learners by using the language for personal enjoyment and enrichment.

"National Standards Report" from *Standards for Foreign Language Learning: Preparing for the 21st Century*. Copyright © 1996 by **National Standards in Foreign Language Education Project**. Reprinted by permission of the publisher.

▲ = Advanced Learners   ◆ = Slower Pace Learners   ● = Special Learning Needs   ■ = Heritage Speakers

Geocultura

The **Geocultura** pages precede the chapter core and highlight different locations throughout the Spanish-speaking world. Levels 1A, 1B, and 1 present eight countries and two U.S. states. Level 2 presents ten cities, and Level 3 presents the Spanish-speaking world divided into five major regions.

The first two pages of each **Geocultura** section explore the geography of the country, city, or region presented. The following pages take a closer look at other characterizing features, such as local cuisine, architecture, festivals and celebrations, art, history, customs, and others.

Geografía

- To familiarize students with the geographic location of the **Geocultura,** present the locator map under the title first. From there, lead students to the location map and have them point out any distinguishing geographical features such as oceans, rivers, lakes, mountain ranges, and so on. This provides the opportunity to compare and contrast the geographical features of the studied country, city, or region with the students' own.
- Next, you might have students scan the surrounding photos and captions and have them find the location of each photo on the map. Then, have students read the captions and comment on them. Point out that the photo will help them understand the caption. Audio for all captions is available in the *¡Exprésate! Online Edition*.
- After students have achieved some familiarity with the geography, you might present the **Almanaque** and the **¿Sabías que...?** fact. Another **¿Sabías que...?** fact provides additional information for the students.
- For comprehension assessment, have students answer the question or questions under **¿Qué tanto sabes?**

A conocer...

- Have students first scan the photos and then have them focus on one section at a time. For orientation, have students find the location of each photo on the map. All sections on these pages lend themselves to comparing and contrasting between the location studied and the place where the students live, or places that they have visited.
- At the end of the **Geocultura** you will find a **Conexión** linking the content to another subject area. The **Conexión** always includes a student activity that can be done in class or assigned as homework. .
- Throughout the chapter—in **Nota cultural**, **Cultura**, **Novela**, and **Integración**—you will find references to the location that expand on the information presented in the **Geocultura**. At these points in the chapter you might want to revisit the **Geocultura** to reinforce and refresh what students have learned, or simply use the map for reference.
- At any point in the chapter, you may want to follow the Traditions, Projects, and Recipes suggestions in each chapter of the *Teacher's Edition* interleaf pages. Each of these is specific to the location covered in the corresponding chapter **Geocultura** and provides opportunities to present additional cultural information.
- The **Geocultura** activities you assign can be easily adapted for Differentiated Instruction. You may want to assign further research or cultural projects to advanced learners or have slower pace learners spend additional time studying the information. Interdisciplinary Links and the topics of the **Geocultura** can be targeted for each of the Multiple Intelligences; for example, you might assign projects focusing on architecture for Logical-Mathematical Intelligences, research on traditional music in each location for Musical Intelligences, Internet research projects based on location-specific flora and fauna for Naturalist Intelligences, and so on.

▲ = Advanced Learners   ◆ = Slower Pace Learners   ● = Special Learning Needs   ■ = Heritage Speakers

- **GeoVisión,** a video counterpart to **Geocultura,** features a local teen presenter who introduces students to highlights of his or her country or city. Each **GeoVisión,** shot on location, allows student to see and hear the sights and sounds of the area and also to hear someone their own age who speaks with the location's regional accent. See *Video Guide* for specific suggestions on how to present **GeoVisión.**

For your reference, here is a chart of the **Geocultura** locations for all levels of *¡Exprésate!*

Chapter	Levels 1A, 1B, 1	Level 2	Level 3
1	Spain	Mexico City	Castilla-La Mancha
2	Puerto Rico	Cuzco	
3	Texas	Santo Domingo	Caribbean
4	Costa Rica	Miami	
5	Chile	San José	Southwestern US/Mexico
6	Mexico	Segovia	
7	Argentina	San Juan	Andean Highlands
8	Florida	Santiago	
9	Dominican Republic	El Paso	Southern Cone
10	Peru	Buenos Aires	

▲ = Advanced Learners   ◆ = Slower Pace Learners   ● = Special Learning Needs   ■ = Heritage Speakers

(xvi)

50-Minute Daily Lesson Plans

¡Empecemos!

DAY 1 50-MINUTE LESSON PLAN

NATIONAL STANDARDS

Chapter Opener

Communication 1.2: Student demonstrates under-standing of simple, clearly spoken, and written language such as simple stories, high-frequency commands, and brief instructions when dealing with familiar topics.

Cultures 2.1: Student demonstrates an understanding of the practices (what people do) and how they are related to the perspectives (how people perceive things) of the cultures studied.

Vocabulario en acción 1

Communication 1.2: Student demonstrates under-standing of simple, clearly spoken, and written language such as simple stories, high-frequency commands, and brief instructions when dealing with familiar topics.

Before starting **Capítulo 1,** you may wish to teach **Geocultura: España,** pp. xxii–3. For teaching suggestions, see pp. xv–xvi of this *Lesson Planner.*

CORE INSTRUCTION

Warm-Up
• (5 min.) See Teacher Note, p. 5.

Chapter Opener
• (5 min.) See Using the Photo, and **Más vocabulario,** p. 4 to discuss the photo on pages 4–5.
• (5 min.) Present **Objetivos,** p. 4.

Vocabulario en acción 1
• (15 min.) To introduce the vocabulary on pp. 6–7, see Teaching **Vocabulario,** p. 6.

• (10 min.) Play Audio CD 1, Tr. 1 for Activity 1, p. 7.
• (5 min.) Have students do Activity 2, p. 7.

Wrap-Up
• (5 min.) Have students practice asking and answering the three questions in Activity 2, p 7.

OPTIONAL RESOURCES
• (5 min.) See Special Learning Needs, p. 7. ●
• (5 min.) Present **Common Error Alert,** p. 6.

Practice Options
• *Lab Book,* pp. 1, 9–10, 31, 32 ▲ ● ■
• *Cuaderno de vocabulario y gramática,* pp. 1–3 ▲ ◆ ●
• *Cuaderno para hispanohablantes,* pp. 1–8, 9 ■
• *Teaching Transparencies:* Map 1; Vocabulary 1.1; *Cuaderno de vocabulario y gramática* Answers, pp. 1–3 ▲ ◆ ●
• *Video Guide,* pp. 1–2, 4–5, 6 ▲ ● ■
• *Interactive Tutor* (Disc 1) or *DVD Tutor* (Disc 1) ▲ ● ■
• Online practice, Chapter 1 (go.hrw.com, Keyword: EXP1A CH1) ▲ ● ■

▲ = Advanced Learners   ◆ = Slower Pace Learners   ● = Special Learning Needs   ■ = Heritage Speakers

¡Empecemos!

DAY 2 50-MINUTE LESSON PLAN

NATIONAL STANDARDS

Vocabulario en acción 1

Communication 1.1: Student engages in oral and written exchanges of learned material to socialize and to provide and obtain information.

Communication 1.2: Student demonstrates understanding of simple, clearly spoken, and written language such as simple stories, high-frequency commands, and brief instructions when dealing with familiar topics.

Communication 1.3: Student presents information using familiar words, phrases, and sentences to listeners and readers.

Cultures 2.1: Student demonstrates an understanding of the practices (what people do) and how they are related to the perspectives (how people perceive things) of the cultures studied.

Comparisons 4.2: Student demonstrates an understanding of the concept of culture through comparisons of the student's own culture and the cultures studied.

CORE INSTRUCTION

Warm-Up
- (2 min.) See Bell Work 1.1, p. 6 or Teaching Transparencies Bell Work 1.1.

Vocabulario en acción 1
- (5 min.) Show the **ExpresaVisión** video Ch. 1, *Video Program* (Videocassette 1) or *DVD Tutor* (Disc 1).
- (5 min.) Present **Nota cultural,** p. 7.
- (10 min.) Have students do Activities 3–4, p. 7.
- (10 min.) To present ¡**Exprésate!,** p. 8, see Teaching ¡**Exprésate!,** p. 8.

- (5 min.) Play Audio CD 1, Tr. 2 for Activity 5, p. 9. ●
- (10 min.) See **Comunicación,** p. 9.

Wrap-Up
- (3 min.) See Comparing and Contrasting, p. 8.

OPTIONAL RESOURCES
- (5 min.) See Slower Pace Learners, p. 7. ◆
- (5 min.) For students with auditory impairments, see Differentiated Instruction, p. 9. ●

Practice Options
- *Lab Book*, pp. 9–10, 32 ▲ ● ■
- *Cuaderno de vocabulario y gramática*, pp. 1–3 ▲ ◆ ●
- *Teaching Transparencies*: Bell Work 1.1; Vocabulary 1.1; *Cuaderno de vocabulario y gramática* Answers, pp. 1–3 ▲ ◆ ●
- *Video Guide*, pp. 4–5, 6 ▲ ● ■
- *Interactive Tutor* (Disc 1) or *DVD Tutor* (Disc 1) ▲ ● ■
- Online practice, Chapter 1 (go.hrw.com, Keyword: EXP1A CH1) ▲ ● ■

▲ = Advanced Learners   ◆ = Slower Pace Learners   ● = Special Learning Needs   ■ = Heritage Speakers

¡Empecemos!

DAY 3 50-MINUTE LESSON PLAN

NATIONAL STANDARDS

Vocabulario en acción 1

Communication 1.1: Student engages in oral and written exchanges of learned material to socialize and to provide and obtain information.

Communication 1.3: Student presents information using familiar words, phrases, and sentences to listeners and readers.

CORE INSTRUCTION

Warm-Up
- (5 min.) Greet students and ask how they are doing, using the expressions in ¡Exprésate!, p. 8.

Vocabulario en acción 1
- (10 min.) Show the **ExpresaVisión** video, Ch. 1, *Video Program* (Videocassette 1) or *DVD Tutor* (Disc 1).
- (5 min.) Do Activity 6 with students, p. 9.
- (20 min.) Have students do Activities 7–8, p. 9.

Wrap-up
- (10 min.) Have volunteers present their conversation from Activity 8 to the class.

OPTIONAL RESOURCES
- (10 min.) See Special Learning Needs, p. 9. ●
- (10 min.) See Advanced Learners, p. 9. ▲

Practice Options
- *Lab Book*, pp. 9–10, 32 ▲ ● ■
- *Cuaderno de vocabulario y gramática*, pp. 1–3 ▲ ◆ ●
- *Teaching Transparencies*: Vocabulary 1.1; *Cuaderno de vocabulario y gramática* Answers, pp. 1–3 ▲ ◆ ●
- *Video Guide*, pp. 4–5, 6 ▲ ● ■
- *Interactive Tutor* (Disc 1) or *DVD Tutor* (Disc 1) ▲ ● ■
- Online practice, Chapter 1 (go.hrw.com, Keyword: EXP1A CH1) ▲ ● ■

▲ = Advanced Learners   ◆ = Slower Pace Learners   ● = Special Learning Needs   ■ = Heritage Speakers

¡Empecemos!

DAY 4 50-MINUTE LESSON PLAN

NATIONAL STANDARDS

Vocabulario en acción 1

Communication 1.2: Student demonstrates understanding of simple, clearly spoken, and written language such as simple stories, high-frequency commands, and brief instructions when dealing with familiar topics.

Communication 1.3: Student presents information using familiar words, phrases, and sentences to listeners and readers.

CORE INSTRUCTION

Warm-Up
- (5 min.) See Bell Work 1.2, p. 10.

Vocabulario en acción 1
- (15 min.) Present ¡**Exprésate!**, p. 10 using Teaching ¡**Exprésate!**, #1–2, p. 10.
- (5 min.) Have students do Activity 9, p. 10.
- (10 min.) To present ¡**Exprésate!**, p. 11, see Teaching ¡**Exprésate!**, #3, p. 10.
- (10 min.) Play Audio CD 1, Tr. 3 for Activity 10, p. 11. ●

Wrap-Up
- (5 min.) Do Activity 10, p. 11 as a class activity. Ask students to bring a few pictures of people for tomorrow.

CORE INSTRUCTION
- (10 min.) See Multiple Intelligences, p. 11. ●

Practice Options
- *Lab Book*, pp. 9–10, 32 ▲ ● ■
- *Cuaderno de vocabulario y gramática*, pp. 1–3 ▲ ◆ ●
- *Teaching Transparencies*: Bell Work 1.2; Vocabulary 1.1; *Cuaderno de vocabulario y gramática* Answers, pp. 1–3 ▲ ◆ ●
- *Video Guide*, pp. 4–5, 6 ▲ ● ■
- *Interactive Tutor* (Disc 1) or *DVD Tutor* (Disc 1) ▲ ● ■
- Online practice, Chapter 1 (go.hrw.com, Keyword: EXP1A CH1) ▲ ● ■

▲ = Advanced Learners   ◆ = Slower Pace Learners   ● = Special Learning Needs   ■ = Heritage Speakers

(4)

CAPÍTULO

1

¡Empecemos!

DAY 5 50-MINUTE LESSON PLAN

NATIONAL STANDARDS

Vocabulario en acción 1

Communication 1.1: Student engages in oral and written exchanges of learned material to socialize and to provide and obtain information.

Communication 1.2: Student demonstrates understanding of simple, clearly spoken, and written language such as simple stories, high-frequency commands, and brief instructions when dealing with familiar topics.

Communication 1.3: Student presents information using familiar words, phrases, and sentences to listeners and readers.

CORE INSTRUCTION

Warm-Up

• (5 min.) Have students introduce the people in the pictures they brought.

Vocabulario en acción 1

• (15 min.) Review **Más vocabulario** and **¡Exprésate!,** pp. 10–11.
• (20 min.) Have students do Activities 11–12, p. 11.
• (15 min.) Review **Vocabulario en acción 1,** pp. 6–11.

Wrap-Up

• Have students do Activity 11 again, this time making up names and countries of origin for each person.

OPTIONAL RESOURCES

• (5 min.) See Advanced Learners, p. 11.) ▲

Practice Options

• *Lab Book,* pp. 9–10, 32 ▲ ● ■
• *Cuaderno de vocabulario y gramática,* pp. 1–3 ▲ ◆ ●
• *Teaching Transparencies*: Vocabulary 1.1; *Cuaderno de vocabulario y gramática* Answers, pp. 1–3 ▲ ◆ ●
• *Video Guide,* pp. 4–5, 6 ▲ ● ■
• *Interactive Tutor* (Disc 1) or *DVD Tutor* (Disc 1) ▲ ● ■
• Online practice, Chapter 1 (go.hrw.com, Keyword: EXP1A CH1) ▲ ● ■

▲ = Advanced Learners   ◆ = Slower Pace Learners   ● = Special Learning Needs   ■ = Heritage Speakers

Holt Spanish 1A

Lesson Planner

¡Empecemos!

DAY 6 50-MINUTE LESSON PLAN

NATIONAL STANDARDS

Vocabulario en acción 1

Communication 1.1: Student engages in oral and written exchanges of learned material to socialize and to provide and obtain information.

Communication 1.2: Student demonstrates understanding of simple, clearly spoken, and written language such as simple stories, high-frequency commands, and brief instructions when dealing with familiar topics.

Communication 1.3: Student presents information using familiar words, phrases, and sentences to listeners and readers.

CORE INSTRUCTION

Warm-Up
• (10 min.) See **Comunicación (TE)**, p. 11.

Vocabulario en acción 1
• (20 min.) Review **Vocabulario en acción 1**, pp. 6–11.

Assessment
• (20 min.) Give **Prueba: Vocabulario 1**.

Practice Options
• *Lab Book*, pp. 9–10, 32 ▲ ● ■
• *Cuaderno de vocabulario y gramática*, pp. 1–3 ▲ ◆ ●
• *Activities for Communication*, pp. 1–2. ▲ ■
• *Teaching Transparencies*: Vocabulary 1.1; *Cuaderno de vocabulario y gramática* Answers, pp. 1–3 ▲ ◆ ●
• *Video Guide*, pp. 4–5, 6 ▲ ● ■
• *Interactive Tutor* (Disc 1) or *DVD Tutor* (Disc 1) ▲ ● ■
• Online practice, Chapter 1 (go.hrw.com, Keyword: EXP1A CH1) ▲ ● ■

Assessment Options
• *Assessment Program*, **Prueba: Vocabulario 1**, pp. 1–2 ▲ ● ■
• Test Generator ▲ ● ■

▲ = Advanced Learners   ◆ = Slower Pace Learners   ● = Special Learning Needs   ■ = Heritage Speakers

¡Empecemos!

DAY 7 50-MINUTE LESSON PLAN

NATIONAL STANDARDS

Gramática en acción 1

Communication 1.2: Student demonstrates understanding of simple, clearly spoken, and written language such as simple stories, high-frequency commands, and brief instructions when dealing with familiar topics.

Communication 1.3: Student presents information using familiar words, phrases, and sentences to listeners and readers.

Comparisons 4.1: Student demonstrates an understanding of the nature of language through comparisons of the student's own language and the language studied.

CORE INSTRUCTION

Warm-Up
- (5 min.) See Bell Work 1.3, p. 12.

Gramática en acción 1
- (10 min.) Show **GramaVisión** (*subject and verbs in sentences*), *Video Program* (Videocassette 1) or *DVD Tutor* (Disc 1).
- (20 min.) Present *Subjects and verbs in sentences*, using Teaching **Gramática**, #1–3, p. 12.
- (5 min.) Have students do Activity 13, p. 12.

Wrap-Up
- (10 min.) Have each student introduce a friend to the class and tell where he or she is from.

OPTIONAL RESOURCES
- (10 min.) Present **Nota cultural**, p. 12.

Practice Options
- *Lab Book*, pp. 9–10 ▲ ● ■
- ***Cuaderno de vocabulario y gramática***, pp. 4–6 ▲ ◆ ●
- ***Cuaderno de actividades***, pp. 1–3. ▲ ● ■
- *Activities for Communication*, pp. 1–2, 55–56 ▲ ■
- *Teaching Transparencies*: Bell Work 1.3; ***Cuaderno de vocabulario y gramática*** Answers, pp. 4–6 ▲ ◆ ●
- *Video Guide*, pp. 4–5 ▲ ● ■
- *Grammar Tutor for Students of Spanish*, pp. 1–2, 168–169 ◆ ●
- *Interactive Tutor* (Disc 1) or *DVD Tutor* (Disc 1) ▲ ● ■
- Online practice, Chapter 1 (go.hrw.com, Keyword: EXP1A CH1) ▲ ● ■

▲ = Advanced Learners   ◆ = Slower Pace Learners   ● = Special Learning Needs   ■ = Heritage Speakers

Holt Spanish 1A

Lesson Planner

¡Empecemos!

DAY 8 50-MINUTE LESSON PLAN

NATIONAL STANDARDS

Gramática en acción 1

Communication 1.1: Student engages in oral and written exchanges of learned material to socialize and to provide and obtain information.

Communication 1.2: Student demonstrates understanding of simple, clearly spoken, and written language such as simple stories, high-frequency commands, and brief instructions when dealing with familiar topics.

Communication 1.3: Student presents information using familiar words, phrases, and sentences to listeners and readers.

CORE INSTRUCTION

Warm-Up

• (5 min.) See Bell Work 1.4, p. 14.

Gramática en acción 1

• (10 min.) Review subjects and verbs in sentences, p. 12.

• (25 min.) Have students do Activities 14–16, p. 13.

Wrap-Up

• (10 min.) See **Comunicación (TE)**, p. 13.

OPTIONAL RESOURCES

• (10 min.) See Slower Pace Learners and Special Learning Needs, p. 13. ◆ ●

Practice Options

• *Lab Book*, pp. 9–10 ▲ ● ■

• *Cuaderno de vocabulario y gramática*, pp. 4–6 ▲ ◆ ●

• *Cuaderno de actividades*, pp. 1–3 ▲ ● ■

• *Activities for Communication*, pp. 1–2, 55–56 ▲ ■

• *Teaching Transparencies*: Bell Work 1.4; *Cuaderno de vocabulario y gramática* Answers, pp. 4–6 ▲ ◆ ●

• *Video Guide*, pp. 4–5 ▲ ● ■

• *Grammar Tutor for Students of Spanish*, pp. 1–2, 168–169 ◆ ●

• *Interactive Tutor* (Disc 1) or *DVD Tutor* (Disc 1) ▲ ● ■

• Online practice, Chapter 1 (go.hrw.com, Keyword: EXP1A CH1) ▲ ● ■

▲ = Advanced Learners   ◆ = Slower Pace Learners   ● = Special Learning Needs   ■ = Heritage Speakers

Holt Spanish 1A

Lesson Planner

¡Empecemos!

DAY 9 50-MINUTE LESSON PLAN

Gramática en acción 1

Communication 1.2: Student demonstrates understanding of simple, clearly spoken, and written language such as simple stories, high-frequency commands, and brief instructions when dealing with familiar topics.

Communication 1.3: Student presents information using familiar words, phrases, and sentences to listeners and readers.

Cultures 2.1: Student demonstrates an understanding of the practices (what people do) and how they are related to the perspectives (how people perceive things) of the cultures studied.

Comparisons 4.1: Student demonstrates an understanding of the nature of language through comparisons of the student's own language and the language studied.

CORE INSTRUCTION

Warm-Up

- (5 min.) Using the pictures they brought for Day 5 or other pictures and the phrases in the word box on page 13, have students describe the people in the pictures.

Gramática en acción 1

- (10 min.) Show **GramaVisión** *(subject pronouns),* *Video Program* (Videocassette 1) or *DVD Tutor* (Disc 1).
- (15 min.) Present *Subject pronouns,* using Teaching **Gramática,** #1–3, p. 14.

- (5 min.) Have students do Activity 17, p. 14.
- (10 min.) Play Audio CD 1, Tr. 4 for Activity 18, p. 15. ●

Wrap-Up

- (5 min.) Have students take turns greeting the people pictured in Activity 18, p. 15.

OPTIONAL RESOURCES

- (5 min.) Have Present Heritage Speakers, p. 14. ■

Practice Options

- *Lab Book,* pp. 9–10 ▲ ● ■
- *Cuaderno de vocabulario y gramática,* pp. 4–6 ▲ ◆ ●
- *Cuaderno de actividades,* pp. 1–3 ▲ ● ■
- *Activities for Communication,* pp. 1–2, 55–56 ▲ ■
- *Teaching Transparencies:* **Cuaderno de vocabulario y gramática** Answers, pp. 4–6 ▲ ◆ ●
- *Video Guide,* pp. 4–5 ▲ ● ■
- *Grammar Tutor for Students of Spanish,* pp.1–2, 168–169 ◆ ●
- *Interactive Tutor* (Disc 1) or *DVD Tutor* (Disc 1) ▲ ● ■
- Online practice, Chapter 1 (go.hrw.com, Keyword: EXP1A CH1) ▲ ● ■

▲ = Advanced Learners   ◆ = Slower Pace Learners   ● = Special Learning Needs   ■ = Heritage Speakers

9

CAPÍTULO

1

¡Empecemos!

DAY 10 50-MINUTE LESSON PLAN

NATIONAL STANDARDS

Gramática en acción 1

Communication 1.1: Student engages in oral and written exchanges of learned material to socialize and to provide and obtain information.

Communication 1.2: Student demonstrates understanding of simple, clearly spoken, and written language such as simple stories, high-frequency commands, and brief instructions when dealing with familiar topics.

Communication 1.3: Student presents information using familiar words, phrases, and sentences to listeners and readers.

CORE INSTRUCTION

Warm-Up

• (5 min.) Review Subject Pronouns, p. 14, using Bell Work 1.5, p. 18.

Gramática en acción 1

• (25 min.) Have students do Activities 19–20, p. 15.

• (15 min.) Review **Gramática en acción 1**, pp. 12–15.

Wrap-Up

(5 min.) Assign the activity in **Comunicación (TE)**, p. 15, for homework.

OPTIONAL RESOURCES

• (5 min.) See Special Learning Needs, p. 15. ●

• (5 min.) See Slower Pace Learners, p. 15. ◆

Practice Options

• *Lab Book*, pp. 9–10 ▲ ● ■

• ***Cuaderno de vocabulario y gramática***, pp. 4–6 ▲ ◆ ●

• ***Cuaderno de actividades***, pp. 1–3 ▲ ● ■

• *Activities for Communication*, pp. 1–2, 55–56 ▲ ■

• *Teaching Transparencies*: Bell Work 1.5; ***Cuaderno de vocabulario y gramática*** Answers pp. 4–6 ▲ ◆ ●

• *Video Guide*, pp. 4–5 ▲ ● ■

• *Grammar Tutor for Students of Spanish*, pp. 1–2, 168–169 ◆ ●

• *Interactive Tutor* (Disc 1) Ch. 1 or *DVD Tutor* (Disc 1) ▲ ● ■

• Online practice, Chapter 1 (go.hrw.com, Keyword: EXP1A CH1) ▲ ● ■

▲ = Advanced Learners ◆ = Slower Pace Learners ● = Special Learning Needs ■ = Heritage Speakers

Holt Spanish 1A

Lesson Planner

¡Empecemos!

NATIONAL STANDARDS

Gramática en acción 1

Communication 1.1: Student engages in oral and written exchanges of learned material to socialize and to provide and obtain information.

Communication 1.2: Student demonstrates understanding of simple, clearly spoken, and written language such as simple stories, high-frequency commands, and brief instructions when dealing with familiar topics.

Communication 1.3: Student presents information using familiar words, phrases, and sentences to listeners and readers.

Cultures 2.1: Student demonstrates an understanding of the practices (what people do) and how they are related to the perspectives (how people perceive things) of the cultures studied.

Comparisons 4.1: Student demonstrates an understanding of the nature of language through comparisons of the student's own language and the language studied.

Cultura

Cultures 2.1: Student demonstrates an understanding of the practices (what people do) and how they are related to the perspectives (how people perceive things) of the cultures studied.

Comparisons 4.2: Student demonstrates an understanding of the concept of culture through comparisons of the student's own culture and the cultures studied.

Communication 1.3: Student presents information using familiar words, phrases, and sentences to listeners and readers.

CORE INSTRUCTION

Warm-Up

- (5 min.) Have volunteers present their interviews from **Comunicación**, p. 15, to the class.

Gramática en acción 1

- (15 min.) Review **Gramática en acción 1**, pp. 12–15.

Assessment

- (20 min.) Give **Prueba: Gramática 1**.

Cultura

- (15 min.) Present **Cultura**, p. 16–17 using Teaching **Cultura**, p. 16, #1–2.

Wrap-Up

- (5 min.) Present **Language Note**, p. 16, and have students act out the greetings shown in the pictures, pp. 16–17.

OPTIONAL RESOURCES

- (5 min.) See Comparing and Contrasting, p. 17.

Practice Options

- *Lab Book*, p. 9–10, 33 ▲ ● ■
- *Cuaderno de vocabulario y gramática*, pp. 4–6 ▲ ◆ ●
- *Cuaderno de actividades*, pp. 1–3 ▲ ● ■
- *Activities for Communication*, pp. 1–2, 55–56 ▲ ■
- *Cuaderno para hispanohablantes*, p. 10 ■
- *Video Guide*, pp. 4–5, 7 ▲ ● ■
- *Grammar Tutor for Students of Spanish*, pp. 1–2, 168–169 ◆ ●
- *Interactive Tutor* (Disc 1) or *DVD Tutor* (Disc 1) ▲ ● ■
- Online practice, Chapter 1 (go.hrw.com, Keyword: EXP1A CH1) ▲ ● ■

Assessment Options

- *Assessment Program*, **Prueba: Gramática 1**, pp. 3–4 ▲ ● ■
- *Assessment Program*, **Prueba: Aplicación 1**, pp. 5–6 ▲ ● ■
- Test Generator ▲ ● ■

▲ = Advanced Learners   ◆ = Slower Pace Learners   ● = Special Learning Needs   ■ = Heritage Speakers

¡Empecemos!

DAY 12 50-MINUTE LESSON PLAN

NATIONAL STANDARDS

Cultura

Communication 1.3: Student presents information using familiar words, phrases, and sentences to listeners and readers.

Cultures 2.1: Student demonstrates an understanding of the practices (what people do) and how they are related to the perspectives (how people perceive things) of the cultures studied.

Comparisons 4.2: Student demonstrates an understanding of the concept of culture through comparisons of the student's own culture and the cultures studied.

CORE INSTRUCTION

Warm-Up

- (5 min.) Review the informal and formal greetings by having pairs of students demonstrate them to the class.

Cultura

- (10 min.) Play the Audio CD 1, Tr. 5, 6, 7, or show **VideoCultura**, Ch. 1. ●
- (10 min.) See Teaching **Cultura**, p. 16, #3.
- (10min.) Present **Comunidad**, p. 17.

Vocabulario en acción 2

- (10 min.) Present **Vocabulario 2**, p.18 using Teaching **Vocabulario**, p.18, #1–2.

Wrap-Up

- (5 min.) Have students make flash cards with the names of numbers 0–10 and have them practice at home.

OPTIONAL RESOURCES

- (10 min.) See Multiple Intelligences, p. 17. ●
- (5 min.) See Advanced Learners, p. 17. ▲
- (5 min.) Present Community Link, p. 17, and assign as homework.
- (10 min.) See Multiple Intelligences, p.17. ●

Practice Options

- *Lab Book*, pp. 11–12, 33, 34 ▲ ● ■
- *Cuaderno de vocabulario y gramática*, pp. 7–9 ▲ ◆ ●
- *Cuaderno para hispanohablantes*, p. 10 ■
- *Video Guide*, pp. 4–5, 7, 8 ▲ ● ■
- *Teaching Transparencies*: **Vocabulario** 1.2, 1.3, 1.4; **Vocabulario y gramática** Answers, pp. 7–9 ▲ ◆ ●
- *Interactive Tutor* (Disc 1) or *DVD Tutor* (Disc 1) ▲ ● ■
- Online practice, Chapter 1 (go.hrw.com, Keyword: EXP1A CH1) ▲ ● ■

▲ = Advanced Learners   ◆ = Slower Pace Learners   ● = Special Learning Needs   ■ = Heritage Speakers

¡Empecemos!

DAY 13 50-MINUTE LESSON PLAN

NATIONAL STANDARDS

Vocabulario en acción 2

Communication 1.2: Student demonstrates understanding of simple, clearly spoken, and written language such as simple stories, high-frequency commands, and brief instructions when dealing with familiar topics.

Communication 1.3: Student presents information using familiar words, phrases, and sentences to listeners and readers.

Cultures 2.1: Student demonstrates an understanding of the practices (what people do) and how they are related to the perspectives (how people perceive things) of the cultures studied.

CORE INSTRUCTION

Warm-Up
• (5 min.) Review numbers 0–10.

Vocabulario en acción 2
• (5 min.) Show **ExpresaVisión,** Ch. 1.
• (10 min.) Review **Vocabulario**, p. 18 using Teaching **Vocabulario**, #3–4, p. 18.
• (10 min.) Have students do Activities 21–22, p. 18.
• (5 min.) Model phrases from **¡Exprésate!,** p. 19.
• (10 min.) Play Audio CD 1, Tr. 8 for Activity 23, p. 19. ●

Wrap-Up
• (5 min.) Present **Practices and Perspectives,** p. 19.

OPTIONAL RESOURCES
• (10 min.) See Special Learning Needs, p. 19. ●
• (5 min.) Have students practice saying their telephone numbers in Spanish.

Practice Options
• *Lab Book*, pp. 11–12, 34 ▲ ● ■
• *Cuaderno de vocabulario y gramática*, pp. 7–9 ▲ ◆ ●
• *Teaching Transparencies*: Vocabulary 1.2, 1.3, 1.4; *Cuaderno de vocabulario y gramática* Answers, pp. 7–9 ▲ ◆ ●
• *Video Guide*, pp. 4–5, 8 ▲ ● ■
• *Interactive Tutor* (Disc 1) or *DVD Tutor* (Disc 1) ▲ ● ■
• Online practice, Chapter 1 (go.hrw.com, Keyword: EXP1A CH1) ▲ ● ■

▲ = Advanced Learners   ◆ = Slower Pace Learners   ● = Special Learning Needs   ■ = Heritage Speakers

¡Empecemos!

DAY 14 50-MINUTE LESSON PLAN

NATIONAL STANDARDS

Vocabulario en acción 2
Communication 1.1: Student engages in oral and written exchanges of learned material to socialize and to provide and obtain information.

Communication 1.2: Student demonstrates understanding of simple, clearly spoken, and written language such as simple stories, high-frequency commands, and brief instructions when dealing with familiar topics.

CORE INSTRUCTION

Warm-Up
(5 min.) Say random numbers from 0–31 and have students write the number on a piece of paper.

Vocabulario en acción 2
- (20 min.) Have students do Activities 24–25, p. 19.
- (20 min.) Present **Vocabulario: ¿Qué hora es?**, p. 20 using Teaching **Vocabulario**, #1–2, p. 20.

Wrap-Up
(5 min.) Present **Comunicación (TE),** p. 19.

OPTIONAL RESOURCES
(10 min.) See Advanced Learners, p. 19. ▲
(5 min.) See Special Learning Needs, p. 21. ●

Practice Options
- *Lab Book*, pp. 11–12, 34 ▲ ● ■
- *Cuaderno de vocabulario y gramática*, pp. 7–9 ▲ ◆ ●
- *Teaching Transparencies*: Vocabulary 1.2, 1.3, 1.4; *Cuaderno de vocabulario y gramática* Answers, pp. 7–9 ▲ ◆ ●
- *Video Guide*, pp. 4–5, 8 ▲ ● ■
- *Interactive Tutor* (Disc 1) or *DVD Tutor* (Disc 1) ▲ ● ■
- Online practice, Chapter 1 (go.hrw.com, Keyword: EXP1A CH1) ▲ ● ■

▲ = Advanced Learners   ◆ = Slower Pace Learners   ● = Special Learning Needs   ■ = Heritage Speakers

Holt Spanish 1A

Lesson Planner

CAPÍTULO

1

¡Empecemos!

DAY 15 50-MINUTE LESSON PLAN

NATIONAL STANDARDS

Vocabulario en acción 2
Communication 1.2: Student demonstrates understanding of simple, clearly spoken, and written language such as simple stories, high-frequency commands, and brief instructions when dealing with familiar topics.

Communication 1.3: Student presents information using familiar words, phrases, and sentences to listeners and readers.

CORE INSTRUCTION

Warm-Up
- (5 min.) Do Bell Work 1.6, p. 20 with students.

Vocabulario en acción 2
- (5 min.) Re-present vocabulary by showing **ExpresaVisión**, Ch. 1.
- (15 min.) Have students do Activities 26–27, p. 20.
- (15 min.) Present **Vocabulario** and **¡Exprésate!,** p. 21 using Teaching **Vocabulario**, #3–4, p. 20.
- (5 min.) Present the seasons, p. 21.

Wrap-Up
- (5 min.) Teach song in **Teacher to Teacher**, p. 21.

OPTIONAL RESOURCES
- (5 min.) See Present **Language Notes**, p. 21.
- (5 min.) See **Comunicación** (TE), p. 21.

Practice Options
- *Lab Book*, pp. 11–12, 34 ▲ ● ■
- ***Cuaderno de vocabulario y gramática***, pp. 7–9 ▲ ◆ ●
- *Teaching Transparencies*: Bell Work 1.6; Vocabulary 1.2, 1.3, 1.4; ***Cuaderno de vocabulario y gramática*** Answers, pp. 7–9 ▲ ◆ ●
- *Video Guide*, pp. 4–5, 8 ▲ ● ■
- *Interactive Tutor* (Disc 1) or *DVD Tutor* (Disc 1) ▲ ● ■
- Online practice, Chapter 1 (go.hrw.com, Keyword: EXP1A CH1) ▲ ● ■

▲ = Advanced Learners   ◆ = Slower Pace Learners   ● = Special Learning Needs   ■ = Heritage Speakers

15

CAPÍTULO

1

¡Empecemos!

DAY 16 50-MINUTE LESSON PLAN

NATIONAL STANDARDS

Vocabulario en acción 2

Communication 1.1: Student engages in oral and written exchanges of learned material to socialize and to provide and obtain information.

Communication 1.2: Student demonstrates understanding of simple, clearly spoken, and written language such as simple stories, high-frequency commands, and brief instructions when dealing with familiar topics.

Communication 1.3: Student presents information using familiar words, phrases, and sentences to listeners and readers.

CORE INSTRUCTION

Warm-Up
- (5 min.) Have students say the days of the week and months of the year in sequence.

Vocabulario en acción 2
- (15 min.) Review giving the date and day of the week, p. 21.
- (15 min.) Have students do Activities 28–29, p. 21.
- Present **El alfabeto** and **¡Exprésate!**, pp. 22–23 using Teaching **Exprésate**, p. 22.

Wrap-Up
- (5 min.) Present **Language Note**, p. 22.

OPTIONAL RESOURCES
- (5 min.) See Slower Pace Learners, p. 21. ◆
- (5 min.) See Special Learning Needs, p. 23. ●

Practice Options
- *Lab Book*, pp. 11–12, 34 ▲ ● ■
- *Cuaderno de vocabulario y gramática*, pp. 7–9 ▲ ◆ ●
- *Teaching Transparencies*: Vocabulary 1.2, 1.3, 1.4; *Cuaderno de vocabulario y gramática* Answers pp. 7–9 ▲ ◆ ●
- *Video Guide*, pp. 4–5, 8 ▲ ● ■
- *Interactive Tutor* (Disc 1) or *DVD Tutor* (Disc 1) ▲ ● ■
- Online practice, Chapter 1 (go.hrw.com, Keyword: EXP1A CH1) ▲ ● ■

▲ = Advanced Learners   ◆ = Slower Pace Learners   ● = Special Learning Needs   ■ = Heritage Speakers

Holt Spanish 1A

Lesson Planner

CAPÍTULO
1

¡Empecemos!

DAY 17 50-MINUTE LESSON PLAN

NATIONAL STANDARDS

Vocabulario en acción 2
Communication 1.2: Student demonstrates understanding of simple, clearly spoken, and written language such as simple stories, high-frequency commands, and brief instructions when dealing with familiar topics.

Communication 1.3: Student presents information using familiar words, phrases, and sentences to listeners and readers.

CORE INSTRUCTION

Warm-Up
- (5 min.) See **Common Error Alert**, p. 23. Write these words on the board for students to practice spelling aloud: **acción, amarillo, perro, flores.**

Vocabulario en acción 2
- (20 min.) Review **El alfabeto** and **¡Exprésate!**, pp. 22–23.
- (10 min.) Play Audio CD 1, Tr. 9 for Activity 30, p. 23. ●
- (10 min.) Have students do Activity 31, p. 23.

Wrap-Up
- (5 min.) Have students spell the names and say aloud the telephone numbers in the cell phone on page 23.

OPTIONAL RESOURCES
(5 min.) See Slower Pace Learners, p. 23. ◆
(10 min.) See **Comunicación** (TE), p. 23.

Practice Options
- *Lab Book*, pp. 11–12, 34 ▲ ● ■
- *Cuaderno de vocabulario y gramática*, pp. 7–9 ▲ ◆ ●
- *Teaching Transparencies*: Vocabulary 1.2, 1.3, 1.4; *Cuaderno de vocabulario y gramática* Answers, pp. 7–9 ▲ ◆ ●
- *Video Guide*, pp. 4–5, 8 ▲ ● ■
- *Interactive Tutor* (Disc 1) or *DVD Tutor* (Disc 1) ▲ ● ■
- Online practice, Chapter 1 (go.hrw.com, Keyword: EXP1A CH1) ▲ ● ■

▲ = Advanced Learners   ◆ = Slower Pace Learners   ● = Special Learning Needs   ■ = Heritage Speakers

(17)

CAPÍTULO
1

¡Empecemos!

DAY 18 50-MINUTE LESSON PLAN

NATIONAL STANDARDS

Vocabulario en acción 2

Communication 1.1: Student engages in oral and written exchanges of learned material to socialize and to provide and obtain information.

Communication 1.2: Student demonstrates understanding of simple, clearly spoken, and written language such as simple stories, high-frequency commands, and brief instructions when dealing with familiar topics.

Communication 1.3: Student presents information using familiar words, phrases, and sentences to listeners and readers.

CORE INSTRUCTION

Warm-Up

• (5 min.) Dictate any five words from the **Vocabulario** letter by letter, and have students write the words you spell.

Vocabulario en acción 2

• (25 min.) Review **Vocabulario en acción 2**, pp. 18–23.
• (15 min.) Have students do Activity 32, p. 23.

Wrap-Up

• (5 min.) Have volunteers present their conversations from Activity 32 to the class.

OPTIONAL RESOURCES

• (10 min.) See Special Learning Needs, p. 23. ●

Practice Options

• *Lab Book*, pp. 11–12, 34 ▲ ● ■
• *Cuaderno de vocabulario y gramática*, pp. 7–9 ▲ ◆ ●
• *Teaching Transparencies*: Vocabulary 1.2, 1.3, 1.4; *Cuaderno de vocabulario y gramática* Answers, pp. 7–9 ▲ ◆ ●
• *Video Guide*, pp. 4–5, 8 ▲ ● ■
• *Interactive Tutor* (Disc 1) or *DVD Tutor* (Disc 1) ▲ ● ■
• Online practice, Chapter 1 (go.hrw.com, Keyword: EXP1A CH1) ▲ ● ■

▲ = Advanced Learners   ◆ = Slower Pace Learners   ● = Special Learning Needs   ■ = Heritage Speakers

18

¡Empecemos!

NATIONAL STANDARDS

Vocabulario en acción 2

Communication 1.1: Student engages in oral and written exchanges of learned material to socialize and to provide and obtain information.

Communication 1.2: Student demonstrates understanding of simple, clearly spoken, and written language such as simple stories, high-frequency commands, and brief instructions when dealing with familiar topics.

Communication 1.3: Student presents information using familiar words, phrases, and sentences to listeners and readers.

CORE INSTRUCTION

Warm-Up
• (5 min.) See Bell Work, 1.7, p. 24.

Vocabulario en acción 2
• (10 min.) Review **Vocabulario en acción 2**, pp. 18–23.

Assessment
• (20 min.) Give **Prueba: Vocabulario 2.**

Gramática en acción 2
• (10 min.) Present the verb **ser**, p. 24 using Teaching **Gramática**, p. 24.

Wrap-Up
• (5 min.) Present and practice song from Teacher to Teacher, p. 25.

OPTIONAL RESOURCES
• (5 min.) Practice song from Teacher to Teacher, p. 21. ●

Practice Options
• *Lab Book*, pp. 11–12, 34 ▲ ● ■
• *Cuaderno de vocabulario y gramática*, pp. 7–9, 10–12 ▲ ◆ ●
• *Cuaderno de actividades*, pp. 5–7 ▲ ● ■
• *Activities for Communication*, pp. 3–4, 55–56 ▲ ■
• *Teaching Transparencies*: Bell Work 1.7; *Cuaderno de vocabulario y gramática* Answers, pp. 7–9, 10–12 ▲ ◆ ●
• *Video Guide*, pp. 4–5 ▲ ● ■
• *TPR Storytelling Book*, pp. 2–3 ▲ ●
• *Grammar Tutor for Students of Spanish*, pp. 3–6, 168–169 ◆ ●
• *Interactive Tutor* (Disc 1) or *DVD Tutor* (Disc 1) ▲ ● ■
• Online practice, Chapter 1 (go.hrw.com, Keyword: EXP1A CH1) ▲ ● ■

Assessment Options
• *Assessment Program*, **Prueba: Vocabulario 2**, pp. 7–8 ▲ ● ■
• *Test Generator* ▲ ● ■

▲ = Advanced Learners   ◆ = Slower Pace Learners   ● = Special Learning Needs   ■ = Heritage Speakers

¡Empecemos!

CAPÍTULO

1

DAY 20 50-MINUTE LESSON PLAN

NATIONAL STANDARDS

Gramática en acción 2

Communication 1.1: Student engages in oral and written exchanges of learned material to socialize and to provide and obtain information.

Communication 1.2: Student demonstrates understanding of simple, clearly spoken, and written language such as simple stories, high-frequency commands, and brief instructions when dealing with familiar topics.

Communication 1.3: Student presents information using familiar words, phrases, and sentences to listeners and readers.

CORE INSTRUCTION

Warm-Up
- (5 min.) Review song to practice the verb **ser**, p. 25.

Gramática en acción 2
- (10 min.) Re-present **ser** by showing **GramaVisión** *(the verb ser)*.
- (25 min.) Have students do Activities 33–36, pp. 24–25.

Wrap-Up
- (10 min.) See **Comunicación (TE)**, p. 25.

OPTIONAL RESOURCES
- (10 min.) See Slower Pace Learners, p. 25. ◆
- (10 min.) See Special Learning Needs, p. 25 ●

Practice Options
- *Lab Book*, pp. 11–12 ▲ ● ■
- *Cuaderno de vocabulario y gramática*, pp. 10–12 ▲ ◆ ●
- *Cuaderno de actividades*, pp. 5–7 ▲ ● ■
- *Activities for Communication*, pp. 3–4, 55–56 ▲ ■
- *Teaching Transparencies*: **Cuaderno de vocabulario y gramática** Answers, pp. 10–12 ▲ ◆ ●
- *Video Guide*, pp. 4–5 ▲ ● ■
- *Grammar Tutor for Students of Spanish*, pp. 3–6, 168–169 ◆ ●
- *Interactive Tutor* (Disc 1) or *DVD Tutor* (Disc 1) ▲ ● ■
- Online practice, Chapter 1 (go.hrw.com, Keyword: EXP1A CH1) ▲ ● ■

▲ = Advanced Learners ◆ = Slower Pace Learners ● = Special Learning Needs ■ = Heritage Speakers

Holt Spanish 1A

Lesson Planner

CAPÍTULO
1

¡Empecemos!

DAY 21 50-MINUTE LESSON PLAN

NATIONAL STANDARDS

Gramática en acción 2
Communication 1.2: Student demonstrates understanding of simple, clearly spoken, and written language such as simple stories, high-frequency commands, and brief instructions when dealing with familiar topics.

CORE INSTRUCTION

Gramática en acción 2

Warm-Up
- (5 min.) See Bell Work, 1.8, p. 26.

Teach
- (15 min.) Present **Gramática en acción,** *Punctuation marks and written accents,* p. 26. See Teaching **Gramática,** #1–3, p. 26.
- (10 min.) Show **GramaVisión** *(punctuation marks and written accents), Video Program* (Videocassette 1) or *DVD Tutor* (Disc 1).
- (10 min.) Have students to Activity 37, p. 26.

Wrap-Up
- (10 min.) Have students work with a partner to check Activity 37, p. 26.

OPTIONAL RESOURCES
- (10 min.) See Advanced Learners, p. 27. ▲

Practice Options
- *Lab Book,* pp. 11–12 ▲ ● ■
- **Cuaderno de vocabulario y gramática,** pp. 10–12 ▲ ◆ ●
- **Cuaderno de actividades,** pp. 5–7 ◆ ●
- *Activities for Communication,* pp. 3–4 ▲ ■
- *Teaching Transparencies:* Bell Work, 1.8; **Cuaderno de vocabulario y gramática** Answers, pp. 10–12 ▲ ◆ ●
- *Video Guide,* pp. 4–5 ▲ ● ■
- *TPR Storytelling Book,* pp. 2–3 ▲ ●
- *Grammar Tutor for Students of Spanish,* pp. 3–6, 168–169 ◆ ●
- *Interactive Tutor* (Disc 1) or *DVD Tutor* (Disc 1) ▲ ● ■
- Online practice, Chapter 1 (go.hrw.com, Keyword: EXP1A CH1) ▲ ● ■

▲ = Advanced Learners   ◆ = Slower Pace Learners   ● = Special Learning Needs   ■ = Heritage Speakers

CAPÍTULO
1

¡Empecemos!

DAY 22 50-MINUTE LESSON PLAN

NATIONAL STANDARDS

Gramática en acción 2

Communication 1.1: Student engages in oral and written exchanges of learned material to socialize and to provide and obtain information.

Communication 1.2: Student demonstrates understanding of simple, clearly spoken, and written language such as simple stories, high-frequency commands, and brief instructions when dealing with familiar topics.

Communication 1.3: Student presents information using familiar words, phrases, and sentences to listeners and readers.

Comparisons 4.1: Student demonstrates an understanding of the nature of language through comparisons of the student's own language and the language studied.

CORE INSTRUCTION

Warm-Up

- (5 min.) Have students tell the class where they are from and their telephone number.

Gramática en acción 2

- (10 min.) Review punctuation marks and accents, p. 26.
- (20 min.) Have students do Activities 38–39, p. 27.
- (10 min.) Review **Gramática en acción 2**, pp. 24–27.

Wrap-Up

- (5 min.) Have students check Activity 38 with a partner. Remind students to prepare for the **Prueba** tomorrow.

OPTIONAL RESOURCES

- (5 min.) See AP Language Examination, p. 27.
- (10 min.) See Special Learning Needs, p. 27. ●

Practice Options

- *Lab Book*, pp. 11–12 ▲ ● ■
- *Cuaderno de vocabulario y gramática*, pp. 10–12 ▲ ◆ ●
- *Cuaderno de actividades*, pp. 5–7 ◆ ●
- *Activities for Communication*, pp. 3–4, 55–56 ▲ ■
- *Teaching Transparencies*: **Cuaderno de vocabulario y gramática** Answers, pp. 10–12 ▲ ◆ ●
- *Video Guide*, pp. 4–5 ▲ ● ■
- *Grammar Tutor for Students of Spanish*, pp. 3–6, 168–169 ◆ ●
- *Interactive Tutor* (Disc 1) or *DVD Tutor* (Disc 1) ▲ ● ■
- Online practice, Chapter 1 (go.hrw.com, Keyword: EXP1A CH1) ▲ ● ■

▲ = Advanced Learners   ◆ = Slower Pace Learners   ● = Special Learning Needs   ■ = Heritage Speakers

¡Empecemos!

DAY 23 50-MINUTE LESSON PLAN

NATIONAL STANDARDS

Gramática en acción 2

Communication 1.1: Student engages in oral and written exchanges of learned material to socialize and to provide and obtain information.

Communication 1.2: Student demonstrates understanding of simple, clearly spoken, and written language such as simple stories, high-frequency commands, and brief instructions when dealing with familiar topics.

Communication 1.3: Student presents information using familiar words, phrases, and sentences to listeners and readers.

Conexiones culturales

Communication 1.2: Student demonstrates understanding of simple, clearly spoken, and written language such as simple stories, high-frequency commands, and brief instructions when dealing with familiar topics.

CORE INSTRUCTION

Warm-Up

- (5 min.) Practice conjugations and uses of **ser,** p. 24.

Gramática en acción 2

- (10 min.) Review **Gramática en acción 2,** pp. 24–27.

Assessment

- (20 min.) Give **Prueba: Gramática 2.**

Conexiones culturales

- (10 min.) Present **Conexiones culturales,** p. 28. See Teach-ing **Conexiones culturales,** #1–2, p. 28.

Wrap-Up

- (5 min.) See Practices and Perspectives, p. 28.

OPTIONAL RESOURCES

- (5 min.) See Advanced Learners, p. 29. ▲

Practice Options

- *Lab Book,* pp. 11–12 ▲ ● ■
- *Cuaderno de vocabulario y gramática,* pp. 10–12 ▲ ◆ ●
- *Cuaderno de actividades,* pp. 5–7 ◆ ●
- *Activities for Communication,* pp. 3–4, 55–56 ▲ ■
- *Teaching Transparencies:* **Cuaderno de vocabulario y gramática** Answers, pp. 10–12; ▲ ◆ ●
- *Video Guide,* pp. 4–5 ▲ ● ■
- *Grammar Tutor for Students of Spanish,* pp. 3–6, 168–169 ◆ ●
- *Interactive Tutor* (Disc 1) or *DVD Tutor* (Disc 1) ▲ ● ■
- Online practice, Chapter 1 (go.hrw.com, Keyword: EXP1A CH1) ▲ ● ■

Assessment Options

- *Assessment Program,* **Pruebas: Gramática 2,** pp. 9–10 and **Aplicación 2,** pp. 11–12
- Test Generator ▲ ● ■

▲ = Advanced Learners   ◆ = Slower Pace Learners   ● = Special Learning Needs   ■ = Heritage Speakers

CAPÍTULO
1

¡Empecemos!

DAY 24 50-MINUTE LESSON PLAN

NATIONAL STANDARDS

Conexiones culturales

Communication 1.2: Student demonstrates understanding of simple, clearly spoken, and written language such as simple stories, high-frequency commands, and brief instructions when dealing with familiar topics.

Cultures 2.1: Student demonstrates an understanding of the practices (what people do) and how they are related to the perspectives (how people perceive things) of the cultures studied.

Comparisons 4.2: Student demonstrates an understanding of the concept of culture through comparisons of the student's own culture and the cultures studied.

Novela en video

Communication 1.2: Student demonstrates understanding of simple, clearly spoken, and written language such as simple stories, high-frequency commands, and brief instructions when dealing with familiar topics.

Connections 3.2: Student uses resources (that may include technology) in the language and cultures being studied to gain access to information.

CORE INSTRUCTION

Warm-Up
- (5 min.) See Comparisons, p. 29.

Conexiones culturales
- (15 min.) Present **Conexión: Matemáticas**, p. 29. See Teaching **Conexiones culturales**, #3–5, p. 28.
- (10 min.) See Special Learning Needs, p. 29. ●

Novela en video
- (15 min.) Present **Novela en video**, p. 30–32. See Teaching **Novela en video**, p. 30. See Advanced Learners ▲ ●

Wrap-Up
- (5 min.) See Connections: Visual Learners, p. 30. ●

OPTIONAL RESOURCES
- (10 min.) See Special Learning Needs, p. 29. ●
- (5 min.) See Advanced Learners, p. 29. ▲

Practice Options
- *Lab Book*, p. 35 ▲ ● ■
- *Video Guide*, pp. 4–5, 9 ▲ ● ■
- *Interactive Tutor* (Disc 1) or *DVD Tutor* (Disc 1) ▲ ● ■
- Online practice, Chapter 1 (go.hrw.com, Keyword: EXP1A CH1) ▲ ● ■

▲ = Advanced Learners   ◆ = Slower Pace Learners   ● = Special Learning Needs   ■ = Heritage Speakers

24

¡Empecemos!

DAY 25 50-MINUTE LESSON PLAN

NATIONAL STANDARDS

Novela en video

Communication 1.2: Student demonstrates understanding of simple, clearly spoken, and written language such as simple stories, high-frequency commands, and brief instructions when dealing with familiar topics.

Connections 3.2: Student uses resources (that may include technology) in the language and cultures being studied to gain access to information.

Leamos y escribamos

Communication 1.2: Student demonstrates understanding of simple, clearly spoken, and written language such as simple stories, high-frequency commands, and brief instructions when dealing with familiar topics.

Comparisons 4.1: Student demonstrates an understanding of the nature of language through comparisons of the student's own language and the language studied.

Comparisons 4.2: Student demonstrates an understanding of the concept of culture through comparisons of the student's own culture and the cultures studied.

CORE INSTRUCTION

Warm-Up
- (5 min.) See Gestures, p. 30.

Novela en video
- (10 min.) Show **VideoNovela**, Ch. 1
- (10 min.) Have students do Activities 1–3, p. 33. See Teaching **Novela en video**, p. 30.

Leamos y escribamos
- (15 min.) Begin **Leamos y escribamos**, p. 34. See Teaching **Leamos**, #1–2, p. 34.

Wrap-Up
- (10 min.) See Comparing and Contrasting, p. 31, and/or **Comunicación**, p. 32.

OPTIONAL RESOURCES
- (5 min.) Using the Strategy, p. 31
- (5 min.) Language Note, p. 32
- (10 min.) Culminating Project, p. 32
- (5 min.) Applying the Strategies, p. 34.
- (5 min.) Heritage Speakers, p.34 ■

Practice Options
- *Lab Book*, p. 35 ▲ ● ■
- *Video Guide*, pp. 4–5, 9 ▲ ● ■
- ***Cuaderno de actividades***, p. 8 ▲ ● ■
- *Student Edition*, **Literatura y variedades**, pp. 228–229 ▲ ● ■
- *Reading Strategies and Skills Handbook*, pp. 65, 14–17 ▲ ● ■
- ***¡Lee conmigo!*** Level 1 Reader ▲ ● ■
- *Audio CD 1*, Tr. 10 ●
- *Interactive Tutor* (Disc 1) or *DVD Tutor* (Disc 1) ▲ ● ■
- Online practice, Chapter 1 (go.hrw.com, Keyword: EXP1A CH1) ▲ ● ■

▲ = Advanced Learners ◆ = Slower Pace Learners ● = Special Learning Needs ■ = Heritage Speakers

¡Empecemos!

DAY 26 50-MINUTE LESSON PLAN

NATIONAL STANDARDS

Leamos y escribamos

Communication 1.2: Student demonstrates understanding of simple, clearly spoken, and written language such as simple stories, high-frequency commands, and brief instructions when dealing with familiar topics.

Communication 1.3: Student presents information using familiar words, phrases, and sentences to listeners and readers.

Communities 5.1: Student uses the language both within and beyond the school setting through activities such as participating in cultural events and using technology to communicate.

CORE INSTRUCTION

Warm-Up

- (5 min.) See Differentiated Instruction for Advanced Learners, p. 35. ▲

Leamos y escribamos

- (15 min.) Present **Leamos**, pp. 34–35. See Teaching **Leamos**, #3, p. 34.
- (20 min.) Present **Escribamos: Taller del escritor**, p. 35. See Teaching **Escribamos**, p. 34.

Wrap-Up

- (10 min.) Give students a copy of the Rubric you will use for assessing the writing assignment and make sure they understand its use.

OPTIONAL RESOURCES

- (5 min.) See Special Learning Needs, p. 35. ●
- (10 min.) Applying the Strategies, p. 34
- (5 min.) Process Writing, p. 35

Practice Options

- *Cuaderno de actividades*, p. 8 ▲ ● ■
- *Student Edition*, **Literatura y variedades,** pp. 228–229
- *Reading Strategies and Skills Handbook,* pp. xi–xii, 65, 14–17 ▲ ● ■
- *¡Lee conmigo!* Level 1 Reader
- *Interactive Tutor* (Disc 1) or *DVD Tutor* (Disc 1) ▲ ● ■
- Online practice, Chapter 1 (go.hrw.com, Keyword: EXP1A CH1) ▲ ● ■

Assessment Options

- *Assessment Program*, **Prueba: Lectura,** p. 13 ▲ ● ■
- *Assessment Program*, **Prueba: Escritura,** p. 14 ▲ ● ■

▲ = Advanced Learners   ◆ = Slower Pace Learners   ● = Special Learning Needs   ■ = Heritage Speakers

Holt Spanish 1A

Lesson Planner

CAPÍTULO

1

¡Empecemos!

DAY 27 50-MINUTE LESSON PLAN

NATIONAL STANDARDS

Leamos y escribamos

Communication 1.3: Student presents information using familiar words, phrases, and sentences to listeners and readers.

Communities 5.1: Student uses the language both within and beyond the school setting through activities such as participating in cultural events and using technology to communicate.

Repaso

Communication 1.2: Student demonstrates understanding of simple, clearly spoken, and written language such as simple stories, high-frequency commands, and brief instructions when dealing with familiar topics.

Communication 1.3: Student presents information using familiar words, phrases, and sentences to listeners and readers.

CORE INSTRUCTION

Leamos y escribamos

Warm-Up

- (10 min.) Have students check their paragraph for **Escribamos** again before publishing it, p. 35.

Repaso

- (10 min.) Point out the summary of the chapter sections (numbers 1–4 in the side columns) p. 36.
- (20 min.) Have students do Activities 1–4, p. 36.

Wrap-Up

- (10 min.) Have students take turns asking and answering with a partner the questions in Activity 4, p. 36.

OPTIONAL RESOURCES

- (10 min.) Teacher to Teacher, p. 36
- (10 min.) Game, p. 39 ●

Practice Options

- *Lab Book*, pp. 11–12, 36 ▲ ● ■
- *Activities for Communication*, pp. 43, 55–56 ▲ ■
- *Teaching Transparencies*: Situation; Picture Sequences ▲ ● ■
- *Video Guide*, pp. 4–5, 10 ▲ ● ■
- *TPR Storytelling Book*, pp. 4–5 ▲ ●
- *Interactive Tutor* (Disc 1) or *DVD Tutor* (Disc 1) ▲ ● ■
- Online practice, Chapter 1 (go.hrw.com, Keyword: EXP1A CH1) ▲ ● ■

▲ = Advanced Learners   ◆ = Slower Pace Learners   ● = Special Learning Needs   ■ = Heritage Speakers

¡Empecemos!

DAY 28 50-MINUTE LESSON PLAN

NATIONAL STANDARDS

Repaso

Communication 1.2: Student demonstrates understanding of simple, clearly spoken, and written language such as simple stories, high-frequency commands, and brief instructions when dealing with familiar topics.

Communication 1.3: Student presents information using familiar words, phrases, and sentences to listeners and readers.

Cultures 2.1: Student demonstrates an understanding of the practices (what people do) and how they are related to the perspectives (how people perceive things) of the cultures studied.

CORE INSTRUCTION

Warm-Up
- (5 min.) Present the Fold-N-Learn project for students to use at home.

Repaso
- (5 min.) Go over points 5–6 on p. 37 as preview for the exam.
- (10 min.) Have students do Activities 5–6, p. 37.
- (5 min.) Play Audio CD 1, Tr. 12 for Activity 7, p. 37 ●
- (10 min.) Have students do Activity 8, p. 37.
- (10 min.) Play Audio CD 1, Tr. 13, 14, 15 for **Letra y sonido**, p. 38. ●

Wrap-Up
- (5 min.) Go over *Repaso de Gramática* 1–2, p. 38.

OPTIONAL RESOURCES
- (10 min.) Chapter Review, pp. 38–39
- (10 min.) Teaching Suggestion, p. 38
- (10 min.) Teacher to Teacher, p. 36
- (10 min.) Game, p. 39 ●

Practice Options
- *Lab Book*, pp. 11–12, 36 ▲ ● ■
- *Activities for Communication*, pp. 43, 55–56 ▲ ■
- *Teaching Transparencies*: Situation; Picture Sequences ▲ ● ■
- *Video Guide*, pp. 4–5, 10 ▲ ● ■
- *TPR Storytelling Book*, pp. 4–5 ▲ ●
- *Interactive Tutor* (Disc 1) or *DVD Tutor* (Disc 1) ▲ ● ■
- Online practice, Chapter 1 (go.hrw.com, Keyword: EXP1A CH1) ▲ ● ■

▲ = Advanced Learners   ◆ = Slower Pace Learners   ● = Special Learning Needs   ■ = Heritage Speakers

28

CAPÍTULO
1

¡Empecemos!

DAY 29 50-MINUTE LESSON PLAN

NATIONAL STANDARDS

Integración

Communication 1.2: Student demonstrates understanding of simple, clearly spoken, and written language such as simple stories, high-frequency commands, and brief instructions when dealing with familiar topics.

Communication 1.3: Student presents information using familiar words, phrases, and sentences to listeners and readers.

CORE INSTRUCTION

Warm-Up

- (5 min.) See Fine Art Connection, Introduction, p. 41.

Integración

- (10 min.) Play Audio CD 1, Tr. 16 for Activity 1, p. 40. ●
- (20 min.) Have students do Activities 2–4, pp. 40–41.

Wrap-Up

- (15 min.) See Test Taking Strategy, p. 36. Also review the **Objetivos**, p. 4, in preparation for exam.

OPTIONAL RESOURCES

- (15 min.) Thinking Critically, p. 41
- (10 min.) Culture Project, p. 40
- (10 min.) Teacher Note, p. 40

Practice Options

- *Lab Book*, pp. 11–12, 36 ▲ ● ■
- *Cuaderno de actividades*, pp. 9–10, 52–53 ◆ ●
- *Teaching Transparencies*: Fine Art, Ch. 1 ▲ ● ■
- Online practice, Chapter 1 (go.hrw.com, Keyword: EXP1A CH1) ▲ ● ■

▲ = Advanced Learners   ◆ = Slower Pace Learners   ● = Special Learning Needs   ■ = Heritage Speakers

¡Empecemos!

DAY 30 50-MINUTE LESSON PLAN

CORE INSTRUCTION

Chapter Assessment
- (50 min.) Give the Chapter Test.

OPTIONAL RESOURCES
- (50 min.) Alternative Assessment (Picture Sequences, Portfolio Suggestions, Performance Assessment) ▲ ● ■
- (50 min.) Test Generator ▲ ● ■

Practice Options
- *Cuaderno de actividades*, pp. 52–53 ◆ ●

Assessment Options
- *Assessment Program*, **Examen: Capítulo 1,** pp. 105–115 ▲ ● ■
- *Assessment Program*, **Examen oral: Capítulo 1,** p. 116 ▲ ●
- *Assessment Program*, **Prueba: Lectura** p. 13 ▲ ● ■
- *Assessment Program*, **Prueba: Escritura** p. 14 ▲ ● ■
- *Assessment Program*, Alternative Assessment, pp. 212, 219, 227 ▲ ● ■
- Test Generator ▲ ● ■

▲ = Advanced Learners   ◆ = Slower Pace Learners   ● = Special Learning Needs   ■ = Heritage Speakers

30

¡A conocernos!

NATIONAL STANDARDS	
Chapter Opener **Communication 1.2:** Student demonstrates understanding of simple, clearly spoken, and written language such as simple stories, high-frequency commands, and brief instructions when dealing with familiar topics.	**Vocabulario 1** **Communication 1.3:** Student presents information using familiar words, phrases, and sentences to listeners and readers.

Before starting **Capítulo 2,** you may wish to teach **Geocultura: Puerto Rico,** pp. 42–45. For teaching suggestions, see pp. xv–xvi of this *Lesson Planner*.

CORE INSTRUCTION

Warm-Up
- (5 min.) See Learning and Pacing Tips, p. 47.

Chapter Opener
- (5 min.) Have students do Bell Work 2.1, p. 48.
- (5 min.) Present information from Using the Photo and **Más vocabulario**, p. 46.
- (5 min.) Present **Objetivos,** p. 46.

Vocabulario en acción 1
- (15 min.) Present **Vocabulario,** pp. 48–49, using Teaching **Vocabulario,** p. 48.
- (10 min.) Present **¡Exprésate!,** p. 49.

Wrap-Up
- (5 min.) Have students give a description of themselves to a partner using the new vocabulary.

OPTIONAL RESOURCES
- (5 min.) See Slower Pace Learners, p. 49. ◆
- (5 min.) See Special Learning Needs, p. 49. ●
- (5 min.) Slower Pace Learners, p. 49 ◆
- (5 min.) Special Learning Needs, p. 49 ●

Practice Options
- *Lab Book*, pp. 2, 13–14, 37, 38 ▲ ● ■
- *Cuaderno de vocabulario y gramática*, pp. 13–15 ▲ ◆ ●
- *Cuaderno para hispanohablantes*, pp. 11–18, 19 ■
- *Teaching Transparencies*: Map 4; Bell Work, 2.1; **Vocabulario** 2.1, 2.2; *Vocabulario y gramática* Answers, pp. 13–15 ▲ ◆ ●
- *Video Guide*, pp. 11–12, 14–15, 16 ▲ ● ■
- *Interactive Tutor* (Disc 1) or *DVD Tutor* (Disc 1) ▲ ● ■
- Online practice, Chapter 2 (go.hrw.com, Keyword: EXP1A CH2) ▲ ● ■

▲ = Advanced Learners   ◆ = Slower Pace Learners   ● = Special Learning Needs   ■ = Heritage Speakers

Holt Spanish 1A

Lesson Planner

¡A conocernos!

NATIONAL STANDARDS

Vocabulario en acción 1

Communication 1.2: Student demonstrates understanding of simple, clearly spoken, and written language such as simple stories, high-frequency commands, and brief instructions when dealing with familiar topics.

Comparisons 4.1: Student demonstrates an understanding of the nature of language through comparisons of the student's own language and the language studied.

Comparisons 4.2: Student demonstrates an understanding of the concept of culture through comparisons of the student's own culture and the cultures studied.

CORE INSTRUCTION

Warm-Up

- (5 min.) Present information from **También se puede decir...**, p. 49.

Vocabulario en acción 1

- (10 min.) Show **ExpresaVisión,** Ch. 2.
- (10 min.) Review **Vocabulario 1** and **¡Exprésate!.**
- (5 min.) Present **Nota cultural,** p. 50.
- (5 min.) Play Audio CD 2, Tr. 1, for Activity 1, p. 50. ●
- (5 min.) Have students do Activity 2, p. 50.

Wrap-Up

- (10 min.) Present the Fold-N-Learn activity, p. 50. Suggest to students that they use it to review for **Prueba: Vocabulario 1.** ●

OPTIONAL RESOURCES

- (5 min.) See Common Error Alert, p. 50.
- (10 min.) TPR, p. 49 ●
- (10 min.) Teacher to Teacher, p. 49

Practice Options

- *Lab Book*, pp. 13–14, 38 ▲ ◆ ●
- *Cuaderno de vocabulario y gramática*, pp. 13–15 ▲ ◆ ●
- *Teaching Transparencies*: **Vocabulario** 2.1, 2.2; *Vocabulario y gramática* Answers, pp. 13–15 ▲ ● ■
- *Video Guide*, pp. 14–15, 16 ▲ ◆ ●
- *Interactive Tutor* (Disc 1) or *DVD Tutor* (Disc 1) ▲ ● ■
- Online practice, Chapter 2 (go.hrw.com, Keyword: EXP1A CH2) ▲ ● ■

▲ = Advanced Learners ◆ = Slower Pace Learners ● = Special Learning Needs ■ = Heritage Speakers

¡Empecemos!

DAY 3 50-MINUTE LESSON PLAN

NATIONAL STANDARDS

Vocabulario en acción 1

Communication 1.1: Student engages in oral and written exchanges of learned material to socialize and to provide and obtain information.

Communication 1.2: Student demonstrates understanding of simple, clearly spoken, and written language such as simple stories, high-frequency commands, and brief instructions when dealing with familiar topics.

Communication 1.3: Student presents information using familiar words, phrases, and sentences to listeners and readers.

CORE INSTRUCTION

Warm-Up

- (5 min.) Present information from Common Error Alert, pp. 50, 51.

Vocabulario en acción 1

- (5 min.) Have students do Bell Work 2.2, p. 54.
- (20 min.) Have students do Activities 3–5, pp. 50–51.
- (15 min.) Present **¡Exprésate!,** p. 52, using Teaching **¡Exprésate!,** p. 52.

Wrap-Up

- (5 min.) Have students do the activity described in **Más práctica,** p. 51.

OPTIONAL RESOURCES

- (5 min.) Have students do Activity 5, p. 51.
- (20 min.) See Slower Pace Learners, p. 51. ◆
- (20 min.) See Multiple Intelligences, p. 51. ●
- (5 min.) Common Error Alert, p. 52
- (5 min.) Slower Pace Learners, p. 51 ◆
- (10 min.) Multiple Intelligences, p. 51 ●
- (10 min.) **Comunicación,** p. 51

Practice Options

- *Lab Book,* pp. 13–14, 38 ▲ ● ■
- *Cuaderno de vocabulario y gramática,* pp. 13–15 ▲ ◆ ●
- *Teaching Transparencies:* Bell Work, 2.2; **Vocabulario** 2.1, 2.2; *Vocabulario y gramática* Answers, pp. 13–15 ▲ ◆ ●
- *Video Guide,* pp. 14–15, 16 ▲ ● ■
- *Interactive Tutor* (Disc 1) or *DVD Tutor* (Disc 1) ▲ ● ■
- Online practice, Chapter 2 (go.hrw.com, Keyword: EXP1A CH2) ▲ ● ■

▲ = Advanced Learners   ◆ = Slower Pace Learners   ● = Special Learning Needs   ■ = Heritage Speakers

¡A conocernos!

NATIONAL STANDARDS

Vocabulario en acción 1

Communication 1.1: Student engages in oral and written exchanges of learned material to socialize and to provide and obtain information.

Communication 1.2: Student demonstrates understanding of simple, clearly spoken, and written language such as simple stories, high-frequency commands, and brief instructions when dealing with familiar topics.

Communication 1.3: Student presents information using familiar words, phrases, and sentences to listeners and readers.

CORE INSTRUCTION

Warm-Up

- (5 min.) Have students do the activity described in Multiple Intelligences, p. 53. ●

Vocabulario en acción 1

- (10 min.) Review **¡Exprésate!**, p. 52.
- (5 min.) Present **Nota cultural,** p. 52.
- (20 min.) Have students do Activities 6–9, pp. 52–53.

Wrap-Up

- (10 min.) Have students do Activity 9, p. 53. Then remind the class to study for **Prueba: Vocabulario 1.**

OPTIONAL RESOURCES

- (5 min.) See Practices and Perspectives, p. 53.
- (10 min.) See Advanced Learners, p. 53. ▲
- (10 min.) Practices and Perspectives, p. 53
- (10 min.) Advanced Learners, p. 53 ▲

Practice Options

- *Lab Book*, pp. 13–14, 38 ▲ ● ■
- *Cuaderno de vocabulario y gramática*, pp. 13–15 ▲ ◆ ●
- *Teaching Transparencies*: **Vocabulario** 2.1, 2.2; *Vocabulario y gramática* Answers, pp. 13–15 ▲ ● ■
- *Video Guide*, pp. 14–15, 16 ▲ ◆ ●
- *Interactive Tutor* (Disc 1) or *DVD Tutor* (Disc 1) ▲ ● ■
- Online practice, Chapter 2 (go.hrw.com, Keyword: EXP1A CH2) ▲ ● ■

▲ = Advanced Learners   ◆ = Slower Pace Learners   ● = Special Learning Needs   ■ = Heritage Speakers

CAPÍTULO
2

¡A conocernos!

DAY 5 50-MINUTE LESSON PLAN

NATIONAL STANDARDS

Vocabulario en acción 1

Communication 1.1: Student engages in oral and written exchanges of learned material to socialize and to provide and obtain information.

Communication 1.2: Student demonstrates understanding of simple, clearly spoken, and written language such as simple stories, high-frequency commands, and brief instructions when dealing with familiar topics.

Communication 1.3: Student presents information using familiar words, phrases, and sentences to listeners and readers.

CORE INSTRUCTION

Warm-Up
- (10 min.) Have students do the activity described in **Comunicación** (TE), p. 53.

Vocabulario en acción 1
- (15 min.) Review **Vocabulario 1,** pp. 48–53.

Assessment
- (20 min.) Give **Prueba: Vocabulario 1.**

Wrap-Up
- (5 min.) Preview **Gramática 1,** pp. 54–59.

OPTIONAL RESOURCES
- You can find alternative quizzes in the Assessment Options listed below.

Practice Options
- *Lab Book*, pp. 13–14, 38 ▲ ● ■
- *Cuaderno de vocabulario y gramática*, pp. 13–15 ▲ ◆ ●
- *Teaching Transparencies*: **Vocabulario** 2.1, 2.2; *Vocabulario y gramática* Answers, pp. 13–15 ▲ ● ■

Assessment Options
- *Assessment Program*: **Prueba: Vocabulario 1,** pp. 21–22 ▲ ● ■
- Test Generator ▲ ● ■

▲ = Advanced Learners   ◆ = Slower Pace Learners   ● = Special Learning Needs   ■ = Heritage Speakers

(35)

¡A conocernos!

DAY 6 50-MINUTE LESSON PLAN

NATIONAL STANDARDS

Gramática en acción 1

Communication 1.2: Student demonstrates understanding of simple, clearly spoken, and written language such as simple stories, high-frequency commands, and brief instructions when dealing with familiar topics.

CORE INSTRUCTION

Warm-Up

- (5 min.) Have students do the activity described in **Más práctica,** p. 54.

Gramática en acción 1

- (15 min.) Present **Gramática: ser** *with adjectives,* p. 54, using Teaching **Gramática,** p. 54.
- (10 min.) Show **GramaVisión** (**ser** *with adjectives*), *Video Program* (Videocassette 1) or *DVD Tutor* (Disc 1).
- (15 min.) Have students do Activities 10–11, pp. 54–55.

Wrap-Up

- (5 min.) Have students share their responses for Activity 10, p. 54.

OPTIONAL RESOURCES

- (15 min.) See Special Learning Needs, p. 55. ●

Practice Options

- *Lab Book,* pp. 13–14 ▲ ● ■
- *Cuaderno de vocabulario y gramática,* pp. 16–18▲ ◆ ●
- *Cuaderno de actividades,* pp. 11–13 ▲ ● ■
- *Activities for Communication,* pp. 5–6, 57–58 ▲ ■
- *Teaching Transparencies:* **Vocabulario y gramática** Answers, pp. 16–18 ▲ ◆ ●
- *Video Guide,* pp. 14–15 ▲ ● ■
- *Grammar Tutor for Students of Spanish,* pp. 7–10, 169–170 ◆ ●
- *Interactive Tutor* (Disc 1) or *DVD Tutor* (Disc 1) ▲ ● ■
- Online practice, Chapter 2 (go.hrw.com, Keyword: EXP1A CH2) ▲ ● ■

▲ = Advanced Learners   ◆ = Slower Pace Learners   ● = Special Learning Needs   ■ = Heritage Speakers

Holt Spanish 1A

Lesson Planner

¡A conocernos!

DAY 7 50-MINUTE LESSON PLAN

NATIONAL STANDARDS

Gramática en acción 1

Communication 1.1: Student engages in oral and written exchanges of learned material to socialize and to provide and obtain information.

Communication 1.2: Student demonstrates understanding of simple, clearly spoken, and written language such as simple stories, high-frequency commands, and brief instructions when dealing with familiar topics.

Communication 1.3: Student presents information using familiar words, phrases, and sentences to listeners and readers.

CORE INSTRUCTION

Warm-Up
- (5 min.) Have students do Bell Work 2.3, p. 56.

Gramática en acción 1
- (5 min.) Review **ser** with adjectives, p. 54.
- (20 min.) Have students do Activities 12–13, p. 55.
- (15 min.) Present **Gramática:** *gender and adjective agreement,* p. 56, using Teaching **Gramática,** p. 56.

Wrap-Up
- (5 min.) Have students do the activity suggested in Advanced Learners, p. 55. ▲

OPTIONAL RESOURCES
- (10 min.)**Comunicación**, p. 55.

Practice Options
- *Lab Book*, pp. 13–14 ▲ ● ■
- *Cuaderno de vocabulario y gramática*, pp. 16–18 ▲ ◆ ●
- *Cuaderno de actividades*, pp. 11–13 ◆ ●
- *Activities for Communication*, pp. 5–6, 57–58 ▲ ■
- *Teaching Transparencies*: Bell Work 2.3; *Vocabulario y gramática* Answers, pp. 16–18 ▲ ● ■
- *Video Guide*, pp. 14–15 ▲ ◆ ●
- *Grammar Tutor for Students of Spanish*, pp. 7–10, 169–170 ◆ ●
- *Interactive Tutor* (Disc 1) or *DVD Tutor* (Disc 1) ▲ ● ■
- Online practice, Chapter 2 (go.hrw.com, Keyword: EXP1A CH2) ▲ ● ■

▲ = Advanced Learners   ◆ = Slower Pace Learners   ● = Special Learning Needs   ■ = Heritage Speakers

¡A conocernos!

DAY 8 50-MINUTE LESSON PLAN

NATIONAL STANDARDS

Gramática en acción 1
Communication 1.1: Student engages in oral and written exchanges of learned material to socialize and to provide and obtain information.

Communication 1.2: Student demonstrates understanding of simple, clearly spoken, and written language such as simple stories, high-frequency commands, and brief instructions when dealing with familiar topics.

Communication 1.3: Student presents information using familiar words, phrases, and sentences to listeners and readers.

CORE INSTRUCTION

Warm-Up
- (15 min.) Have students do Activity 17, p. 57. To do the activity, they should prepare pairs of index cards as indicated in **Comunicación** (TE), p. 57.

Gramática en acción 1
- (5 min.) Have students do Bell Work, 2.4, p. 58.
- (10 min.) Show **GramaVisión** *(gender and adjective agreement), Video Program* (Videocassette 1) or *DVD Tutor* (Disc 1).
- (15 min.) Have students to Activities 14–17, pp. 56–57.

Wrap-Up
- (5 min.) Use the index cards made during the Warm-Up to do Activity 17, p. 57.

OPTIONAL RESOURCES
- (5 min.) See Slower Pace Learners, p. 57. ◆
- (5 min.) See Special Learning Needs, p. 57. ●

Practice Options
- *Lab Book*, pp. 13–14 ▲ ● ■
- *Cuaderno de vocabulario y gramática*, pp. 16–18 ▲ ◆ ●
- *Cuaderno de actividades*, pp. 11–13 ▲ ● ■
- *Activities for Communication*, pp. 5–6, 57–58 ▲ ■
- *Teaching Transparencies*: Bell Work, 2.4; *Vocabulario y gramática* Answers, pp. 16–18 ▲ ◆ ●
- *Video Guide*, pp. 14–15 ▲ ● ■
- *Grammar Tutor for Students of Spanish*, pp. 7–10, 169–170 ◆ ●
- *Interactive Tutor* (Disc 1) or *DVD Tutor* (Disc 1) ▲ ● ■
- Online practice, Chapter 2 (go.hrw.com, Keyword: EXP1A CH2) ▲ ● ■

▲ = Advanced Learners ◆ = Slower Pace Learners ● = Special Learning Needs ■ = Heritage Speakers

Holt Spanish 1A

Lesson Planner

¡A conocernos!

DAY 9 50-MINUTE LESSON PLAN

NATIONAL STANDARDS

Gramática en acción 1
Communication 1.2: Student demonstrates understanding of simple, clearly spoken, and written language such as simple stories, high-frequency commands, and brief instructions when dealing with familiar topics.

Communication 1.3: Student presents information using familiar words, phrases, and sentences to listeners and readers.

CORE INSTRUCTION

Warm-Up
- (5 min.) Name some famous people (or show pictures) and ask volunteers to describe them.

Gramática en acción 1
- (15 min.) Present **Gramática:** *Question formation,* p. 58, using Teaching **Gramática,** p. 58.
- (10 min.) Show **GramaVisión** *(question formation),* *Video Program* (Videocassette 1) or *DVD Tutor* (Disc 1).
- (10 min.) Play Audio CD 2, Tr. 2 for Activity 18, p. 58. ●
- (5 min.) Have students do Activity 19, p. 58.

Wrap-Up
- (5 min.) Have students do the activity described in Advanced Learners, p. 59. ▲

OPTIONAL RESOURCES
- (5 min.) See Special Learning Needs, p. 59. ●

Practice Options
- *Lab Book*, pp. 13–14 ▲ ● ■
- *Cuaderno de vocabulario y gramática*, pp. 16–18 ▲ ◆ ●
- *Cuaderno de actividades*, pp. 11–13 ◆ ●
- *Activities for Communication*, pp. 5–6, 57–58 ▲ ■
- *Teaching Transparencies*: *Vocabulario y gramática* Answers, pp. 16–18 ▲ ◆ ●
- *Video Guide*, pp. 14–15 ▲ ● ■
- *Grammar Tutor for Students of Spanish*, pp. 7–10, 169–170 ◆ ●
- *Interactive Tutor* (Disc 1) or *DVD Tutor* (Disc 1) ▲ ● ■
- Online practice, Chapter 2 (go.hrw.com, Keyword: EXP1A CH2) ▲ ● ■

▲ = Advanced Learners   ◆ = Slower Pace Learners   ● = Special Learning Needs   ■ = Heritage Speakers

¡A conocernos!

DAY 10 50-MINUTE LESSON PLAN

NATIONAL STANDARDS

Gramática en acción 1

Communication 1.1: Student engages in oral and written exchanges of learned material to socialize and to provide and obtain information.

Communication 1.2: Student demonstrates understanding of simple, clearly spoken, and written language such as simple stories, high-frequency commands, and brief instructions when dealing with familiar topics.

Communication 1.3: Student presents information using familiar words, phrases, and sentences to listeners and readers.

Cultures 2.1: Student demonstrates an understanding of the practices (what people do) and how they are related to the perspectives (how people perceive things) of the cultures studied.

Comparisons 4.2: Student demonstrates an understanding of the concept of culture through comparisons of the student's own culture and the cultures studied.

CORE INSTRUCTION

Warm-Up

- (5 min.) Present Common Error Alert, p. 59.

Gramática en acción 1

- (15 min.) Have students do Activities 20–22, p. 59.
- (5 min.) Present **Nota cultural,** p. 59.
- (15 min.) Review **Gramática 1,** pp. 54–56.

Wrap-Up

- (10 min.) Have students write an answer to the e-mail in Activity 21, p. 59. Then remind them to study for **Prueba: Gramática 1.**

OPTIONAL RESOURCES

- (10 min.) Have students do Activity 22, p. 59.
- (15 min.) **Comunicación,** p. 59

Practice Options

- *Lab Book,* pp. 13–14 ▲ ● ■
- *Cuaderno de vocabulario y gramática,* pp. 16–18 ▲ ◆ ●
- *Cuaderno de actividades,* pp. 11–13 ▲ ● ■
- *Activities for Communication,* pp. 5–6, 57–58 ▲ ■
- *Teaching Transparencies: Vocabulario y gramática* Answers, pp. 16–18 ▲ ● ■
- *Video Guide,* pp. 14–15 ▲ ◆ ●
- *Grammar Tutor for Students of Spanish,* pp. 7–10, 169–170 ◆ ●
- *Interactive Tutor* (Disc 1) or *DVD Tutor* (Disc 1) ▲ ● ■
- Online practice, Chapter 2 (go.hrw.com, Keyword: EXP1A CH2) ▲ ● ■

▲ = Advanced Learners   ◆ = Slower Pace Learners   ● = Special Learning Needs   ■ = Heritage Speakers

¡A conocernos!

DAY 11 50-MINUTE LESSON PLAN

NATIONAL STANDARDS

Gramática en acción 1
Communication 1.1: Student engages in oral and written exchanges of learned material to socialize and to provide and obtain information.
Communication 1.2: Student demonstrates understanding of simple, clearly spoken, and written language such as simple stories, high-frequency commands, and brief instructions when dealing with familiar topics.
Communication 1.3: Student presents information using familiar words, phrases, and sentences to listeners and readers.

Cultura
Cultures 2.1: Student demonstrates an understanding of the practices (what people do) and how they are related to the perspectives (how people perceive things) of the cultures studied.
Comparisons 4.2: Student demonstrates an understanding of the concept of culture through comparisons of the student's own culture and the cultures studied.
Comparisons 4C: Student demonstrates an understanding of the influence of one language and culture on another.

CORE INSTRUCTION

Warm-Up
- (5 min.) Play Twenty Questions with your students. Give statements about famous people using forms of **ser** with adjectives and have students guess at the identities of the people.

Gramática en acción 1
- (10 min.) Review **Gramática 1,** pp. 57–59.

Assessment
- (20 min.) Give **Prueba: Gramática 1.**

Cultura
- (10 min.) Present **Cultura,** pp. 60–61, using Teaching **Cultura,** #s 1–2, p. 60.

Wrap-Up
- (5 min.) See Language to Language, p. 61.

OPTIONAL RESOURCES
- (10 min.) Map Activities, p. 60

Practice Options
- *Lab Book*, pp. 13–14, 39 ▲ ● ■
- *Cuaderno de vocabulario y gramática*, pp. 16–18 ▲ ◆ ●
- *Cuaderno de actividades*, pp. 11–13, 14 ▲ ● ■
- *Activities for Communication*, pp. 5–6, 57–58 ▲ ■
- *Cuaderno para hispanohablantes,* p.20 ■
- *Teaching Transparencies*: *Vocabulario y gramática* Answers, pp. 16–18 ▲ ◆ ●
- *Video Guide*, pp. 14–15, 17 ▲ ● ■
- *Grammar Tutor for Students of Spanish,* pp. 7–10, 169–170 ◆ ●

- *Interactive Tutor* (Disc 1) or *DVD Tutor* (Disc 1) ▲ ● ■
- Online practice, Chapter 2 (go.hrw.com, Keyword: EXP1A CH2)▲ ● ■

Assessment Options
- *Assessment Program*: **Prueba: Gramática 1,** pp. 23–24 ▲ ● ■
- *Assessment Program*: **Prueba: Aplicación 1,** pp. 25–26, 37 ▲ ● ■
- *Audio CD 2*, Tr. 15 ●
- Test Generator ▲ ● ■

▲ = Advanced Learners   ◆ = Slower Pace Learners   ● = Special Learning Needs   ■ = Heritage Speakers

¡A conocernos!

DAY 12 50-MINUTE LESSON PLAN

NATIONAL STANDARDS

Cultura

Communication 1.1: Student engages in oral and written exchanges of learned material to socialize and to provide and obtain information.

Communication 1.2: Student demonstrates understanding of simple, clearly spoken, and written language such as simple stories, high-frequency commands, and brief instructions when dealing with familiar topics.

Cultures 2.1: Student demonstrates an understanding of the practices (what people do) and how they are related to the perspectives (how people perceive things) of the cultures studied.

Comparisons 4.2: Student demonstrates an understanding of the concept of culture through comparisons of the student's own culture and the cultures studied.

CORE INSTRUCTION

Warm-Up
- (10 min.) Review the information about **Luis** and **Andrea,** pp. 60–61.

Cultura
- (10 min.) Show **VideoCultura,** Ch. 2.
- (10 min.) See Teaching **Cultura,** #s 3–4, p. 60.

Vocabulario en acción 2
- (15 min.) Present **Vocabulario** and **¡Exprésate!,** pp. 62–63, using Teaching **Vocabulario,** p. 62.

Wrap-Up
- (5 min.) Have students tell a partner three things they like from the new vocabulary words.

OPTIONAL RESOURCES
- (15 min.) See Advanced Learners, p. 61. ▲
- (15 min.) See Multiple Intelligences, p. 61. ●
- (10 min.) See Special Learning Needs, p. 63. ●
- (5 min.) See Language to Language, p. 63.
- (10 min.) Community Link, p. 61
- (10 min.) Advanced Learners, p. 61 ▲
- (10 min.) Multiple Intelligences, p. 61 ●
- (10 min.) Special Learning Needs, p. 63 ●
- (5 min.) Language to Language, p. 63

Practice Options
- *Lab Book,* pp.15–16, 39, 40 ▲ ● ■
- *Cuaderno de vocabulario y gramática,* pp. 19–21 ▲ ◆ ●
- *Cuaderno para hispanohablantes,* p. 20
- *Teaching Transparencies:* **Vocabulario** 2.3, 2.4; *Vocabulario y gramática* Answers, pp. 19–21 ▲ ● ■
- *Video Guide,* pp. 14–15, 17, 18 ▲ ◆ ●
- *Interactive Tutor* (Disc 1) or *DVD Tutor* (Disc 1) ▲ ● ■
- Online practice, Chapter 2 (go.hrw.com, Keyword: EXP1A CH2) ▲ ● ■

▲ = Advanced Learners   ◆ = Slower Pace Learners   ● = Special Learning Needs   ■ = Heritage Speakers

¡A conocernos!

DAY 13 50-MINUTE LESSON PLAN

NATIONAL STANDARDS

Vocabulario en acción 2

Communication 1.2: Student demonstrates understanding of simple, clearly spoken, and written language such as simple stories, high-frequency commands, and brief instructions when dealing with familiar topics.

Cultures 2.1: Student demonstrates an understanding of the practices (what people do) and how they are related to the perspectives (how people perceive things) of the cultures studied.

Comparisons 4.2: Student demonstrates an understanding of the concept of culture through comparisons of the student's own culture and the cultures studied.

CORE INSTRUCTION

Warm-Up
- (5 min.) Have students do Bell Work 2.5, p. 62.

Vocabulario en acción 2
- (10 min.) Show **ExpresaVisión,** Ch. 2.
- (20 min.) Review **Vocabulario 2,** pp. 62–63.
- (10 min.) Present **Nota cultural,** p. 64.

Wrap-Up
- (5 min.) Present **También se puede decir…** , p. 63. Then have students use the new words and say in Spanish whether they like or dislike those things.

OPTIONAL RESOURCES
- (10 min.) See TPR, p. 63. ●
- (10 min.) See Slower Pace Learners, p. 63. ◆
- (10 min.) See Special Learning Needs, p. 63. ●

Practice Options
- *Lab Book*, pp.15–16, 40 ▲ ● ■
- *Cuaderno de vocabulario y gramática*, pp. 19–21 ▲ ◆ ●
- *Teaching Transparencies*: Bell Work, 2.5; **Vocabulario** 2.3, 2.4; *Vocabulario y gramática* Answers, pp. 19–21 ▲ ◆ ●
- *Video Guide*, pp. 14–15, 18 ▲ ● ■
- *Interactive Tutor* (Disc 1) or *DVD Tutor* (Disc 1) ▲ ● ■
- Online practice, Chapter 2 (go.hrw.com, Keyword: EXP1A CH2) ▲ ● ■

▲ = Advanced Learners   ◆ = Slower Pace Learners   ● = Special Learning Needs   ■ = Heritage Speakers

¡A conocernos!

DAY 14 50-MINUTE LESSON PLAN

NATIONAL STANDARDS

Vocabulario en acción 2

Communication 1.2: Student demonstrates understanding of simple, clearly spoken, and written language such as simple stories, high-frequency commands, and brief instructions when dealing with familiar topics.

Communication 1.3: Student presents information using familiar words, phrases, and sentences to listeners and readers.

Cultures 2.2: Student demonstrates an understanding of the products (what people create) and how they are related to the perspectives (how people perceive things) of the cultures studied.

CORE INSTRUCTION

Warm-Up
• (5 min.) Have students do Bell Work 2.6, p. 68.

Vocabulario en acción 2
• (10 min.) Have students do Activity 23, p. 64.
• (10 min.) Play Audio CD 2, Tr. 6, for Activity 24, p. 64. ●
• (15 min.) Have students do Activities 25–26, pp. 64–65.

Wrap-Up
• (10 min.) Have students play Game, p. 64. ●

OPTIONAL RESOURCES
• (10 min.) See Products and Perspectives, p. 65.

Practice Options
• *Lab Book*, pp.15–16, 40 ▲ ● ■
• *Cuaderno de vocabulario y gramática*, pp. 19–21 ▲ ◆ ●
• *Teaching Transparencies*: Bell Work, 2.6; **Vocabulario** 2.3, 2.4; *Vocabulario y gramática* Answers, pp. 19–21 ▲ ◆ ●
• *Video Guide*, pp. 14–15, 18 ▲ ● ■
• *Interactive Tutor* (Disc 1) or *DVD Tutor* (Disc 1) ▲ ● ■
• Online practice, Chapter 2 (go.hrw.com, Keyword: EXP1A CH2) ▲ ● ■

▲ = Advanced Learners   ◆ = Slower Pace Learners   ● = Special Learning Needs   ■ = Heritage Speakers

Holt Spanish 1A

Lesson Planner

¡A conocernos!

DAY 15 50-MINUTE LESSON PLAN

NATIONAL STANDARDS

Vocabulario en acción 2
Communication 1.1: Student engages in oral and written exchanges of learned material to socialize and to provide and obtain information.

Communication 1.2: Student demonstrates understanding of simple, clearly spoken, and written language such as simple stories, high-frequency commands, and brief instructions when dealing with familiar topics.

Communication 1.3: Student presents information using familiar words, phrases, and sentences to listeners and readers.

CORE INSTRUCTION

Warm-Up
- (5 min.) Have students ask the questions in Activity 25, p. 64, to a partner and answer each other.

Vocabulario en acción 2
- (10 min.) Have students do Activity 27, p. 65.
- (15 min.) Present **¡Exprésate!,** p. 66, using Teaching **¡Exprésate!,** p. 66.
- (10 min.) Have students do Activities 28–29, pp. 66–67.

Wrap-Up
- (10 min.) See Advanced Learners, p. 65. ▲

OPTIONAL RESOURCES
- (15 min.) Have students do Activity 27, p. 65.
- (10 min.) See Special Learning Needs, p. 65. ●
- (10 min.) See Multicultural Link, p. 66.
- (10 min.) **Comunicación**, p. 65.
- (10 min.) Multicultural Link, p. 66.

Practice Options
- *Lab Book*, pp.15–16, 40 ▲ ● ■
- *Cuaderno de vocabulario y gramática*, pp. 19–21 ▲ ◆ ●
- *Teaching Transparencies*: Bell Work, 2.6; **Vocabulario** 2.3, 2.4; *Vocabulario y gramática* Answers, pp. 19–21 ▲ ◆ ●
- *Video Guide*, pp. 14–15, 18 ▲ ● ■
- *Interactive Tutor* (Disc 1) or *DVD Tutor* (Disc 1) ▲ ● ■
- Online practice, Chapter 2 (go.hrw.com, Keyword: EXP1A CH2) ▲ ● ■

▲ = Advanced Learners   ◆ = Slower Pace Learners   ● = Special Learning Needs   ■ = Heritage Speakers

¡Empecemos!

DAY 16 50-MINUTE LESSON PLAN

NATIONAL STANDARDS

Vocabulario en acción 2

Communication 1.1: Student engages in oral and written exchanges of learned material to socialize and to provide and obtain information.

Communication 1.2: Student demonstrates understanding of simple, clearly spoken, and written language such as simple stories, high-frequency commands, and brief instructions when dealing with familiar topics.

Communication 1.3: Student presents information using familiar words, phrases, and sentences to listeners and readers.

CORE INSTRUCTION

Warm-Up

- (5 min.) Have a few students perform the interviews they prepared in Advanced Learners, p. 65. ▲

Vocabulario en acción 2

- (5 min.) Review **¡Exprésate!,** p. 66.
- (15 min.) Have students do Activities 30–31, p. 67.
- (15 min.) Review **Vocabulario 2,** pp. 62–67.

Wrap-Up

- (10 min.) Have students do the activity described in Advanced Learners, p. 67. Then remind the class to study for **Prueba: Vocabulario 2.** ▲

OPTIONAL RESOURCES

- (10 min.) Have students do Activity 31, p. 67.
- (20 min.) See Multiple Intelligences, p. 67. ●
- (10 min.) **Comunicación(TE),** p. 67.
- (10 min.) Multiple Intelligences, p. 67. ●

Practice Options

- *Lab Book,* pp. 15–16, 40 ▲ ● ■
- *Cuaderno de vocabulario y gramática*, pp. 19–21 ▲ ◆ ●
- *Teaching Transparencies*: *Vocabulario y gramática* Answers, pp. 19–21 ▲ ◆ ●
- *Video Guide,* pp. 14–15, 18 ▲ ● ■
- *Interactive Tutor* (Disc 1) or *DVD Tutor* (Disc 1) ▲ ● ■
- Online practice, Chapter 2 (go.hrw.com, Keyword: EXP1A CH2) ▲ ● ■

▲ = Advanced Learners   ◆ = Slower Pace Learners   ● = Special Learning Needs   ■ = Heritage Speakers

¡A conocernos!

DAY 17 50-MINUTE LESSON PLAN

NATIONAL STANDARDS

Vocabulario en acción 2

Communication 1.1: Student engages in oral and written exchanges of learned material to socialize and to provide and obtain information.

Communication 1.2: Student demonstrates understanding of simple, clearly spoken, and written language such as simple stories, high-frequency commands, and brief instructions when dealing with familiar topics.

Communication 1.3: Student presents information using familiar words, phrases, and sentences to listeners and readers.

Gramática en acción 2

Comparisons 4.1: Student demonstrates an understanding of the nature of language through comparisons of the student's own language and the language studied.

CORE INSTRUCTION

Warm-Up

- (5 min.) Have students do the first part of **Comunicación (TE),** p. 65.

Vocabulario en acción 2

- (10 min.) Review **Vocabulario 2,** pp. 62–67.

Assessment

- (20 min.) Give **Prueba: Vocabulario 2.**

Gramática en acción 2

- (10 min.) Present **Gramática:** *Nouns and definite articles,* p. 68, using Teaching **Gramática,** p. 68.

Wrap-Up

- (5 min.) See Thinking Critically, p. 69.

OPTIONAL RESOURCES

- (10 min.) Multiple Intelligences, p. 69. ●
- You can find alternative quizzes in the Assessment Options listed below.

Practice Options

- *Lab Book,* pp. 15–16, 40 ▲ ◆ ●
- ***Cuaderno de vocabulario y gramática***, pp. 19–21, 22–24 ▲ ◆ ●
- ***Cuaderno de actividades***, pp. 15–17 ▲ ● ■
- *Activities for Communication,* pp. 7–8, 57–58 ▲ ■
- *Teaching Transparencies*: ***Vocabulario y gramática*** Answers, pp. 19–21, 22–24 ▲ ◆ ●
- *Video Guide,* pp. 14–15, 18 ▲ ● ■
- *Grammar Tutor for Students of Spanish,* pp. 11–14, 169–170 ◆ ●
- *Interactive Tutor* (Disc 1) or *DVD Tutor* (Disc 1) ▲ ● ■
- Online practice, Chapter 2 (go.hrw.com, Keyword: EXP1A CH2) ▲ ● ■

Assessment Options

- *Assessment Program*: **Prueba: Vocabulario 2**, pp. 27–28 ▲ ● ■
- Test Generator ▲ ● ■

▲ = Advanced Learners   ◆ = Slower Pace Learners   ● = Special Learning Needs   ■ = Heritage Speakers

¡A conocernos!

DAY 18 50-MINUTE LESSON PLAN

NATIONAL STANDARDS

Gramática en acción 2

Communication 1.2: Student demonstrates understanding of simple, clearly spoken, and written language such as simple stories, high-frequency commands, and brief instructions when dealing with familiar topics.

Communication 1.3: Student presents information using familiar words, phrases, and sentences to listeners and readers.

CORE INSTRUCTION

Warm-Up

- (5 min.) Write ten vocabulary words on the board and have students provide the definite articles that accompany them.

Gramática en acción 2

- (10 min.) Show **GramaVisión** *(nouns and definite articles), Video Program* (Videocassette 1) or *DVD Tutor* (Disc 1).
- (15 min.) Review nouns and definite articles.
- (15 min.) Have students do Activities 32–33, pp. 68–69.

Wrap-Up

- (5 min.) Ask some students to read sentences from Activity 33 aloud.

OPTIONAL RESOURCES

- (25 min.) Have students practice with activities in the *Interactive Tutor,* Ch. 2.

Practice Options

- *Lab Book,* pp. 15–16 ▲ ● ■
- **Cuaderno de vocabulario y gramática**, pp. 22–24 ▲ ◆ ●
- **Cuaderno de actividades**, pp. 15–17 ▲ ● ■
- *Activities for Communication,* pp. 7–8, 57–58 ▲ ■
- *Teaching Transparencies*: **Vocabulario y gramática** Answers, pp. 22–24 ▲ ◆ ●
- *Video Guide,* pp. 14–15 ▲ ● ■
- *Grammar Tutor for Students of Spanish,* pp. 11–14, 169–170 ● ■
- *Interactive Tutor* (Disc 1) or *DVD Tutor* (Disc 1) ▲ ● ■
- Online practice, Chapter 2 (go.hrw.com, Keyword: EXP1A CH2) ▲ ● ■

▲ = Advanced Learners   ◆ = Slower Pace Learners   ● = Special Learning Needs   ■ = Heritage Speakers

CAPÍTULO

¡A conocernos!

2

DAY 19 50-MINUTE LESSON PLAN

NATIONAL STANDARDS

Gramática en acción 2

Communication 1.1: Student engages in oral and written exchanges of learned material to socialize and to provide and obtain information.

Communication 1.2: Student demonstrates understanding of simple, clearly spoken, and written language such as simple stories, high-frequency commands, and brief instructions when dealing with familiar topics.

Communication 1.3: Student presents information using familiar words, phrases, and sentences to listeners and readers.

Comparisons 4.1: Student demonstrates an understanding of the nature of language through comparisons of the student's own language and the language studied.

CORE INSTRUCTION

Warm-Up

- (10 min.) Have students do Bell Work 2.7, p. 70.

Gramática en acción 2

- (15 min.) Have students do Activities 34–35, pp. 69.
- (20 min.) Present **Gramática:** *The verb* **gustar,** **¿por qué?,** *and* **porque,** p. 70, using Teaching **Gramática,** p. 70.

Wrap-Up

- (5 min.) Present Common Error Alert, p. 71.

OPTIONAL RESOURCES

- (10 min.) Have students do Activity 35, p. 69.
- (10 min.) **Comunicación (TE),** p. 69

Practice Options

- *Lab Book,* pp. 15–16 ▲ ● ■
- *Cuaderno de vocabulario y gramática,* pp. 22–24 ▲ ◆ ●
- *Cuaderno de actividades,* pp. 15–17 ▲ ● ■
- *Activities for Communication,* pp. 7–8, 57–58 ▲ ■
- *Teaching Transparencies:* Bell Work 2.7; *Vocabulario y gramática* Answers, pp. 22–24 ▲ ◆ ●
- *Video Guide,* pp. 14–15 ▲ ● ■
- *Grammar Tutor for Students of Spanish,* pp. 11–14, 169–170 ◆ ●
- *Interactive Tutor* (Disc 1) or *DVD Tutor* (Disc 1) ▲ ● ■
- Online practice, Chapter 2 (go.hrw.com, Keyword: EXP1A CH2) ▲ ● ■

▲ = Advanced Learners   ◆ = Slower Pace Learners   ● = Special Learning Needs   ■ = Heritage Speakers

¡A conocernos!

DAY 20 50-MINUTE LESSON PLAN

NATIONAL STANDARDS

Gramática en acción 2

Communication 1.1: Student engages in oral and written exchanges of learned material to socialize and to provide and obtain information.

Communication 1.2: Student demonstrates understanding of simple, clearly spoken, and written language such as simple stories, high-frequency commands, and brief instructions when dealing with familiar topics.

Communication 1.3: Student presents information using familiar words, phrases, and sentences to listeners and readers.

Cultures 2.1: Student demonstrates an understanding of the practices (what people do) and how they are related to the perspectives (how people perceive things) of the cultures studied.

CORE INSTRUCTION

Warm-Up

- (5 min.) Have students share answers from Activity 34, p. 69.

Gramática en acción 2

- (10 min.) Show **GramaVisión (gustar, por qué?** *and* **porque),** *Video Program* (Videocassette 1) or *DVD Tutor* (Disc 1).
- (10 min.) Review **gustar, ¿por qué?,** and **porque.**
- (5 min.) Play Audio CD 2, Tr. 7, for Activity 36, p. 70. ●
- (15 min.) Have students do Activities 37–38, p. 71.

Wrap-Up

- (5 min.) Present information in Practices and Perspectives, p. 71.

OPTIONAL RESOURCES

- (5 min.) See Common Error Alert, p. 71.

Practice Options

- *Lab Book*, pp. 15–16 ▲ ● ■
- *Cuaderno de vocabulario y gramática*, pp. 22–24 ▲ ◆ ●
- *Cuaderno de actividades*, pp. 15–17 ▲ ● ■
- *Activities for Communication*, pp. 7–8, 57–58 ▲ ■
- *Teaching Transparencies*: *Vocabulario y gramática* Answers, pp. 22–24 ▲ ◆ ●
- *Video Guide*, pp. 14–15 ▲ ● ■
- *Grammar Tutor for Students of Spanish*, pp. 11–14, 169–170 ▲ ●
- *Interactive Tutor* (Disc 1) or *DVD Tutor* (Disc 1) ▲ ● ■
- Online practice, Chapter 2 (go.hrw.com, Keyword: EXP1A CH2) ▲ ● ■

▲ = Advanced Learners   ◆ = Slower Pace Learners   ● = Special Learning Needs   ■ = Heritage Speakers

Holt Spanish 1A

Lesson Planner

CAPÍTULO

2

¡A conocernos!

DAY 21 50-MINUTE LESSON PLAN

NATIONAL STANDARDS

Gramática en acción 2

Communication 1.1: Student engages in oral and written exchanges of learned material to socialize and to provide and obtain information.

Communication 1.2: Student demonstrates understanding of simple, clearly spoken, and written language such as simple stories, high-frequency commands, and brief instructions when dealing with familiar topics.

Communication 1.3: Student presents information using familiar words, phrases, and sentences to listeners and readers.

CORE INSTRUCTION

Warm-Up
- (5 min.) Have students do Bell Work 2.8, p. 72.

Gramática en acción 2
- (15 min.) Have students do Activity 39, p. 71.
- (15 min.) Present **Gramática:** *The preposition* **de,** p. 72, using Teaching **Gramática,** p. 72.
- (5 min.) Have students do Activity 40, p. 72.

Wrap-Up
- (10 min.) Have students do the first part of **Comunicación (TE)**, p. 73. ▲

OPTIONAL RESOURCES
- (5 min.) See Special Learning Needs, p. 71. ●
- (5 min.) See Special Learning Needs, p. 73. ●
- (10 min.) Special Learning Needs, p. 71 ●
- (10 min.) **Comunicación (TE)**, p. 71

Practice Options
- *Lab Book*, pp. 15–16 ▲ ● ■
- *Cuaderno de vocabulario y gramática*, pp. 22–24 ▲ ◆ ●
- *Cuaderno de actividades*, pp. 15–17 ▲ ● ■
- *Activities for Communication*, pp. 7–8, 57–58 ▲ ■
- *Teaching Transparencies*: Bell Work 2.8; *Vocabulario y gramática* Answers, pp. 22–24 ▲ ◆ ●
- *Video Guide*, pp. 14–15 ▲ ● ■
- *Grammar Tutor for Students of Spanish*, pp. 11–14, 169–170 ● ■
- *Interactive Tutor* (Disc 1) or *DVD Tutor* (Disc 1) ▲ ● ■
- Online practice, Chapter 2 (go.hrw.com, Keyword: EXP1A CH2) ▲ ● ■

▲ = Advanced Learners   ◆ = Slower Pace Learners   ● = Special Learning Needs   ■ = Heritage Speakers

51

¡A conocernos!

DAY 22 50-MINUTE LESSON PLAN

NATIONAL STANDARDS

Gramática en acción 2

Communication 1.1: Student engages in oral and written exchanges of learned material to socialize and to provide and obtain information.

Communication 1.2: Student demonstrates understanding of simple, clearly spoken, and written language such as simple stories, high-frequency commands, and brief instructions when dealing with familiar topics.

Communication 1.3: Student presents information using familiar words, phrases, and sentences to listeners and readers.

CORE INSTRUCTION

Warm-Up

- (5 min.) Have students complete the activity in **Comunicación (TE)**, p.73.

Gramática en acción 2

- (5 min.) Show **GramaVisión** (*the preposition de*), *Video Program* (Videocassette 1) or *DVD Tutor* (Disc 1).
- (5 min.) Have students do Activity 41, p. 73.
- (10 min.) Play Audio CD 2, Tr. 8, for Activity 42, p. 73. ●
- (10 min.) Have students do Activity 43, p. 73.
- (10 min.) Review **Gramática 2,** pp. 68–73.

Wrap-Up

- (5 min.) Share and check answers to Activity 41, p. 73. Remind students to study for **Prueba: Gramática 2.**

OPTIONAL RESOURCES

- (15 min.) See Slower Pace Learners, p. 73. ◆
- (10 min.) Have students do Activity 43, p. 73.
- (5 min.) See AP Language Examination, p. 73.

Practice Options

- *Lab Book*, pp. 15–16 ▲ ● ■
- *Cuaderno de vocabulario y gramática*, pp. 22–24 ▲ ◆ ●
- *Cuaderno de actividades*, pp. 15–17 ▲ ● ■
- *Activities for Communication*, pp. 7–8, 57–58 ▲ ■
- *Teaching Transparencies*: *Vocabulario y gramática* Answers, pp. 22–24 ▲ ◆ ●
- *Video Guide*, pp. 14–15 ▲ ● ■
- *Grammar Tutor for Students of Spanish*, pp. 11–14, 169–170 ◆ ●
- *Interactive Tutor* (Disc 1) or *DVD Tutor* (Disc 1) ▲ ● ■
- Online practice, Chapter 2 (go.hrw.com, Keyword: EXP1A CH2) ▲ ● ■

▲ = Advanced Learners   ◆ = Slower Pace Learners   ● = Special Learning Needs   ■ = Heritage Speakers

Holt Spanish 1A

Lesson Planner

CAPÍTULO
2

¡A conocernos!

DAY 23 50-MINUTE LESSON PLAN

NATIONAL STANDARDS

Gramática en acción 2

Communication 1.1: Student engages in oral and written exchanges of learned material to socialize and to provide and obtain information.

Communication 1.2: Student demonstrates understanding of simple, clearly spoken, and written language such as simple stories, high-frequency commands, and brief instructions when dealing with familiar topics.

Communication 1.3: Student presents information using familiar words, phrases, and sentences to listeners and readers.

Conexiones culturales

Connections 3.2: Student uses resources (that may include technology) in the language and cultures being studied to gain access to information.

Connections 3.1: Student uses the language to obtain, reinforce, or expand knowledge of other subject areas.

CORE INSTRUCTION

Warm-Up
• (5 min.) Have students do Bell Work 2.6, p. 68.

Gramática en acción 2
• (10 min.) Review **Gramática 2,** pp. 68–73.

Assessment
• (20 min.) Give **Prueba: Gramática 2.**

Conexiones culturales
• (10 min.) Present **Conexiones culturales,** p. 74, using Teaching **Conexiones culturales,** #s 1–2, p. 74.

Wrap-Up
• (5 min.) Remind students of the countries where Spanish is spoken by pointing them out on a map and having students repeat the name of each one.

OPTIONAL RESOURCES
• (10 min.) **Más práctica,** p. 75.

Practice Options
• *Lab Book,* pp. 15–16 ▲ ● ■
• ***Cuaderno de vocabulario y gramática,*** pp. 22–24 ▲ ◆ ●
• ***Cuaderno de actividades,*** pp. 15–17 ▲ ● ■
• *Activities for Communication,* pp. 7–8, 57–58 ▲ ■
• *Teaching Transparencies:* ***Vocabulario y gramática*** Answers, pp. 22–24 ▲ ◆ ●
• *Video Guide,* pp. 14–15 ▲ ● ■
• *Grammar Tutor for Students of Spanish,* pp. 11–14, 169–170 ◆ ●

• *Interactive Tutor* (Disc 1) or *DVD Tutor* (Disc 1) ▲ ● ■
• Online practice, Chapter 2 (go.hrw.com, Keyword: EXP1A CH2) ▲ ● ■

Assessment Options
• *Assessment Program*: **Prueba: Gramática 2,** pp. 29–30 ▲ ● ■
• *Assessment Program*: **Prueba: Aplicación 2,** pp. 31–32, 38 ▲ ● ■
• *Audio CD 2,* Tr. 16 ●
• Test Generator ▲ ● ■

▲ = Advanced Learners   ◆ = Slower Pace Learners   ● = Special Learning Needs   ■ = Heritage Speakers

(53)

¡A conocernos!

DAY 24 50-MINUTE LESSON PLAN

NATIONAL STANDARDS

Conexiones culturales
Communication 1.1: Student engages in oral and written exchanges of learned material to socialize and to provide and obtain information.

Connections 3.2: Student uses resources (that may include technology) in the language and cultures being studied to gain access to information.

Connections 3.1: Student uses the language to obtain, reinforce, or expand knowledge of other subject areas.

Novela en video
Communication 1.2: Student demonstrates understanding of simple, clearly spoken, and written language such as simple stories, high-frequency commands, and brief instructions when dealing with familiar topics.

Connections 3.2: Student uses resources (that may include technology) in the language and cultures being studied to gain access to information.

CORE INSTRUCTION

Warm-Up
- (5 min.) Have students find Bolivia, Guatemala, the Dominican Republic, and Spain on the maps on pages R2–R6.

Conexiones culturales
- (30 min.) Present **Conexiones culturales,** p. 74–75, using Teaching **Conexiones culturales,** #s 3–5, p. 74.

Novela en video
- (10 min.) Present **Novela en video,** using Teaching **Novela en video,** #s 1–2, p. 76.

Wrap-Up
- (5 min.) Have students do the activity described in Visual Learners, p. 76.

OPTIONAL RESOURCES
- (20 min.) See Slower Pace Learners, p. 75. ◆
- (30 min.) See Multiple Intelligences, p. 75. ●
- (20 min.) Multiple Intelligences, p. 75 ●
- (20 min.) Culminating Project. p. 78.

Practice Options
- *Lab Book,* p. 41 ▲ ● ■
- *Video Guide,* pp. 14–15, 19 ▲ ● ■
- *Interactive Tutor* (Disc 1) or *DVD Tutor* (Disc 1) ▲ ● ■
- Online practice, Chapter 2 (go.hrw.com, Keyword: EXP1A CH2) ▲ ● ■

▲ = Advanced Learners   ◆ = Slower Pace Learners   ● = Special Learning Needs   ■ = Heritage Speakers

54

¡A conocernos!

DAY 25 50-MINUTE LESSON PLAN

NATIONAL STANDARDS

Novela en video

Communication 1.2: Student demonstrates understanding of simple, clearly spoken, and written language such as simple stories, high-frequency commands, and brief instructions when dealing with familiar topics.

Communication 1.3: Student presents information using familiar words, phrases, and sentences to listeners and readers.

Cultures 2.1: Student demonstrates an understanding of the practices (what people do) and how they are related to the perspectives (how people perceive things) of the cultures studied.

Comparisons 4.2: Student demonstrates an understanding of the concept of culture through comparisons of the student's own culture and the cultures studied.

Leamos y escribamos

Communication 1.2: Student demonstrates understanding of simple, clearly spoken, and written language such as simple stories, high-frequency commands, and brief instructions when dealing with familiar topics.

Communication 1.3: Student presents information using familiar words, phrases, and sentences to listeners and readers.

CORE INSTRUCTION

Warm-Up
- (10 min.) Have students do Activities 1–2, p. 79.

Novela en video
- (15 min.) Present **Novela en video,** pp. 76–79, using Teaching **Novela en video,** #s 3–4, p. 76.
- (5 min.) Discuss Gestures, p. 78, and Language Note, p. 77.

Leamos y escribamos
- (15 min.) Present **Leamos,** p. 80, using Teaching **Leamos,** #s 1–3, p. 80.

Wrap-Up
- (5 min.) See Applying the Strategies, p. 80.

OPTIONAL RESOURCES
- (10 min.) Play Audio CD 2, Tr. 9, for Activity A, p. 80. ●
- (10 min.) See Multiple Intelligences, p. 81. ●

Practice Options
- *Lab Book*, p. 41 ▲ ● ■
- *Video Guide*, pp. 14–15, 19, 103–109 ▲ ● ■
- ***Cuaderno de actividades***, p. 18 ▲ ● ■
- *Student Edition*, **Literatura y variedades**, pp. 230–231 ▲ ● ■
- *Reading Strategies and Skills Handbook*, pp. xi–xii, 66, 22–25 ▲ ● ■
- ***¡Lee conmigo!*** Level 1 Reader ▲ ■
- *Interactive Tutor* (Disc 1) or *DVD Tutor* (Disc 1) ▲ ● ■
- Online practice, Chapter 2 (go.hrw.com, Keyword: EXP1A CH2) ▲ ● ■

▲ = Advanced Learners   ◆ = Slower Pace Learners   ● = Special Learning Needs   ■ = Heritage Speakers

CAPÍTULO
2

¡A conocernos!

DAY 26 50-MINUTE LESSON PLAN

NATIONAL STANDARDS

Leamos y escribamos

Communication 1.2: Student demonstrates understanding of simple, clearly spoken, and written language such as simple stories, high-frequency commands, and brief instructions when dealing with familiar topics.

Communication 1.3: Student presents information using familiar words, phrases, and sentences to listeners and readers.

Connections 3.2: Student uses resources (that may include technology) in the language and cultures being studied to gain access to information.

CORE INSTRUCTION

Warm-Up

- (10 min.) Have students reread **Leamos,** p. 80.

Leamos y escribamos

- (15 min.) Present the remainder of **Leamos,** using Teaching **Leamos,** #4, p. 80.
- (20 min.) Present **Taller del escritor,** p. 81, using Teaching **Escribamos,** p. 80.

Wrap-Up

- (5 min.) Review with students the rubric you intend to use to evaluate the **Taller del escritor** assignment. See Writing Assignment, p. 81.

OPTIONAL RESOURCES

- (10 min.) See Advanced Learners, p. 81. ▲
- (25 min.) See Additional Reading, pp. 230–231.

Practice Options

- *Cuaderno de actividades*, p. 18 ▲ ● ■
- *Student Edition,* **Literatura** *y variedades*, pp. 230–231 ▲ ● ■
- *Reading Strategies and Skills Handbook,* pp. xi–xii, 66, 22–25 ▲ ● ■
- *¡Lee conmigo!* Level 1 Reader ▲ ■
- *Interactive Tutor* (Disc 1) or *DVD Tutor* (Disc 1) ▲ ● ■
- Online practice, Chapter 2 (go.hrw.com, Keyword: EXP1A CH2) ▲ ● ■

Assessment Options

- *Assessment Program,* **Prueba: Lectura,** pp. 33, 39 ▲ ● ■
- *Assessment Program,* **Prueba: Escritura,** pp. 34, 39 ▲ ● ■

▲ = Advanced Learners ◆ = Slower Pace Learners ● = Special Learning Needs ■ = Heritage Speakers

Holt Spanish 1A

Lesson Planner

¡A conocernos!

NATIONAL STANDARDS

Repaso

Communication 1.1: Student engages in oral and written exchanges of learned material to socialize and to provide and obtain information.

Communication 1.2: Student demonstrates understanding of simple, clearly spoken, and written language such as simple stories, high-frequency commands, and brief instructions when dealing with familiar topics.

Communication 1.3: Student presents information using familiar words, phrases, and sentences to listeners and readers.

CORE INSTRUCTION

Warm-Up

- (5 min.) Ask students the following questions: **¿Qué día es hoy? / ¿Cuándo es tu cumpleaños?**

Repaso

Review

- (25 min.) Have students do Activities 1–4 of **Repaso,** pp. 82–83.
- (15 min.) Play Game, p. 83. ●

Wrap-Up

- (5 min.) Present the activity described in Fold-N-Learn, p. 82. Suggest to students that they use the activity to review for the Chapter Test.

OPTIONAL RESOURCES

- (15 min.) See Teacher to Teacher, p. 82.

Practice Options

- *Lab Book,* pp. 15–16, 42 ▲ ● ■
- *Activities for Communication,* pp. 44, 55–57 ▲ ■
- *Teaching Transparencies:* Situation; Picture Sequences ▲ ● ■
- *Video Guide,* pp. 14–15, 20 ▲ ● ■
- *TPR Storytelling Book,* pp. 10–11 ▲ ●
- *Interactive Tutor* (Disc 1) or *DVD Tutor* (Disc 1) ▲ ● ■
- Online practice, Chapter 2 (go.hrw.com, Keyword: EXP1A CH2) ▲ ● ■

▲ = Advanced Learners   ◆ = Slower Pace Learners   ● = Special Learning Needs   ■ = Heritage Speakers

¡A conocernos!

DAY 28 50-MINUTE LESSON PLAN

NATIONAL STANDARDS

Repaso

Communication 1.2: Student demonstrates understanding of simple, clearly spoken, and written language such as simple stories, high-frequency commands, and brief instructions when dealing with familiar topics.

Communication 1.3: Student presents information using familiar words, phrases, and sentences to listeners and readers.

Communities 5.1: Student uses the language both within and beyond the school setting through activities such as participating in cultural events and using technology to communicate.

CORE INSTRUCTION

Warm-Up
- (5 min.) Review the answers to Activity 4, p. 83.

Repaso
- (10 min.) Have students do Activity 5, p. 83.
- (10 min.) Play Audio CD 2, Tr. 11, for Activity 6, p. 83. ●
- (15 min.) Have students do Activity 7, p. 83.
- (5 min.) Play Audio CD 2, Tr. 12, 13, 14, for **Letra y sonido,** p. 84. ●

Wrap-Up
- (5 min.) Read aloud from AP Language Examination, p. 83, as students look at the pictures for Activity 7, p. 83.

OPTIONAL RESOURCES
- (15 min.) See Language Arts Link, p. 85.

Practice Options
- *Lab Book,* pp. 15–16, 42 ▲ ● ■
- *Activities for Communication,* pp. 44, 55–57 ▲ ■
- *Teaching Transparencies:* Situation; Picture Sequences ▲ ● ■
- *Video Guide,* pp. 14–15, 20 ▲ ● ■
- *TPR Storytelling Book,* pp. 10–11 ▲ ●
- *Interactive Tutor* (Disc 1) or *DVD Tutor* (Disc 1) ▲ ● ■
- Online practice, Chapter 2 (go.hrw.com, Keyword: EXP1A CH2) ▲ ● ■

▲ = Advanced Learners   ◆ = Slower Pace Learners   ● = Special Learning Needs   ■ = Heritage Speakers

Holt Spanish 1A

Lesson Planner

¡A conocernos!

DAY 29 50-MINUTE LESSON PLAN

NATIONAL STANDARDS

Integración
Communication 1.1: Student engages in oral and written exchanges of learned material to socialize and to provide and obtain information.

Communication 1.2: Student demonstrates understanding of simple, clearly spoken, and written language such as simple stories, high-frequency commands, and brief instructions when dealing with familiar topics.

Communication 1.3: Student presents information using familiar words, phrases, and sentences to listeners and readers.

CORE INSTRUCTION

Warm-Up
- (5 min.) Have students look at the photos for Activity 1, p. 86, and think of some Spanish phrases or sentences that describe each one.

Integración
- (10 min.) Play Audio CD 2, Tr. 17, for Activity 1, p. 86. ●
- (30 min.) Have students do Activities 2–4, pp. 86–87.

Wrap-Up
- (5 min.) Point out the review material in the side columns of pp. 82–83 and 84–85. Remind students this material will help them study for the Chapter Test.

OPTIONAL RESOURCES
- (15 min.) See **Más práctica**, p. 86.
- (35 min.) See Culture Project, p. 86.
- (45 min.) See Fine Art Connection, p. 87.

Practice Options
- *Lab Book*, pp. 15–16 ▲ ● ■
- *Cuaderno de actividades*, pp. 19–20, 54–55 ▲ ● ■
- *Teaching Transparencies*: Fine Art, Chapter 2 ▲ ● ■
- Online practice, Chapter 2 (go.hrw.com, Keyword: EXP1A CH2) ▲ ● ■

▲ = Advanced Learners ◆ = Slower Pace Learners ● = Special Learning Needs ■ = Heritage Speakers

Holt Spanish 1A

Lesson Planner

CAPÍTULO
2

¡A conocernos!

DAY 30 50-MINUTE LESSON PLAN

CORE INSTRUCTION

Assessment
- (50 min.) Give the Chapter 2 Test.

OPTIONAL RESOURCES
- You may also choose from the other modes of assessment listed in the Assessment Options box below.

Assessment Options
- *Assessment Program:* **Examen, Capítulo 2,** pp. 117–127 ▲ ● ■
- *Assessment Program:* **Examen oral,** p. 128 ▲ ● ■
- *Assessment Program:* Alternative Assessment, pp. 213, 219, 226 ▲ ● ■
- *Audio CD 2,* Tr. 18–19 ●
- Test Generator ▲ ● ■

▲ = Advanced Learners   ◆ = Slower Pace Learners   ● = Special Learning Needs   ■ = Heritage Speakers

Holt Spanish 1A

Lesson Planner

CAPÍTULO
3

¿Qué te gusta hacer?

DAY 1 50-MINUTE LESSON PLAN

NATIONAL STANDARDS

Chapter Opener

Communication 1.2: Student demonstrates understanding of simple, clearly spoken, and written language such as simple stories, high-frequency commands, and brief instructions when dealing with familiar topics.

Communication 1.3: Student presents information using familiar words, phrases, and sentences to listeners and readers.

Vocabulario en acción 1

Communication 1.3: Student presents information using familiar words, phrases, and sentences to listeners and readers.

Comparisons 4.3: Student demonstrates an understanding of the influence of one language and culture on another.

Before starting **Capítulo 3,** you may wish to teach **Geocultura: Texas,** pp. 88–91. For teaching suggestions, see pp. xv–xvi of this *Lesson Planner.*

CORE INSTRUCTION

Warm-Up

- (5 min.) See Learning and Pacing Tips, p. 93.

Chapter Opener

- (5 min.) Present information from Using the Photo and **Más vocabulario,** p. 92.
- (5 min.) Present **Objetivos,** p. 92.

Vocabulario en acción 1

- (25 min.) Present **Vocabulario 1,** pp. 94–95, using Teaching **Vocabulario,** p. 94.

Wrap-Up

- (10 min.) Have students do the activity described in Advanced Learners, p. 95. ▲

OPTIONAL RESOURCES

- (5 min.) See Language Note, p. 95.
- (5 min.) See Special Learning Needs, p. 95. ●

Practice Options

- *Lab Book,* pp. 3, 17–18, 43, 44 ▲ ● ■
- ***Cuaderno de vocabulario y gramática,*** pp. 25–27 ▲ ◆ ●
- ***Cuaderno para hispanohablantes,*** pp. 21–30, 31 ■
- *Teaching Transparencies:* Map 6; **Vocabulario** 3.1, 3.2; Situation; ***Vocabulario y gramática*** Answers, pp. 25–27 ▲ ● ■
- *Video Guide,* pp. 21–22, 24–25, 26 ▲ ● ■
- *TPR Storytelling Book,* pp. 12–13 ▲ ●
- Online practice, Chapter 3 (go.hrw.com, Keyword: EXP1A CH3) ▲ ● ■

▲ = Advanced Learners   ◆ = Slower Pace Learners   ● = Special Learning Needs   ■ = Heritage Speakers

¿Qué te gusta hacer?

DAY 2 50-MINUTE LESSON PLAN

NATIONAL STANDARDS

Vocabulario en acción 1

Communication 1.2: Student demonstrates understanding of simple, clearly spoken, and written language such as simple stories, high-frequency commands, and brief instructions when dealing with familiar topics.

CORE INSTRUCTION

Warm-Up
- (5 min.) Have students do Bell Work 3.1, p. 94.

Vocabulario en acción 1
- (10 min.) Show **ExpresaVisión,** Ch. 3.
- (10 min.) Review **Vocabulario 1** and **¡Exprésate!,** pp. 94–95.
- (5 min.) Present **Nota cultural,** p. 96.
- (10 min.) Play Audio CD 3, Tr. 1, for Activity 1, p. 96. ●

Wrap-Up
- (10 min.) Have students do the Fold-N-Learn activity, p. 96. ●

OPTIONAL RESOURCES
- (15 min.) See TPR, p. 95.
- (5 min.) Special Learning Needs, p. 95 ●
- (5 min.) Language Note, p. 95

Practice Options
- *Lab Book,* pp. 17–18, 44 ▲ ● ■
- *Cuaderno de vocabulario y gramática,* pp. 25–27 ▲ ◆ ●
- *Teaching Transparencies:* Bell Work 3.1; **Vocabulario** 3.1, 3.2; *Vocabulario y gramática* Answers, pp. 25–27 ▲ ◆ ●
- *Video Guide,* pp. 24–25, 26 ▲ ● ■
- *Interactive Tutor* (Disc 1) or *DVD Tutor* (Disc 1) ▲ ● ■
- Online practice, Chapter 3 (go.hrw.com, Keyword: EXP1A CH3) ▲ ● ■

▲ = Advanced Learners   ◆ = Slower Pace Learners   ● = Special Learning Needs   ■ = Heritage Speakers

¡Empecemos!

DAY 3 50-MINUTE LESSON PLAN

NATIONAL STANDARDS

Vocabulario en acción 1

Communication 1.1: Student engages in oral and written exchanges of learned material to socialize and to provide and obtain information.

Communication 1.2: Student demonstrates understanding of simple, clearly spoken, and written language such as simple stories, high-frequency commands, and brief instructions when dealing with familiar topics.

Communication 1.3: Student presents information using familiar words, phrases, and sentences to listeners and readers.

CORE INSTRUCTION

Warm-Up
- (5 min.) Review **Vocabulario 1.**

Vocabulario en acción 1
- (25 min.) Have students do Activities 2–5, pp. 96–97.
- (10 min.) Present **¡Exprésate!,** p. 98, using Teaching **¡Exprésate!,** p. 98.

Wrap-Up
- (10 min.) Have students do Activity 5, p. 97.

OPTIONAL RESOURCES
- (5 min.) See Language Note, p. 97.
- (5 min.) See Slower Pace Learners, p. 97. ◆
- (25 min.) See Multiple Intelligences, p. 97. ●
- (10 min.) See Slower Learners, p. 97 ◆

Practice Options
- *Lab Book,* pp. 17–18, 44 ▲ ● ■
- *Cuaderno de vocabulario y gramática,* pp. 25–27 ▲ ◆ ●
- *Teaching Transparencies:* **Vocabulario** 3.1, 3.2; *Vocabulario y gramática* Answers, pp. 25–27 ▲ ◆ ●
- *Video Guide,* pp. 24–25, 26 ▲ ● ■
- *Interactive Tutor* (Disc 1) or *DVD Tutor* (Disc 1) ▲ ● ■
- Online practice, Chapter 3 (go.hrw.com, Keyword: EXP1A CH3) ▲ ● ■

▲ = Advanced Learners   ◆ = Slower Pace Learners   ● = Special Learning Needs   ■ = Heritage Speakers

Lesson Planner

¿Qué te gusta hacer?

DAY 4 50-MINUTE LESSON PLAN

NATIONAL STANDARDS

Vocabulario en acción 1

Communication 1.1: Student engages in oral and written exchanges of learned material to socialize and to provide and obtain information.

Communication 1.2: Student demonstrates understanding of simple, clearly spoken, and written language such as simple stories, high-frequency commands, and brief instructions when dealing with familiar topics.

CORE INSTRUCTION

Warm-Up
- (5 min.) Have students practice phrases from **¡Exprésate!,** p. 98, aloud with a partner.

Vocabulario en acción 1
- (5 min.) Have students do Bell Work 3.2, p. 100.
- (10 min.) Review **¡Exprésate!,** p. 98.
- (25 min.) Have students do Activities 6–9, pp. 98–99.

Wrap-Up
- (5 min.) Have students do the activity described in **Más práctica,** p. 99. Then remind the class to study for **Prueba: Vocabulario 1.**

OPTIONAL RESOURCES
- (5 min.) See Common Error Alert, p. 99.
- (5 min.) See **Comunicación (TE)**, p. 99.

Practice Options
- *Lab Book*, pp. 17–18, 44 ▲ ● ■
- *Cuaderno de vocabulario y gramática*, pp. 25–27 ▲ ◆ ●
- *Teaching Transparencies:* Bell Work 3.2; **Vocabulario** 3.1, 3.2; *Vocabulario y gramática* Answers, pp. 25–27 ▲ ◆ ●
- *Video Guide*, pp. 24–25, 26 ▲ ● ■
- *Interactive Tutor* (Disc 1) or *DVD Tutor* (Disc 1) ▲ ● ■
- Online practice, Chapter 3 (go.hrw.com, Keyword: EXP1A CH3) ▲ ● ■

▲ = Advanced Learners   ◆ = Slower Pace Learners   ● = Special Learning Needs   ■ = Heritage Speakers

¿Qué te gusta hacer?

DAY 5 50-MINUTE LESSON PLAN

NATIONAL STANDARDS

Vocabulario en acción 1

Communication 1.1: Student engages in oral and written exchanges of learned material to socialize and to provide and obtain information.

Communication 1.2: Student demonstrates understanding of simple, clearly spoken, and written language such as simple stories, high-frequency commands, and brief instructions when dealing with familiar topics.

Communication 1.3: Student presents information using familiar words, phrases, and sentences to listeners and readers.

CORE INSTRUCTION

Warm-Up

- (10 min.) Have students create a calendar for themselves for the week. They should list the days by their names in Spanish and an activity that they'll be doing every day.

Vocabulario en acción 1

- (15 min.) Review **Vocabulario 1,** pp. 94–99.

Assessment

- (20 min.) Give **Prueba: Vocabulario 1.**

Wrap-Up

- (5 min.) Have students do Bell Work 3.2, p. 100.

OPTIONAL RESOURCES

- (5 min.) See Advanced Learners, p. 99. ▲
- (5 min.) See Special Learning Needs, p. 99. ●
- You can find alternative quizzes in the Assessment Options listed below.

Practice Options

- *Lab Book*, pp. 17–18, 44 ▲ ● ■
- *Cuaderno de vocabulario y gramática*, pp. 25–27 ▲ ◆ ●
- *Teaching Transparencies:* **Vocabulario** 3.1, 3.2; *Vocabulario y gramática* Answers, pp. 25–27 ▲ ◆ ●
- *Video Guide*, pp. 24–25, 26 ▲ ● ■
- *Interactive Tutor* (Disc 1) or *DVD Tutor* (Disc 1) ▲ ● ■
- Online practice, Chapter 3 (go.hrw.com, Keyword: EXP1A CH3) ▲ ● ■

Assessment Options

- *Assessment Program*: **Prueba, Vocabulario 1,** pp. 41–42 ▲ ● ■
- Test Generator ▲ ● ■

▲ = Advanced Learners   ◆ = Slower Pace Learners   ● = Special Learning Needs   ■ = Heritage Speakers

¿Qué te gusta hacer?

DAY 6 50-MINUTE LESSON PLAN

NATIONAL STANDARDS

Gramática en acción 1
Communication 1.1: Student engages in oral and written exchanges of learned material to socialize and to provide and obtain information.

Communication 1.2: Student demonstrates understanding of simple, clearly spoken, and written language such as simple stories, high-frequency commands, and brief instructions when dealing with familiar topics.

CORE INSTRUCTION

Warm-Up
- (5 min.) Ask a few students **¿Te gusta... ?** questions to review using **gustar** with nouns.

Gramática en acción 1
- (15 min.) Present **Gramática: Gustar** *with infinitives,* p. 100, using Teaching **Gramática,** p. 100.
- (10 min.) Show **GramaVisión** (**gustar** *with infinitives*), *Video Program* (Videocassette 2) or *DVD Tutor* (Disc 1).
- (15 min.) Have students do Activities 10–11, pp. 100–101.

Wrap-Up
- (5 min.) Have students share answers to Activity 11, p. 101.

OPTIONAL RESOURCES
- (15 min.) See Teacher to Teacher, p. 101.

Practice Options
- *Lab Book,* pp. 17–18 ▲ ● ■
- *Cuaderno de vocabulario y gramática,* pp. 28–30 ▲ ◆ ●
- *Cuaderno de actividades,* pp. 21–23 ▲ ● ■
- *Activities for Communication,* pp. 9–10, 59–60 ▲ ■
- *Teaching Transparencies: Vocabulario y gramática* Answers, pp. 28–30 ▲ ● ■
- *Video Guide,* pp. 24–25 ▲ ◆ ●
- *Grammar Tutor for Students of Spanish,* pp. 15–18, 170–171 ◆ ●
- *TPR Storytelling Book,* pp. 12–13 ▲ ● ■
- *Interactive Tutor* (Disc 1) or *DVD Tutor* (Disc 1) ▲ ● ■
- Online practice, Chapter 3 (go.hrw.com, Keyword: EXP1A CH3) ▲ ● ■

▲ = Advanced Learners   ◆ = Slower Pace Learners   ● = Special Learning Needs   ■ = Heritage Speakers

¿Qué te gusta hacer?

DAY 7 50-MINUTE LESSON PLAN

NATIONAL STANDARDS

Gramática en acción 1

Communication 1.1: Student engages in oral and written exchanges of learned material to socialize and to provide and obtain information.

Communication 1.2: Student demonstrates understanding of simple, clearly spoken, and written language such as simple stories, high-frequency commands, and brief instructions when dealing with familiar topics.

Communication 1.3: Student presents information using familiar words, phrases, and sentences to listeners and readers.

CORE INSTRUCTION

Warm-Up
- (5 min.) Have students do Bell Work 3.3, p. 102.

Gramática en acción 1
- (15 min.) Have students do Activities 12–13, p. 101.
- (20 min.) Present **Gramática:** *Pronouns after prepositions*, p. 102, using Teaching **Gramática,** p. 102.

Wrap-Up
- (10 min.) Have students do the activity described in Advanced Learners, p. 101. ▲

OPTIONAL RESOURCES
- (5 min.) See Special Learning Needs, p. 101. ●
- (10 min.) See Multiple Intelligences, p. 103. ●
- (10 min.) **Comunicación**, p. 101

Practice Options
- *Lab Book*, pp. 17–18 ▲ ● ■
- *Cuaderno de vocabulario y gramática*, pp. 28–30 ▲ ◆ ●
- *Cuaderno de actividades*, pp. 21–23 ▲ ● ■
- *Activities for Communication*, pp. 9–10, 59–60 ▲ ■
- *Teaching Transparencies:* Bell Work 3.3; *Vocabulario y gramática* Answers, pp. 28–30 ▲ ◆ ●
- *Video Guide*, pp. 24–25 ▲ ● ■
- *Grammar Tutor for Students of Spanish*, pp. 15–18, 170–171 ● ■
- *TPR Storytelling Book*, pp. 12–13 ▲ ● ■
- *Interactive Tutor* (Disc 1) or *DVD Tutor* (Disc 1) ▲ ● ■
- Online practice, Chapter 3 (go.hrw.com, Keyword: EXP1A CH3) ▲ ● ■

▲ = Advanced Learners   ◆ = Slower Pace Learners   ● = Special Learning Needs   ■ = Heritage Speakers

Holt Spanish 1A

Lesson Planner

¿Qué te gusta hacer?

CAPÍTULO 3

DAY 8 50-MINUTE LESSON PLAN

NATIONAL STANDARDS

Gramática en acción 1

Communication 1.2: Student demonstrates understanding of simple, clearly spoken, and written language such as simple stories, high-frequency commands, and brief instructions when dealing with familiar topics.

CORE INSTRUCTION

Warm-Up
- (5 min.) Have students do Bell Work 3.4, p. 104.

Gramática en acción 1
- (10 min.) Show **GramaVisión** (*pronouns after prepositions*), *Video Program* (Videocassette 3) or *DVD Tutor* (Disc 1).
- (30 min.) Have students do Activities 14–17, pp. 102–103.

Wrap-Up
- (5 min.) Have students get in small groups and read the letter from Activity 14 aloud.

OPTIONAL RESOURCES
- (5 min.) See Slower Pace Learners, p. 103. ◆
- (5 min.) See Heritage Speakers, p. 103. ■
- (15 min.) See **Comunicación** (TE), p. 103.

Practice Options
- *Lab Book*, pp. 17–18 ▲ ● ■
- ***Cuaderno de vocabulario y gramática***, pp. 28–30 ▲ ◆ ●
- ***Cuaderno de actividades***, pp. 21–23 ▲ ● ■
- *Activities for Communication*, pp. 9–10, 59–60 ▲ ■
- *Teaching Transparencies:* Bell Work 3.4; ***Vocabulario y gramática*** Answers, pp. 28–30 ▲ ◆ ●
- *Video Guide*, pp. 24–25 ▲ ● ■
- *Grammar Tutor for Students of Spanish*, pp. 15–18, 170–171 ◆ ●
- *TPR Storytelling Book*, pp. 12–13 ▲ ●
- *Interactive Tutor* (Disc 1) or *DVD Tutor* (Disc 1) ▲ ● ■
- Online practice, Chapter 3 (go.hrw.com, Keyword: EXP1A CH3) ▲ ● ■

▲ = Advanced Learners   ◆ = Slower Pace Learners   ● = Special Learning Needs   ■ = Heritage Speakers

¿Qué te gusta hacer?

DAY 9 50-MINUTE LESSON PLAN

NATIONAL STANDARDS

Gramática en acción 1

Communication 1.1: Student engages in oral and written exchanges of learned material to socialize and to provide and obtain information.

Communication 1.2: Student demonstrates understanding of simple, clearly spoken, and written language such as simple stories, high-frequency commands, and brief instructions when dealing with familiar topics.

Cultures 2.1: Student demonstrates an understanding of the practices (what people do) and how they are related to the perspectives (how people perceive things) of the cultures studied.

Comparisons 4.2: Student demonstrates an understanding of the concept of culture through comparisons of the student's own culture and the cultures studied.

CORE INSTRUCTION

Warm-Up

- (5 min.) Have students review and practice introducing each other to an adult.

Gramática en acción 1

- (10 min.) Present **Gramática:** *Present tense of* **querer** *with infinitives,* p. 104, using Teaching **Gramática,** p. 104.
- (10 min.) Show **GramaVisión (querer** *with infinitives), Video Program* (Videocassette 2) or *DVD Tutor* (Disc 1).
- (10 min.) Have students do Activities 18–19, p. 104.

- (10 min.) Present **Nota cultural,** p. 104.

Wrap-Up

- (5 min.) Have students work with a partner to read aloud the completed conversation in Activity 19.

OPTIONAL RESOURCES

- (5 min.) Have students practice with activities from the *Interactive Tutor,* Ch. 3.

Practice Options

- *Lab Book,* pp. 17–18 ▲ ● ■
- *Cuaderno de vocabulario y gramática,* pp. 28–30 ▲ ◆ ●
- *Cuaderno de actividades,* pp. 21–23 ▲ ● ■
- *Activities for Communication,* pp. 9–10, 59–60 ▲ ■
- *Teaching Transparencies:* **Vocabulario y gramática** Answers, pp. 28–30 ▲ ◆ ●
- *Video Guide,* pp. 24–25 ▲ ● ■
- *Grammar Tutor for Students of Spanish,* pp. 15–18, 170–171 ◆ ●
- *TPR Storytelling Book,* pp. 12–13 ▲ ●
- *Interactive Tutor* (Disc 1) or *DVD Tutor* (Disc 1) ▲ ● ■
- Online practice, Chapter 3 (go.hrw.com, Keyword: EXP1A CH3) ▲ ● ■

▲ = Advanced Learners   ◆ = Slower Pace Learners   ● = Special Learning Needs   ■ = Heritage Speakers

¿Qué te gusta hacer?

DAY 10 50-MINUTE LESSON PLAN

NATIONAL STANDARDS

Gramática en acción 1

Communication 1.1: Student engages in oral and written exchanges of learned material to socialize and to provide and obtain information.

Communication 1.2: Student demonstrates understanding of simple, clearly spoken, and written language such as simple stories, high-frequency commands, and brief instructions when dealing with familiar topics.

Communication 1.3: Student presents information using familiar words, phrases, and sentences to listeners and readers.

CORE INSTRUCTION

Warm-Up

- (5 min.) Have students do Bell Work 3.5, p. 108.

Gramática en acción 1

- (10 min.) Have students do Activity 20, p. 105.
- (10 min.) Play Audio CD 3, Tr. 2, for Activity 21, p. 105. ●
- (10 min.) Have students do Activity 22, p. 105.
- (10 min.) Review **Gramática 1,** pp. 100–105.

Wrap-Up

- (5 min.) Have students do the activity described in **Comunicación (TE)**, p. 105. Then remind the class to study for **Prueba: Gramática 1.**

OPTIONAL RESOURCES

- (15 min.) See Slower Pace Learners, p. 105. ◆
- (5 min.) See Special Learning Needs, p. 105. ●

Practice Options

- *Lab Book*, pp. 17–18 ▲ ● ■
- *Cuaderno de vocabulario y gramática*, pp. 28–30 ▲ ◆ ●
- *Cuaderno de actividades*, pp. 21–23 ▲ ● ■
- *Activities for Communication*, pp. 9–10, 59–60 ▲ ■
- *Teaching Transparencies:* Bell Work 3.5; *Vocabulario y gramática* Answers, pp. 28–30 ▲ ◆ ●
- *Video Guide*, pp. 24–25 ▲ ● ■
- *Grammar Tutor for Students of Spanish*, pp. 15–18, 170–171 ◆ ●
- *TPR Storytelling Book*, pp. 12–13 ▲ ●
- *Interactive Tutor* (Disc 1) or *DVD Tutor* (Disc 1) ▲ ● ■
- Online practice, Chapter 3 (go.hrw.com, Keyword: EXP1A CH3) ▲ ● ■

▲ = Advanced Learners   ◆ = Slower Pace Learners   ● = Special Learning Needs   ■ = Heritage Speakers

Holt Spanish 1A

Lesson Planner

¿Qué te gusta hacer?

DAY 11 50-MINUTE LESSON PLAN

NATIONAL STANDARDS

Gramática en acción 1

Communication 1.1: Student engages in oral and written exchanges of learned material to socialize and to provide and obtain information.

Communication 1.2: Student demonstrates understanding of simple, clearly spoken, and written language such as simple stories, high-frequency commands, and brief instructions when dealing with familiar topics.

Communication 1.3: Student presents information using familiar words, phrases, and sentences to listeners and readers.

Cultura

Communication 1.2: Student demonstrates understanding of simple, clearly spoken, and written language such as simple stories, high-frequency commands, and brief instructions when dealing with familiar topics.

CORE INSTRUCTION

Warm-Up
• (5 min.) Ask students the following question: **¿Qué quieres hacer hoy?**

Gramática en acción 1
• (5 min.) Review **Gramática 1,** pp. 100–105.

Assessment
• (20 min.) Give **Prueba: Gramática 1.**

Cultura
• (10 min.) Present **Cultura,** pp. 106–107, using Teaching **Cultura,** p. 106, #s 1–2.

Wrap-Up
• (5 min.) Have students do #1 of the Map Activities, p. 106.

OPTIONAL RESOURCES
• (5 min.) See Language Note, p. 107.
• (5 min.) See Heritage Speakers, p. 107. ■

Practice Options
• *Lab Book,* p. 45 ▲ ● ■
• *Cuaderno de vocabulario y gramática,* pp. 28–30 ▲ ● ■
• *Cuaderno de actividades,* p. 24 ▲ ● ■
• *Cuaderno para hispanohablantes,* p. 32 ■
• *Activities for Communication,* pp. 9–10, 59–60
• *Teaching Transparencies: Vocabulario y gramática* Answers, pp. 28–30 ▲ ◆ ●
• *Video Guide,* pp. 24–25, 27 ▲ ● ■
• *Grammar Tutor for Students of Spanish,* pp. 15–18, 170–171 ◆ ●
• *TPR Storytelling Book,* pp. 12–13 ▲ ●
• *Interactive Tutor* (Disc 1) or *DVD Tutor* (Disc 1) ▲ ● ■
• Online practice, Chapter 3 (go.hrw.com, Keyword: EXP1A CH3) ▲ ● ■

Assessment Options
• *Assessment Program*: **Prueba: Gramática 1,** pp. 43–44 ▲ ● ■
• *Assessment Program*: **Prueba: Aplicación 1,** pp. 45–56 ▲ ● ■
• *Audio CD 3,* Tr. 16 ●
• Test Generator ▲ ● ■

▲ = Advanced Learners   ◆ = Slower Pace Learners   ● = Special Learning Needs   ■ = Heritage Speakers

Holt Spanish 1A

Lesson Planner

¿Qué te gusta hacer?

DAY 12 50-MINUTE LESSON PLAN

NATIONAL STANDARDS

Cultura

Communication 1.2: Student demonstrates understanding of simple, clearly spoken, and written language such as simple stories, high-frequency commands, and brief instructions when dealing with familiar topics.

Cultures 2.1: Student demonstrates an understanding of the practices (what people do) and how they are related to the perspectives (how people perceive things) of the cultures studied.

Comparisons 4.2: Student demonstrates an understanding of the concept of culture through comparisons of the student's own culture and the cultures studied.

Communities 5.2: Student shows evidence of becoming a lifelong learner by using the language for personal enrichment and career development.

Vocabulario en acción 2

Communication 1.2: Student demonstrates understanding of simple, clearly spoken, and written language such as simple stories, high-frequency commands, and brief instructions when dealing with familiar topics.

CORE INSTRUCTION

Warm-Up

- (5 min.) Present Language Note, p. 107.

Cultura

- (15 min.) Present **Cultura,** pp. 106–107, using Teaching **Cultura,** p. 106, #3.
- (5 min.) Present and have students begin **Comunidad,** p. 107.

Vocabulario en acción 2

- (15 min.) Present **Vocabulario 2,** pp. 108–109. See Teaching **Vocabulario,** #s 1–2, p. 108.

Wrap-Up

- (5 min.) Present Common Error Alert, p. 108.

OPTIONAL RESOURCES

- (25 min.) See Advanced Learners, p. 107. ▲
- (10 min.) See Multiple Intelligences, p. 107.
- (10 min.) Community Link, p. 107

Practice Options

- *Lab Book,* pp. 19–20, 45, 46 ▲ ● ■
- *Cuaderno de vocabulario y gramática*, pp. 31–33 ▲ ◆ ●
- *Cuaderno de actividades*, p. 24 ▲ ● ■
- *Cuaderno para hispanohablantes*, p. 32 ■
- *Teaching Transparencies:* **Vocabulario** 3.3, 3.4; *Vocabulario y gramática* Answers, pp. 31–33 ▲ ◆ ●
- *Video Guide,* pp. 24–25, 27, 28 ▲ ● ■
- *Interactive Tutor* (Disc 1) or *DVD Tutor* (Disc 1) ▲ ● ■
- Online practice, Chapter 3 (go.hrw.com, Keyword: EXP1A CH3) ▲ ● ■

▲ = Advanced Learners   ◆ = Slower Pace Learners   ● = Special Learning Needs   ■ = Heritage Speakers

CAPÍTULO
3

¿Qué te gusta hacer?

DAY 13 50-MINUTE LESSON PLAN

NATIONAL STANDARDS

Vocabulario en acción 2

Communication 1.1: Student engages in oral and written exchanges of learned material to socialize and to provide and obtain information.

Communication 1.2: Student demonstrates understanding of simple, clearly spoken, and written language such as simple stories, high-frequency commands, and brief instructions when dealing with familiar topics.

Communication 1.3: Student presents information using familiar words, phrases, and sentences to listeners and readers.

Comparisons 4.2: Student demonstrates an understanding of the concept of culture through comparisons of the student's own culture and the cultures studied.

CORE INSTRUCTION

Warm-Up
• (5 min.) See Slower Pace Learners, p. 109. ◆

Vocabulario en acción 2
• (10 min.) Show **ExpresaVisión,** Ch. 3.
• (10 min.) Review **Vocabulario 2,** pp. 108–113.
• (15 min.) Present **Vocabulario,** pp. 108–109, using Teaching **Vocabulario,** #s 3–4, p. 108.
• (5 min.) Present **Nota cultural,** p. 110.

Wrap-Up
• (5 min.) Present **También se puede decir… ,** p. 109.

OPTIONAL RESOURCES
• (15 min.) See TPR, p. 109. ●
• (10 min.) See Multiple Intelligences, p. 109. ●

Practice Options
• *Lab Book*, pp. 19–20, 46 ▲ ● ■
• *Cuaderno de vocabulario y gramática*, pp. 31–33 ▲ ◆ ●
• *Teaching Transparencies:* **Vocabulario** 3.3, 3.4; *Vocabulario y gramática* Answers, pp. 31–33 ▲ ◆ ●
• *Video Guide*, pp. 24–25, 28 ▲ ● ■
• *Interactive Tutor* (Disc 1) or *DVD Tutor* (Disc 1) ▲ ● ■
• Online practice, Chapter 3 (go.hrw.com, Keyword: EXP1A CH3) ▲ ● ■

▲ = Advanced Learners   ◆ = Slower Pace Learners   ● = Special Learning Needs   ■ = Heritage Speakers

Holt Spanish 1A   Lesson Planner

¿Qué te gusta hacer?

DAY 14 50-MINUTE LESSON PLAN

NATIONAL STANDARDS

Vocabulario en acción 2

Communication 1.1: Student engages in oral and written exchanges of learned material to socialize and to provide and obtain information.

Communication 1.2: Student demonstrates understanding of simple, clearly spoken, and written language such as simple stories, high-frequency commands, and brief instructions when dealing with familiar topics.

Communication 1.3: Student presents information using familiar words, phrases, and sentences to listeners and readers.

CORE INSTRUCTION

Warm-Up
- (5 min.) Have students do the activity described in Advanced Learners, p. 111. ▲

Vocabulario en acción 2
- (10 min.) Review **Vocabulario 2** and **¡Exprésate!**, pp. 108–109.
- (30 min.) Have students do Activities 23–26, pp. 110–111.

Wrap-Up
- (5 min.) Have students do the activity described in **Más práctica,** p. 111.

OPTIONAL RESOURCES
- (15 min.) See Game, p. 110.
- (15 min.) See **Comunicación** (TE), p. 111.
- (15 min.) See Multiple Intelligences, p. 111. ●

Practice Options
- *Lab Book*, pp. 19–20, 46 ▲ ● ■
- *Cuaderno de vocabulario y gramática*, pp. 31–33 ▲ ◆ ●
- *Teaching Transparencies:* **Vocabulario** 3.3, 3.4; *Vocabulario y gramática* Answers, pp. 31–33 ▲ ◆ ●
- *Video Guide*, pp. 24–25, 28 ▲ ● ■
- *Interactive Tutor* (Disc 1) or *DVD Tutor* (Disc 1) ▲ ● ■
- Online practice, Chapter 3 (go.hrw.com, Keyword: EXP1A CH3) ▲ ● ■

▲ = Advanced Learners   ◆ = Slower Pace Learners   ● = Special Learning Needs   ■ = Heritage Speakers

¿Qué te gusta hacer?

DAY 15 50-MINUTE LESSON PLAN

NATIONAL STANDARDS

Vocabulario en acción 2
Communication 1.2: Student demonstrates understanding of simple, clearly spoken, and written language such as simple stories, high-frequency commands, and brief instructions when dealing with familiar topics.

CORE INSTRUCTION

Warm-Up
- (5 min.) Have students review the answers to Activity 24, p. 110.

Vocabulario en acción 2
- (20 min.) Present **¡Exprésate!,** p. 112, using Teaching **¡Exprésate!,** p. 112.
- (10 min.) Play Audio CD 3, Tr. 6, for Activity 27, p. 112. ●
- (10 min.) Have students do Activity 28, p. 112.

Wrap-Up
- (5 min.) Review **Más vocabulario,** p. 112.

OPTIONAL RESOURCES
- (5 min.) See Practices and Perspectives, p. 110.

Practice Options
- *Lab Book,* pp. 19–20, 46 ▲ ● ■
- *Cuaderno de vocabulario y gramática*, pp. 31–33 ▲ ◆ ●
- *Teaching Transparencies:* **Vocabulario** 3.3, 3.4; *Vocabulario y gramática* Answers, pp. 31–33 ▲ ◆ ●
- *Video Guide,* pp. 24–25, 28 ▲ ● ■
- *Interactive Tutor* (Disc 1) or *DVD Tutor* (Disc 1) ▲ ● ■
- Online practice, Chapter 3 (go.hrw.com, Keyword: EXP1A CH3) ▲ ● ■

▲ = Advanced Learners   ◆ = Slower Pace Learners   ● = Special Learning Needs   ■ = Heritage Speakers

75

¡Empecemos!

DAY 16 50-MINUTE LESSON PLAN

NATIONAL STANDARDS

Vocabulario en acción 2

Communication 1.1: Student engages in oral and written exchanges of learned material to socialize and to provide and obtain information.

Communication 1.2: Student demonstrates understanding of simple, clearly spoken, and written language such as simple stories, high-frequency commands, and brief instructions when dealing with familiar topics.

Communication 1.3: Student presents information using familiar words, phrases, and sentences to listeners and readers.

CORE INSTRUCTION

Warm-Up
• (5 min.) Have students do Bell Work 3.6, p. 114.

Vocabulario en acción 2
• (5 min.) Review ¡Exprésate!, p. 112.
• (20 min.) Have students do Activities 29–30, p. 113.
• (10 min.) Review **Vocabulario 2,** pp. 108–113.

Wrap-Up
• (10 min.) Have students do the activity described in Extension, p. 113. Then remind the class to study for **Prueba: Vocabulario 2.**

OPTIONAL RESOURCES
• (15 min.) See **Más práctica,** p. 113.
• (20 min.) See Slower Pace Learners, p. 113. ◆
• (10 min.) See Special Learning Needs, p. 113. ●

Practice Options
• *Lab Book,* pp. 19–20, 46 ▲ ● ■
• *Cuaderno de vocabulario y gramática,* pp. 31–33 ▲ ◆ ●
• *Teaching Transparencies:* Bell Work 3.6; **Vocabulario** 3.3, 3.4; *Vocabulario y gramática* Answers, pp. 31–33 ▲ ◆ ●
• *Video Guide,* pp. 24–25, 28 ▲ ● ■
• *Interactive Tutor* (Disc 1) or *DVD Tutor* (Disc 1) ▲ ● ■
• Online practice, Chapter 3 (go.hrw.com, Keyword: EXP1A CH3) ▲ ● ■

▲ = Advanced Learners   ◆ = Slower Pace Learners   ● = Special Learning Needs   ■ = Heritage Speakers

¿Qué te gusta hacer?

NATIONAL STANDARDS

Vocabulario en acción 2

Communication 1.1: Student engages in oral and written exchanges of learned material to socialize and to provide and obtain information.

Communication 1.2: Student demonstrates understanding of simple, clearly spoken, and written language such as simple stories, high-frequency commands, and brief instructions when dealing with familiar topics.

Communication 1.3: Student presents information using familiar words, phrases, and sentences to listeners and readers.

Gramática en acción 2

Communication 1B: Student demonstrates understanding of simple, clearly spoken, and written language such as simple stories, high-frequency commands, and brief instructions when dealing with familiar topics.

CORE INSTRUCTION

Warm-Up
• (5 min.) Ask students **¿Qué haces los fines de semana?**

Vocabulario en acción 2
• (5 min.) Review **Vocabulario 2,** pp. 108–113.

Assessment
• (20 min.) Give **Prueba: Vocabulario 2.**

Gramática en acción 2
• (15 min.) Present **Gramática:** *Present tense of regular* **-ar** verbs, p. 114, using Teaching **Gramática,** p. 114.

Wrap-Up
• (5 min.) Take a survey of the class. Ask students to raise their hands to indicate whether each of the following statements is true about them: **Estudio mucho los fines de semana. / Bailo muy bien. / Hablo por teléfono todos los días. / Después de clases, descanso un poco en casa.**

OPTIONAL RESOURCES
• (15 min.) See Language to Language, p. 115.
• You can find alternative quizzes in the Assessment Options listed below.

Practice Options
• *Lab Book,* pp. 19–20, 46 ▲ ● ■
• ***Cuaderno de vocabulario y gramática,*** pp. 31–33, 34–36 ▲ ◆ ●
• ***Cuaderno de actividades,*** pp. 25–27 ▲ ● ■
• *Activities for Communication,* pp. 11–12, 59–60 ▲ ■
• *Teaching Transparencies:* **Vocabulario** 3.3, 3.4; **Vocabulario y gramática** Answers, pp. 31–33, 34–36 ▲ ◆ ●
• *Video Guide,* pp. 24–25, 28 ▲ ● ■
• *TPR Storytelling Book,* pp. 14–15 ▲ ●

• *Grammar Tutor for Students of Spanish,* pp. 19–20, 170–171 ◆ ●
• *Interactive Tutor* (Disc 1) or *DVD Tutor* (Disc 1) ▲ ● ■
• Online practice, Chapter 3 (go.hrw.com, Keyword: EXP1A CH3) ▲ ● ■

Assessment Options
• *Assessment Program:* **Prueba: Vocabulario 2,** pp. 47–48 ▲ ● ■
• Test Generator ▲ ● ■

▲ = Advanced Learners   ◆ = Slower Pace Learners   ● = Special Learning Needs   ■ = Heritage Speakers

CAPÍTULO

3

¿Qué te gusta hacer?

DAY 18 50-MINUTE LESSON PLAN

NATIONAL STANDARDS

Gramática en acción 2

Communication 1.1: Student engages in oral and written exchanges of learned material to socialize and to provide and obtain information.

Communication 1.2: Student demonstrates understanding of simple, clearly spoken, and written language such as simple stories, high-frequency commands, and brief instructions when dealing with familiar topics.

CORE INSTRUCTION

Warm-Up
- (5 min.) Have students work with a partner and read to each other from the personal agendas they made for Extension, Activity 29.

Gramática en acción 2
- (10 min.) Show **GramaVisión** *(present tense of regular -ar verbs)*, *Video Program* (Videocassette 2) or *DVD Tutor* (Disc 1).
- (15 min.) Review the present-tense conjugation of regular **-ar** verbs, p. 114.

- (15 min.) Have students do Activities 31–32, pp. 114–115.

Wrap-Up
- (5 min.) Have volunteers read aloud some sentences from Activity 32, p. 115.

OPTIONAL RESOURCES
- (5 min.) See Slower Pace Learners, p. 115. ◆

Practice Options
- *Lab Book*, pp. 19–20 ▲ ● ■
- *Cuaderno de vocabulario y gramática*, pp. 34–36 ▲ ◆ ●
- *Cuaderno de actividades*, pp. 25–27 ▲ ● ■
- *Activities for Communication*, pp. 11–12, 59–60 ▲ ■
- *Teaching Transparencies: **Vocabulario y gramática** Answers*, pp. 34–36 ▲ ◆ ●
- *Video Guide*, pp. 24–25 ▲ ● ■
- *TPR Storytelling Book*, pp. 14–15 ▲ ●
- *Grammar Tutor for Students of Spanish*, pp. 19–20, 170–171 ◆ ●
- *Interactive Tutor* (Disc 1) or *DVD Tutor* (Disc 1) ▲ ● ■
- Online practice, Chapter 3 (go.hrw.com, Keyword: EXP1A CH3) ▲ ● ■

▲ = Advanced Learners   ◆ = Slower Pace Learners   ● = Special Learning Needs   ■ = Heritage Speakers

Holt Spanish 1A

Lesson Planner

CAPÍTULO
3

¿Qué te gusta hacer?

DAY 19 50-MINUTE LESSON PLAN

Gramática en acción 2
Communication 1.1: Student engages in oral and written exchanges of learned material to socialize and to provide and obtain information.

Communication 1.2: Student demonstrates understanding of simple, clearly spoken, and written language such as simple stories, high-frequency commands, and brief instructions when dealing with familiar topics.

CORE INSTRUCTION

Warm-Up
- (5 min.) Have students do Bell Work 3.7, p. 116.

Gramática en acción 2
- (20 min.) Have students do Activities 33–34, p. 115.
- (20 min.) Present **Gramática:** *Present tense of* **ir** *and* **jugar,** p. 116, using Teaching **Gramática,** p. 116.

Wrap-Up
- (5 min.) Present Language to Language, p. 115.

OPTIONAL RESOURCES
- (5 min.) For students with visual impairments, see Special Learning Needs, p. 115. ●
- (15 min.) See **Comunicación** (TE), p. 115.

Practice Options
- *Lab Book*, pp. 19–20 ▲ ● ■
- *Cuaderno de vocabulario y gramática*, pp. 34–36 ▲ ◆ ●
- *Cuaderno de actividades*, pp. 25–27 ▲ ● ■
- *Activities for Communication*, pp. 11–12, 59–60 ▲ ■
- *Teaching Transparencies:* Bell Work 3.7; *Vocabulario y gramática* Answers, pp. 34–36 ▲ ◆ ●
- *Video Guide*, pp. 24–25 ▲ ● ■
- *TPR Storytelling Book*, pp. 14–15 ▲ ●
- *Grammar Tutor for Students of Spanish*, pp. 19–20, 170–171 ◆ ●
- *Interactive Tutor* (Disc 1) or *DVD Tutor* (Disc 1) ▲ ● ■
- Online practice, Chapter 3 (go.hrw.com, Keyword: EXP1A CH3) ▲ ● ■

▲ = Advanced Learners   ◆ = Slower Pace Learners   ● = Special Learning Needs   ■ = Heritage Speakers

Holt Spanish 1A

Lesson Planner

¿Qué te gusta hacer?

DAY 20 50-MINUTE LESSON PLAN

NATIONAL STANDARDS

Gramática en acción 2

Communication 1.1: Student engages in oral and written exchanges of learned material to socialize and to provide and obtain information.

Communication 1.2: Student demonstrates understanding of simple, clearly spoken, and written language such as simple stories, high-frequency commands, and brief instructions when dealing with familiar topics.

Communication 1.3: Student presents information using familiar words, phrases, and sentences to listeners and readers.

Comparisons 4.2: Student demonstrates an understanding of the concept of culture through comparisons of the student's own culture and the cultures studied.

CORE INSTRUCTION

Warm-Up

- (5 min.) Ask students to tell a partner what sports they play and when they play them.

Gramática en acción 2

- (10 min.) Show **GramaVisión** (**ir, jugar**), *Video Program* (Videocassette 2) or *DVD Tutor* (Disc 1).
- (10 min.) Review the present tense of **jugar** and **ir,** p. 116.
- (15 min.) Have students do Activities 35–37, pp. 116–117.
- (5 min.) Present **Nota cultural,** p. 117.

Wrap-Up

- (5 min.) Have students compare the answers they wrote for Activity 37, p. 117.

OPTIONAL RESOURCES

- (5 min.) See Special Learning Needs, p. 117. ●

Practice Options

- *Lab Book*, pp. 19–20 ▲ ● ■
- *Cuaderno de vocabulario y gramática*, pp. 34–36 ▲ ◆ ●
- *Cuaderno de actividades*, pp. 25–27 ▲ ● ■
- *Activities for Communication*, pp. 11–12, 59–60 ▲ ■
- *Teaching Transparencies: Vocabulario y gramática* Answers, pp. 34–36 ▲ ◆ ●
- *Video Guide*, pp. 24–25 ▲ ● ■
- *TPR Storytelling Book*, pp. 14–15 ▲ ●
- *Grammar Tutor for Students of Spanish*, pp. 19–20, 170–171 ◆ ●
- *Interactive Tutor* (Disc 1) or *DVD Tutor* (Disc 1) ▲ ● ■
- Online practice, Chapter 3 (go.hrw.com, Keyword: EXP1A CH3) ▲ ● ■

▲ = Advanced Learners   ◆ = Slower Pace Learners   ● = Special Learning Needs   ■ = Heritage Speakers

**CAPÍTULO
3**

¿Qué te gusta hacer?

DAY 21 50-MINUTE LESSON PLAN

NATIONAL STANDARDS

Gramática en acción 2
Communication 1.1: Student engages in oral and written exchanges of learned material to socialize and to provide and obtain information.

Communication 1.2: Student demonstrates understanding of simple, clearly spoken, and written language such as simple stories, high-frequency commands, and brief instructions when dealing with familiar topics.

CORE INSTRUCTION

Warm-Up
- (5 min.) Have students do Bell Work 3.8, p. 118.

Gramática en acción 2
- (15 min.) Have students do Activity 38, p. 117.
- (20 min.) Present **Gramática:** *Weather expressions*, p. 118, using Teaching **Gramática,** p. 118.
- (5 min.) Have students do Activity 39, p. 118.

Wrap-Up
- (5 min.) Have students practice weather expressions aloud with a partner.

OPTIONAL RESOURCES
- (15 min.) See Advanced Learners, p. 117. ▲
- (15 min.) See **Comunicación (TE),** p. 117.

Practice Options
- *Lab Book*, pp. 19–20 ▲ ● ■
- ***Cuaderno de vocabulario y gramática***, pp. 34–36 ▲ ◆ ●
- ***Cuaderno de actividades***, pp. 25–27 ▲ ● ■
- *Activities for Communication*, pp. 11–12, 59–60 ▲ ■
- *Teaching Transparencies:* Bell Work 3.8; ***Vocabulario y gramática*** Answers, pp. 34–36 ▲ ◆ ●
- *Video Guide*, pp. 24–25 ▲ ● ■
- *TPR Storytelling Book*, pp. 14–15 ▲ ●
- *Grammar Tutor for Students of Spanish*, pp. 19–20, 170–171 ◆ ●
- *Interactive Tutor* (Disc 1) or *DVD Tutor* (Disc 1) ▲ ● ■
- Online practice, Chapter 3 (go.hrw.com, Keyword: EXP1A CH3) ▲ ● ■

▲ = Advanced Learners ◆ = Slower Pace Learners ● = Special Learning Needs ■ = Heritage Speakers

Holt Spanish 1A

Lesson Planner

¿Qué te gusta hacer?

DAY 22 50-MINUTE LESSON PLAN

NATIONAL STANDARDS

Gramática en acción 2

Communication 1.1: Student engages in oral and written exchanges of learned material to socialize and to provide and obtain information.

Communication 1.2: Student demonstrates understanding of simple, clearly spoken, and written language such as simple stories, high-frequency commands, and brief instructions when dealing with familiar topics.

Communication 1.3: Student presents information using familiar words, phrases, and sentences to listeners and readers.

CORE INSTRUCTION

Warm-Up

- (5 min.) Have students describe today's weather.

Gramática en acción 2

- (10 min.) Show **GramaVisión** *(weather expressions), Video Program* (Videocassette 2) or *DVD Tutor* (Disc 1).
- (10 min.) Play Audio CD 3, Tr. 7, for Activity 40, p. 119. ●
- (15 min.) Have students do Activities 41–42, p. 119.
- (5 min.) Review **Gramática 2,** pp. 114–119.

Wrap-Up

- (5 min.) Have students write a sentence about each picture in Activity 40. Then remind the class to study for **Prueba: Gramática 2.**

OPTIONAL RESOURCES

- (5 min.) See Advanced Learners, p. 119. ▲
- (5 min.) See Multiple Intelligences, p. 119. ●
- (15 min.) See **Comunicación** (TE), p. 119.

Practice Options

- *Lab Book*, pp. 19–20 ▲ ● ■
- *Cuaderno de vocabulario y gramática*, pp. 34–36 ▲ ◆ ●
- *Cuaderno de actividades*, pp. 25–27 ▲ ● ■
- *Activities for Communication*, pp. 11–12, 59–60 ▲ ■
- *Teaching Transparencies: Vocabulario y gramática* Answers, pp. 34–36 ▲ ◆ ●
- *Video Guide*, pp. 24–25 ▲ ● ■
- *TPR Storytelling Book*, pp. 14–15 ▲ ●
- *Grammar Tutor for Students of Spanish*, pp. 19–20, 170–171 ◆ ●
- *Interactive Tutor* (Disc 1) or *DVD Tutor* (Disc 1) ▲ ● ■
- Online practice, Chapter 3 (go.hrw.com, Keyword: EXP1A CH3) ▲ ● ■

▲ = Advanced Learners   ◆ = Slower Pace Learners   ● = Special Learning Needs   ■ = Heritage Speakers

¿Qué te gusta hacer?

DAY 23 50-MINUTE LESSON PLAN

NATIONAL STANDARDS

Gramática en acción 2

Communication 1.1: Student engages in oral and written exchanges of learned material to socialize and to provide and obtain information.

Communication 1.2: Student demonstrates understanding of simple, clearly spoken, and written language such as simple stories, high-frequency commands, and brief instructions when dealing with familiar topics.

Communication 1.3: Student presents information using familiar words, phrases, and sentences to listeners and readers.

Conexiones culturales

Communication 1.2: Student demonstrates understanding of simple, clearly spoken, and written

language such as simple stories, high-frequency commands, and brief instructions when dealing with familiar topics.

Cultures 2.2: Student demonstrates an understanding of the products (what people create) and how they are related to the perspectives (how people perceive things) of the cultures studied.

Connections 3.1: Student uses the language to obtain, reinforce, or expand knowledge of other subject areas.

Comparisons 4.2: Student demonstrates an understanding of the concept of culture through comparisons of the student's own culture and the cultures studied.

CORE INSTRUCTION

Warm-Up

- (5 min.) Ask students to complete the following sentences: **Cuando hace calor, yo… / Cuando hace frío, yo… / Cuando llueve, yo…**

Gramática en acción 2

- (5 min.) Review **Gramática 2,** pp. 114–119.

Assessment

- (20 min.) Give **Prueba: Gramática 2.**

Conexiones culturales

- (15 min.) Present **Conexiones culturales**, pp. 120–121, using Teaching **Conexiones culturales**, #s 1–3, p. 120.

Wrap-Up

- (5 min.) Present Practices and Products, p. 120.

OPTIONAL RESOURCES

- You can find alternative quizzes in the Assessment Options listed below.

Practice Options

- *Lab Book*, pp. 19–20 ▲ ● ■
- ***Cuaderno de vocabulario y gramática***, pp. 34–36 ▲ ◆ ●
- ***Cuaderno de actividades***, pp. 25–27 ▲ ● ■
- *Activities for Communication*, pp. 11–12, 59–60 ▲ ■
- *Teaching Transparencies: **Vocabulario y gramática*** Answers, pp. 34–36 ▲ ◆ ●
- *Video Guide*, pp. 24–25 ▲ ● ■
- *TPR Storytelling Book*, pp. 14–15 ▲ ●
- *Grammar Tutor for Students of Spanish*, pp. 19–20, 170–171 ◆ ●

- *Interactive Tutor* (Disc 1) or *DVD Tutor* (Disc 1) ▲ ● ■
- Online practice, Chapter 3 (go.hrw.com, Keyword: EXP1A CH3) ▲ ● ■

Assessment Options

- *Assessment Program*: **Prueba: Gramática 2**, pp. 43–44 ▲ ● ■
- *Assessment Program*: **Prueba: Aplicación 2**, pp. 45–56 ▲ ● ■
- *Audio CD 3*, Tr. 17 ●
- Test Generator ▲ ● ■

▲ = Advanced Learners   ◆ = Slower Pace Learners   ● = Special Learning Needs   ■ = Heritage Speakers

83

¿Qué te gusta hacer?

DAY 24 50-MINUTE LESSON PLAN

NATIONAL STANDARDS

Conexiones culturales

Communication 1.3: Student presents information using familiar words, phrases, and sentences to listeners and readers.

Cultures 2.1: Student demonstrates an understanding of the practices (what people do) and how they are related to the perspectives (how people perceive things) of the cultures studied.

Connections 3.1: Student uses the language to obtain, reinforce, or expand knowledge of other subject areas.

Novela en video

Communication 1.2: Student demonstrates understanding of simple, clearly spoken, and written language such as simple stories, high-frequency commands, and brief instructions when dealing with familiar topics.

CORE INSTRUCTION

Warm-Up

- (5 min.) Have the class preview the pictures on p. 121 before reading.

Conexiones culturales

- (20 min.) Present **Conexiones culturales,** pp. 120–212, using Teaching **Conexiones culturales,** #s 4–6, p. 120.

Novela en video

- (20 min.) Present **Novela en video,** pp. 122–125, using Teaching **Novela en video,** #1–2, p. 122.

Wrap-Up

- (5 min.) Present Gestures, p. 122.

OPTIONAL RESOURCES

- (5 min.) See Language Note, p. 121.
- (10 min.) See Advanced Learners, p. 121. ▲
- (10 min.) See Multiple Intelligences, p. 121. ●
- (15 min.) See Visual Learners, p. 122. ●
- (20 min.) Science Link, p. 121

Practice Options

- *Lab Book,* p. 47 ▲ ● ■
- *Video Guide,* pp. 24–25, 29 ▲ ● ■
- *Interactive Tutor* (Disc 1) or *DVD Tutor* (Disc 1) ▲ ● ■
- Online practice, Chapter 3 (go.hrw.com, Keyword: EXP1A CH3) ▲ ● ■

▲ = Advanced Learners   ◆ = Slower Pace Learners   ● = Special Learning Needs   ■ = Heritage Speakers

Holt Spanish 1A

Lesson Planner

CAPÍTULO
3

¿Qué te gusta hacer?

DAY 25 50-MINUTE LESSON PLAN

NATIONAL STANDARDS

Novela en video

Communication 1.2: Student demonstrates understanding of simple, clearly spoken, and written language such as simple stories, high-frequency commands, and brief instructions when dealing with familiar topics.

Leamos y escribamos

Communication 1.2: Student demonstrates understanding of simple, clearly spoken, and written language such as simple stories, high-frequency commands, and brief instructions when dealing with familiar topics.

Communication 1.3: Student presents information using familiar words, phrases, and sentences to listeners and readers.

Connections 3.2: Student uses resources (that may include technology) in the language and cultures being studied to gain access to information.

CORE INSTRUCTION

Warm-Up

- (5 min.) Ask students to recap in English what they've seen so far of the **VideoNovela** for this chapter.

Novela en video

- (10 min.) Show scenes 1–2 of the **VideoNovela** again.
- (15 min.) Present the remainder of the **Novela en video,** pp. 122–125, using Teaching **Novela en video,** #s 3–4, p. 122.

Leamos y escribamos

- (10 min.) Present **Leamos,** p. 126, using Teaching **Leamos,** #s 1–2, p. 126.

Wrap-Up

- (5 min.) Have volunteers read parts of the story aloud, p. 126.

OPTIONAL RESOURCES

- (5 min.) See Culminating Project, p. 124.
- (5 min.) See Slower Pace Learners, p. 127. ◆
- (5 min.) See Special Learning Needs, p. 127. ●
- (5 min.) Play Audio CD 3, Tr. 8 for **Los cuatro elementos** p. 126. ●

Practice Options

- *Lab Book,* p. 47 ▲ ● ■
- *Video Guide,* pp. 24–25, 29 ▲ ● ■
- ***Cuaderno de actividades,*** p. 28 ▲ ● ■
- *Student Edition,* **Literatura y variedades,** pp. 232–233
- *Reading Strategies and Skills Handbook,* pp. xi–xii, 67–68, 50–53 ▲ ● ■
- ***¡Lee conmigo!*** Level 1 Reader ▲ ■
- *Interactive Tutor* (Disc 1) or *DVD Tutor* (Disc 1) ▲ ● ■
- Online practice, Chapter 3 (go.hrw.com, Keyword: EXP1A CH3) ▲ ● ■

▲ = Advanced Learners   ◆ = Slower Pace Learners   ● = Special Learning Needs   ■ = Heritage Speakers

Holt Spanish 1A

Lesson Planner

¿Qué te gusta hacer?

DAY 26 50-MINUTE LESSON PLAN

NATIONAL STANDARDS

Leamos y escribamos

Communication 1.2: Student demonstrates understanding of simple, clearly spoken, and written language such as simple stories, high-frequency commands, and brief instructions when dealing with familiar topics.

Communication 1.3: Student presents information using familiar words, phrases, and sentences to listeners and readers.

Cultures 2.1: Student demonstrates an understanding of the practices (what people do) and how they are related to the perspectives (how people perceive things) of the cultures studied.

Connections 3.1: Student uses the language to obtain, reinforce, or expand knowledge of other subject areas.

Comparisons 4.2: Student demonstrates an understanding of the concept of culture through comparisons of the student's own culture and the cultures studied.

CORE INSTRUCTION

Warm-Up
• (5 min.) Have students reread **Leamos,** p. 126.

Leamos y escribamos
• (15 min.) Present the remainder of **Leamos,** p. 126, using Teaching **Leamos,** #3, p. 126.
• (10 min.) Present **Taller del escritor,** p. 127, using Teaching **Escribamos,** #s 1–2, p. 126.
• (15 min.) Have students do **Escribamos,** Steps 1–2, p. 127.

Wrap-Up
• (5 min.) Present the information from Computer Science Link, p. 127.

OPTIONAL RESOURCES
• (5 min.) See Additional Practice, pp. 386–387.

Practice Options
• *Cuaderno de actividades*, p. 28 ▲ ● ■
• *Student Edition*, **Literatura y variedades**, pp. 232–233
• *Reading Strategies and Skills Handbook*, pp. xi–xii, 67–68, 50–53 ▲ ● ■
• *¡Lee conmigo!* Level 1 Reader ▲ ■
• *Interactive Tutor* (Disc 1) or *DVD Tutor* (Disc 1) ▲ ● ■
• Online practice, Chapter 3 (go.hrw.com, Keyword: EXP1A CH3) ▲ ● ■

Assessment Options
• *Assessment Program,* **Prueba: Lectura,** pp. 53, 59 ▲ ● ■
• *Assessment Program,* **Prueba: Escritura,** pp. 54, 59 ▲ ● ■

▲ = Advanced Learners   ◆ = Slower Pace Learners   ● = Special Learning Needs   ■ = Heritage Speakers

86

CAPÍTULO

3

¿Qué te gusta hacer?

DAY 27 50-MINUTE LESSON PLAN

NATIONAL STANDARDS

Leamos y escribamos

Communication 1.3: Student presents information using familiar words, phrases, and sentences to listeners and readers.

Repaso

Communication 1.1: Student engages in oral and written exchanges of learned material to socialize and to provide and obtain information.

Communication 1.2: Student demonstrates understanding of simple, clearly spoken, and written language such as simple stories, high-frequency commands, and brief instructions when dealing with familiar topics.

CORE INSTRUCTION

Warm-Up

- (5 min.) Have students review their letters and make any last-minute corrections that they think are needed.

Leamos y escribamos

- (10 min.) Have students do **Escribamos,** Step 3, p. 127.

Repaso

- (5 min.) Review chapter vocabulary with *Teaching Transparencies 4.1–4.4.*
- (25 min.) Have students do Activities 1–4, pp. 128–129.

Wrap-Up

- (5 min.) Have students check their work for Activity 4 with a partner.

OPTIONAL RESOURCES

- (5 min.) See Science Link, p. 128.
- (25 min.) See Fold-N-Learn, p. 128. ●

Practice Options

- *Lab Book*, pp. 19–20, 48 ▲ ● ■
- *Activities for Communication*, pp. 45, 59–60 ▲ ■
- *Teaching Transparencies:* Situation; Picture Sequences ▲ ● ■
- *Video Guide*, pp. 24–25, 30 ▲ ● ■
- *TPR Storytelling Book*, pp. 16–17 ▲ ●
- *Interactive Tutor* (Disc 1) or *DVD Tutor* (Disc 1) ▲ ● ■
- Online practice, Chapter 3 (go.hrw.com, Keyword: EXP1A CH3) ▲ ● ■

▲ = Advanced Learners   ◆ = Slower Pace Learners   ● = Special Learning Needs   ■ = Heritage Speakers

Holt Spanish 1A

Lesson Planner

87

CAPÍTULO

3

¿Qué te gusta hacer?

DAY 28 50-MINUTE LESSON PLAN

NATIONAL STANDARDS

Repaso

Communication 1.2: Student demonstrates understanding of simple, clearly spoken, and written language such as simple stories, high-frequency commands, and brief instructions when dealing with familiar topics.

Communication 1.3: Student presents information using familiar words, phrases, and sentences to listeners and readers.

Cultures 2.1: Student demonstrates an understanding of the practices (what people do) and how they are related to the perspectives (how people perceive things) of the cultures studied.

Comparisons 4.2: Student demonstrates an understanding of the concept of culture through comparisons of the student's own culture and the cultures studied.

CORE INSTRUCTION

Warm-Up

- (5 min.) Have students read aloud their answers to Activities 1–2, p. 128.

Repaso

- (5 min.) Have students do Activity 5, p. 129.
- (10 min.) Play Audio CD 3, Tr. 10, for Activity 6, p. 129. ●
- (15 min.) Have students do Activity 7, p. 129.
- (10 min.) Play Audio CD 3, Tr. 11, 12, 13, for **Letra y sonido,** p. 130. ●

Wrap-Up

- (5 min.) Have students make up sentences that include the following words: **quiero, queremos, voy, vamos, hablo, hablamos.** They should say the sentences aloud to the class.

OPTIONAL RESOURCES

- (5 min.) See Common Error Alert, p. 130.
- (20 min.) See Teacher to Teacher, p. 131.

Practice Options

- *Lab Book*, pp. 19–20, 48 ▲ ● ■
- *Activities for Communication*, pp. 45, 59–60 ▲ ■
- *Teaching Transparencies:* Situation; Picture Sequences ▲ ● ■
- *Video Guide*, pp. 24–25, 30 ▲ ● ■
- *TPR Storytelling Book*, pp. 16–17 ▲ ●
- *Interactive Tutor* (Disc 1) or *DVD Tutor* (Disc 1) ▲ ● ■
- Online practice, Chapter 3 (go.hrw.com, Keyword: EXP1A CH3) ▲ ● ■

▲ = Advanced Learners   ◆ = Slower Pace Learners   ● = Special Learning Needs   ■ = Heritage Speakers

Holt Spanish 1A

Lesson Planner

¿Qué te gusta hacer?

DAY 29 50-MINUTE LESSON PLAN

NATIONAL STANDARDS

Integración

Communication 1.1: Student engages in oral and written exchanges of learned material to socialize and to provide and obtain information.

Communication 1.2: Student demonstrates understanding of simple, clearly spoken, and written language such as simple stories, high-frequency commands, and brief instructions when dealing with familiar topics.

Communication 1.3: Student presents information using familiar words, phrases, and sentences to listeners and readers.

CORE INSTRUCTION

Warm-Up

- (5 min.) Look at the pictures on p. 132 and have students predict what they might hear on the recording.

Integración

- (10 min.) Play Audio CD 3, Tr. 14, for Activity 1, p. 132. ●
- (30 min.) Have students do Activities 2–5, pp. 132–133.

Wrap-Up

- (5 min.) Present Fine Art Connection: Introduction and Extension, p. 133. Then remind the class to study for the Chapter Test.

OPTIONAL RESOURCES

- (25 min.) See **Más práctica,** p. 132.

Practice Options

- *Lab Book*, pp. 19–20 ▲ ● ■
- *Cuaderno de actividades,* pp. 29–30, 56–57 ▲ ● ■
- *Activities for Communication*, pp. 45, 59–60 ▲ ■
- *Teaching Transparencies:* Fine Art, Chapter 3 ▲ ● ■
- Online practice, Chapter 3 (go.hrw.com, Keyword: EXP1A CH3) ▲ ● ■

▲ = Advanced Learners   ◆ = Slower Pace Learners   ● = Special Learning Needs   ■ = Heritage Speakers

Holt Spanish 1A

Lesson Planner

¿Qué te gusta hacer?

DAY 30 50-MINUTE LESSON PLAN

CORE INSTRUCTION

Assessment
- (50 min.) Give the Chapter 3 Test.

OPTIONAL RESOURCES
- You may also choose from the other modes of assessment listed in the Assessment Options box below.

Assessment Options
- *Assessment Program*: **Examen: Capítulo 3,** pp. 129–139 ▲ ● ■
- *Assessment Program*: **Examen oral: Capítulo 3,** p. 140 ▲ ● ■
- *Assessment Program*: Alternative Assessment, pp. 214, 220, 227 ▲ ● ■
- Audio CD 3, Tr. 18–19 ●
- *Assessment Program*: **Examen parcial: Capítulos 1–3,** p. 141–155 ▲ ● ■
- Audio CD 3, Tr. 20–21 ●
- *Test Generator* ▲ ● ■
- *Interactive Tutor* (Disc 1) or *DVD Tutor* (Disc 1) ▲ ● ■
- Online practice, Chapter 3 (go.hrw.com, Keyword: EXP1A CH3) ▲ ● ■

▲ = Advanced Learners   ◆ = Slower Pace Learners   ● = Special Learning Needs   ■ = Heritage Speakers

Teacher's Name _____ Class _____ Date _____

La vida escolar

DAY 1 50-MINUTE LESSON PLAN

NATIONAL STANDARDS

Chapter Opener
Communication 1.2: Student demonstrates understanding of simple, clearly spoken, and written
language such as simple stories, high-frequency
commands, and brief instructions when dealing
with familiar topics.

Vocabulario en acción 1
Communication 1.3: Student presents information
using familiar words, phrases, and sentences to
listeners and readers.
Comparisons 4.2: Student demonstrates an understanding of the concept of culture through
comparisons of the student's own culture and the
cultures studied.

Before starting **Capítulo 4,** you may wish to teach **Geocultura: Costa Rica,** pp. 134–137. For teaching
suggestions, see pp. xv–xvi of this *Lesson Planner.*

CORE INSTRUCTION

Warm-Up
• (5 min.) See Learning and Pacing Tips, p. 139.

Chapter Opener
• (5 min.) Present information from Using the
Photo and **Más vocabulario,** p. 138.
• (5 min.) Present **Objetivos,** p. 138.

Vocabulario en acción 1
• (30min.) Present **Vocabulario,** pp. 140–141,
using Teaching **Vocabulario,** p. 140.

Wrap-Up
• (5 min.) Present **También se puede decir...** and
Common Error Alert, p. 141.

OPTIONAL RESOURCES
• (15 min.) See Multiple Intelligences, p. 141. ●

Practice Options
• *Lab Book,* pp. 4, 21–22, 49, 50 ▲ ● ■
• *Cuaderno de vocabulario y gramática,* pp. 37–39 ▲ ◆ ●
• *Cuaderno para hispanohablantes,* pp. 33–42, 43
• *Teaching Transparencies:* Map 4; **Vocabulario** 4.1, 4.2; Situation; *Vocabulario
y gramática* Answers, pp. 37–39 ▲ ◆ ●
• *Video Guide,* pp. 31, 32, 34–35, 36 ▲ ● ■
• *Interactive Tutor* (Disc 1) or *DVD Tutor* (Disc 1) ▲ ● ■
• Online practice, Chapter 4 (go.hrw.com, Keyword: EXP1A CH4) ▲ ● ■

▲ = Advanced Learners   ◆ = Slower Pace Learners   ● = Special Learning Needs   ■ = Heritage Speakers

Holt Spanish 1A

CAPÍTULO
4

La vida escolar

DAY 2 50-MINUTE LESSON PLAN

NATIONAL STANDARDS

Vocabulario en acción 1

Communication 1.2: Student demonstrates understanding of simple, clearly spoken, and written language such as simple stories, high-frequency commands, and brief instructions when dealing with familiar topics.

Cultures 2.1: Student demonstrates an understanding of the practices (what people do) and how they are related to the perspectives (how people perceive things) of the cultures studied.

CORE INSTRUCTION

Warm-Up
- (5 min.) Have students do Bell Work 4.1, p. 140.

Vocabulario en acción 1
- (10 min.) Show **ExpresaVisión,** Ch. 4.
- (5 min.) Review **Vocabulario 1,** pp. 140–141.
- (10 min.) Present **¡Exprésate!,** p. 141.
- (5 min.) Present **Nota cultural,** p. 142.
- (10 min.) Play Audio CD 4, Tr. 1, for Activity 1, p. 142. ●

Wrap-Up
- (5 min.) Have students do the first part of the activity described in Advanced Learners, p. 141. ▲

OPTIONAL RESOURCES
- (5 min.) See Fold-N-Learn, p. 142. ●
- (10 min.) TPR, p. 141 ●

Practice Options
- *Lab Book,* pp. 21–22, 50 ▲ ● ■
- *Cuaderno de vocabulario y gramática*, pp. 37–39 ▲ ◆ ●
- *Teaching Transparencies:* Bell Work 4.1; **Vocabulario** 4.1, 4.2; *Vocabulario y gramática* Answers, pp. 37–39 ▲ ◆ ●
- *Video Guide,* pp. 34–35, 36 ▲ ● ■
- *Interactive Tutor* (Disc 1) or *DVD Tutor* (Disc 1) ▲ ● ■
- Online practice, Chapter 4 (go.hrw.com, Keyword: EXP1A CH4) ▲ ● ■

▲ = Advanced Learners   ◆ = Slower Pace Learners   ● = Special Learning Needs   ■ = Heritage Speakers

Lesson Planner

CAPÍTULO
4

¡Empecemos!

DAY 3 50-MINUTE LESSON PLAN

NATIONAL STANDARDS

Vocabulario en acción 1

Communication 1.1: Student engages in oral and written exchanges of learned material to socialize and to provide and obtain information.

Communication 1.2: Student demonstrates understanding of simple, clearly spoken, and written language such as simple stories, high-frequency commands, and brief instructions when dealing with familiar topics.

Communication 1.3: Student presents information using familiar words, phrases, and sentences to listeners and readers.

CORE INSTRUCTION

Warm-Up

- (5 min.) Review the vocabulary words, on pp. 140–141 by pointing to objects around the classroom and asking students **¿Qué es esto?**

Vocabulario en acción 1

- (5 min.) Have students do Bell Work 4.2, p. 146.
- (35 min.) Have students do Activities 2–6, pp. 142–143.

Wrap-Up

- (5 min.) Have students do the activity described in **Más práctica,** p. 142.

OPTIONAL RESOURCES

- (5 min.) See Language Note, p. 143.
- (5 min.) See Practices and Perspectives, p. 143.
- (20 min.) See **Comunicación** (TE), p. 143.
- (15 min.) See Slower Pace Learners, p. 143. ◆
- (25 min.) See Multiple Intelligences, p. 143. ●

Practice Options

- *Lab Book*, pp. 21–22, 50 ▲ ● ■
- *Cuaderno de vocabulario y gramática*, pp. 37–39 ▲ ◆ ●
- *Teaching Transparencies:* Bell Work 4.2; **Vocabulario** 4.1, 4.2; *Vocabulario y gramática* Answers, pp. 37–39 ▲ ◆ ●
- *Video Guide*, pp. 34–35, 36 ▲ ● ■
- *Interactive Tutor* (Disc 1) or *DVD Tutor* (Disc 1) ▲ ● ■
- Online practice, Chapter 4 (go.hrw.com, Keyword: EXP1A CH4) ▲ ● ■

▲ = Advanced Learners   ◆ = Slower Pace Learners   ● = Special Learning Needs   ■ = Heritage Speakers

La vida escolar

DAY 4 50-MINUTE LESSON PLAN

NATIONAL STANDARDS

Vocabulario en acción 1

Communication 1.1: Student engages in oral and written exchanges of learned material to socialize and to provide and obtain information.

Communication 1.2: Student demonstrates understanding of simple, clearly spoken, and written language such as simple stories, high-frequency commands, and brief instructions when dealing with familiar topics.

Communication 1.3: Student presents information using familiar words, phrases, and sentences to listeners and readers.

CORE INSTRUCTION

Warm-Up
- (5 min.) Have students read aloud sentences they wrote for Activity 5, p. 143.

Vocabulario en acción 1
- (10 min.) Present **¡Exprésate!,** p. 144, using Teaching **¡Exprésate!,** p. 144.
- (10 min.) Present **Nota cultural,** p. 145.
- (20 min.) Have students do Activities 7–9, pp. 144–145.

Wrap-Up
- (5 min.) Pull items out of a student backpack. As each item is pulled out, students should say the name of the item in Spanish. Then remind the class to study for **Prueba: Vocabulario 1.**

OPTIONAL RESOURCES
- (15 min.) See Teacher to Teacher, p. 145.
- (15 min.) See **Comunicación** (TE), p. 145.
- (25 min.) See Special Learning Needs, p. 145. ●

Practice Options
- *Lab Book*, pp. 21–22, 50 ▲ ● ■
- *Cuaderno de vocabulario y gramática*, pp. 37–39 ▲ ◆ ●
- *Teaching Transparencies:* **Vocabulario** 4.1, 4.2; *Vocabulario y gramática* Answers, pp. 37–39 ▲ ◆ ●
- *Video Guide*, pp. 34–35, 36 ▲ ● ■
- *Interactive Tutor* (Disc 1) or *DVD Tutor* (Disc 1) ▲ ● ■
- Online practice, Chapter 4 (go.hrw.com, Keyword: EXP1A CH4) ▲ ● ■

▲ = Advanced Learners ◆ = Slower Pace Learners ● = Special Learning Needs ■ = Heritage Speakers

CAPÍTULO
4

La vida escolar

DAY 5 50-MINUTE LESSON PLAN

NATIONAL STANDARDS

Vocabulario en acción 1

Communication 1.1: Student engages in oral and written exchanges of learned material to socialize and to provide and obtain information.

Communication 1.2: Student demonstrates understanding of simple, clearly spoken, and written language such as simple stories, high-frequency commands, and brief instructions when dealing with familiar topics.

Communication 1.3: Student presents information using familiar words, phrases, and sentences to listeners and readers.

CORE INSTRUCTION

Warm-Up
- (5 min.) Have students read the paragraphs from Activity 8, p. 144, aloud with a partner.

Vocabulario en acción 1
- (10 min.) Have students do Activity 10, p. 145.
- (10 min.) Review **Vocabulario 1,** pp. 140–145.

Assessment
- (20 min.) Give **Prueba: Vocabulario 1.**

Wrap-Up
- (5 min.) Have students do the activity described in Slower Pace Learners, p. 145. ◆

OPTIONAL RESOURCES
- You can find alternative quizzes in the Assessment Options listed below.

Practice Options
- *Lab Book*, pp. 21–22, 50 ▲ ● ■
- *Cuaderno de vocabulario y gramática*, pp. 37–39 ▲ ◆ ●
- *Teaching Transparencies:* **Vocabulario** 4.1, 4.2; *Vocabulario y gramática* Answers, pp. 37–39 ▲ ◆ ●
- *Video Guide*, pp. 34–35, 36 ▲ ● ■
- *Interactive Tutor* (Disc 1) or *DVD Tutor* (Disc 1) ▲ ● ■
- Online practice, Chapter 4 (go.hrw.com, Keyword: EXP1A CH4) ▲ ● ■

Assessment Options
- *Assessment Program*: **Prueba: Vocabulario 1**, pp. 61–62 ▲ ● ■
- Test Generator ▲ ● ■

▲ = Advanced Learners   ◆ = Slower Pace Learners   ● = Special Learning Needs   ■ = Heritage Speakers

(95)

CAPÍTULO
4

La vida escolar

DAY 6 50-MINUTE LESSON PLAN

NATIONAL STANDARDS

Gramática en acción 1

Communication 1.2: Student demonstrates understanding of simple, clearly spoken, and written language such as simple stories, high-frequency commands, and brief instructions when dealing with familiar topics.

Comparisons 4.1: Student demonstrates an understanding of the nature of language through comparisons of the student's own language and the language studied.

CORE INSTRUCTION

Warm-Up
- (5 min.) See Teaching **Gramática**, #1, p. 146.

Gramática en acción 1
- (20 min.) Present **Gramática:** *Indefinite articles;* **¿cuánto?, mucho,** *and* **poco,** p. 146, using Teaching **Gramática**, #s 2–4, p. 146.
- (10 min.) Show **GramaVisión** (*indefinite articles;* **¿cuánto?, mucho,** *and* **poco**), *Video Program* (Videocassette 2) or *DVD Tutor* (Disc 1).
- (10 min.) Have students do Activities 11–12, pp. 146–147.

Wrap-Up
- (5 min.) Present Common Error Alert, p. 147.

OPTIONAL RESOURCES
- (15 min.) See **Comunicación** (TE), p. 147.

Practice Options
- *Lab Book*, pp. 21–22 ▲ ● ■
- *Cuaderno de vocabulario y gramática*, pp. 40–42 ▲ ◆ ●
- *Cuaderno de actividades*, pp. 31–33 ▲ ● ■
- *Activities for Communication*, pp. 13–14, 61–62 ▲ ■
- *Teaching Transparencies:* **Vocabulario y gramática** Answers, pp. 40–42 ▲ ◆ ●
- *Video Guide*, pp. 34–35 ▲ ● ■
- *Grammar Tutor for Students of Spanish*, pp. 21–22, 171–172 ◆ ●
- *TPR Storytelling Book*, pp. 18–19 ▲ ●
- *Interactive Tutor* (Disc 1) or *DVD Tutor* (Disc 1) ▲ ● ■
- Online practice, Chapter 4 (go.hrw.com, Keyword: EXP1A CH4) ▲ ● ■

▲ = Advanced Learners   ◆ = Slower Pace Learners   ● = Special Learning Needs   ■ = Heritage Speakers

Holt Spanish 1A

Lesson Planner

Teacher's Name _____ Class _____ Date _____

La vida escolar

DAY 7 50-MINUTE LESSON PLAN

Gramática en acción 1

Communication 1.1: Student engages in oral and written exchanges of learned material to socialize and to provide and obtain information.

Communication 1.2: Student demonstrates understanding of simple, clearly spoken, and written language such as simple stories, high-frequency commands, and brief instructions when dealing with familiar topics.

Communication 1.3: Student presents information using familiar words, phrases, and sentences to listeners and readers.

Comparisons 4.1: Student demonstrates an understanding of the nature of language through comparisons of the student's own language and the language studied.

CORE INSTRUCTION

Warm-Up
• (5 min.) Have students do Bell Work 4.3, p. 148.

Gramática en acción 1
• (5 min.) Have students do Activity 13, p. 147.
• (10 min.) Play Audio CD 4, Tr. 2, for Activity 14, p. 147. ●
• (10 min.) Have students do Activity 15, p. 147.
• (15 min.) Present **Gramática:** *The present tense* of **tener** *and some* **tener** *idioms,* p. 148, using Teaching **Gramática,** p. 148.

Wrap-Up
• (5 min.) Present Heritage Speakers and Language to Language, p. 149. ■

OPTIONAL RESOURCES
• (25 min.) See Advanced Learners, p. 147. ▲
• (15 min.) Multiple Intelligences, p. 147 ●

Practice Options
• *Lab Book,* pp. 21–22 ▲ ● ■
• *Cuaderno de vocabulario y gramática,* pp. 40–42 ▲ ● ■
• *Cuaderno de actividades,* pp. 31–33 ▲ ● ■
• *Activities for Communication,* pp. 13–14, 61–62 ▲ ■
• *Teaching Transparencies:* Bell Work 4.3; *Vocabulario y gramática* Answers, pp. 40–42 ▲ ● ■
• *Video Guide,* pp. 34–36 ▲ ● ■
• *Grammar Tutor for Students of Spanish,* pp. 21–22, 171–172 ◆ ●
• *TPR Storytelling Book,* pp. 18–19 ▲ ●
• *Interactive Tutor* (Disc 1) or *DVD Tutor* (Disc 1) ▲ ● ■
• Online practice, Chapter 4 (go.hrw.com, Keyword: EXP1A CH4) ▲ ● ■

▲ = Advanced Learners ◆ = Slower Pace Learners ● = Special Learning Needs ■ = Heritage Speakers

Lesson Planner
97

CAPÍTULO

4

La vida escolar

DAY 8 50-MINUTE LESSON PLAN

NATIONAL STANDARDS

Gramática en acción 1
Communication 1.1: Student engages in oral and written exchanges of learned material to socialize and to provide and obtain information.

Communication 1.2: Student demonstrates understanding of simple, clearly spoken, and written language such as simple stories, high-frequency commands, and brief instructions when dealing with familiar topics.

CORE INSTRUCTION

Warm-Up
- (5 min.) Have students do Bell Work 4.4, p. 150.

Gramática en acción 1
- (15 min.) Show **GramaVisión** (**tener** *and some* **tener** idioms*), Video Program* (Videocassette 2) or *DVD Tutor* (Disc 1) and review **tener** and **tener** idioms.
- (10 min.) Play Audio CD 4, Tr. 3, for Activity 16, p. 148. ●
- (15 min.) Have students do Activities 17–19, p. 149.

Wrap-Up
- (5 min.) Have students compare sentences from Activity 18, p. 149.

OPTIONAL RESOURCES
- (20 min.) See Advanced Learners, p. 149. ▲
- (15 min.) See Special Learning Needs, p. 149. ●
- (20 min.) See **Comunicación** (TE), p. 149.

Practice Options
- *Lab Book*, pp. 21–22 ▲ ● ■
- **Cuaderno de vocabulario y gramática**, pp. 40–42 ▲ ◆ ●
- **Cuaderno de actividades**, pp. 31–33 ▲ ● ■
- *Activities for Communication*, pp. 13–14, 61–62 ▲ ■
- *Teaching Transparencies:* Bell Work 4.4; **Vocabulario y gramática** Answers, pp. 40–42 ▲ ◆ ●
- *Video Guide*, pp. 34–35 ▲ ● ■
- *Grammar Tutor for Students of Spanish*, pp. 21–22, 171–172 ◆ ●
- *TPR Storytelling Book*, pp. 18–19 ▲ ●
- *Interactive Tutor* (Disc 1) or *DVD Tutor* (Disc 1) ▲ ● ■
- Online practice, Chapter 4 (go.hrw.com, Keyword: EXP1A CH4) ▲ ● ■

▲ = Advanced Learners ◆ = Slower Pace Learners ● = Special Learning Needs ■ = Heritage Speakers

Holt Spanish 1A

Lesson Planner

La vida escolar

NATIONAL STANDARDS

Gramática en acción 1
Communication 1.1: Student engages in oral and written exchanges of learned material to socialize and to provide and obtain information.

Communication 1.2: Student demonstrates understanding of simple, clearly spoken, and written language such as simple stories, high-frequency commands, and brief instructions when dealing with familiar topics.

CORE INSTRUCTION

Warm-Up
- (5 min.) Ask students to answer the following questions with words and gestures: **¿Tienes hambre? / ¿Tienes sed? / ¿Tienes ganas de descansar? / ¿Tienes un bolígrafo?**

Gramática en acción 1
- (10 min.) Present **Gramática:** *The verb* **venir** *and* **a** + *time*, p. 150, using Teaching **Gramática,** p. 150.
- (10 min.) Show **GramaVisión** *(***venir** *and* **a** + *time), Video Program* (Videocassette 2) or *DVD Tutor* (Disc 1).
- (10 min.) Play Audio CD 4, Tr. 4, for Activity 20, p. 150. ●
- (10 min.) Have students do Activity 21, p. 150.

Wrap-Up
- (5 min.) Have students use Activity 21 to create a few questions to ask of a partner.

OPTIONAL RESOURCES
- (10 min.) See Slower Pace Learners, p. 151. ◆
- (5 min.) See Special Learning Needs, p. 151. ●

Practice Options
- *Lab Book*, pp. 21–22 ▲ ● ■
- *Cuaderno de vocabulario y gramática*, pp. 40–42 ▲ ◆ ●
- *Cuaderno de actividades*, pp. 31–33 ▲ ● ■
- *Activities for Communication*, pp. 13–14, 62–62 ▲ ■
- *Teaching Transparencies: Vocabulario y gramática* Answers, pp. 40–42 ▲ ◆ ●
- *Video Guide*, pp. 34–35 ▲ ● ■
- *Grammar Tutor for Students of Spanish*, pp. 21–22, 171–172 ◆ ●
- *TPR Storytelling Book*, pp. 18–19 ▲ ●
- *Interactive Tutor* (Disc 1) or *DVD Tutor* (Disc 1) ▲ ● ■
- Online practice, Chapter 4 (go.hrw.com, Keyword: EXP1A CH4) ▲ ● ■

▲ = Advanced Learners   ◆ = Slower Pace Learners   ● = Special Learning Needs   ■ = Heritage Speakers

La vida escolar

DAY 10 50-MINUTE LESSON PLAN

NATIONAL STANDARDS

Gramática en acción 1

Communication 1.1: Student engages in oral and written exchanges of learned material to socialize and to provide and obtain information.

Communication 1.2: Student demonstrates understanding of simple, clearly spoken, and written language such as simple stories, high-frequency commands, and brief instructions when dealing with familiar topics.

Communication 1.3: Student presents information using familiar words, phrases, and sentences to listeners and readers.

Cultures 2.2: Student demonstrates an understanding of the products (what people create) and how they are related to the perspectives (how people perceive things) of the cultures studied.

Connections 3.2: Student uses resources (that may include technology) in the language and cultures being studied to gain access to information.

CORE INSTRUCTION

Warm-Up
- (5 min.) Have students do Bell Work 4.5, p. 154.

Gramática en acción 1
- (20 min.) Have students do Activities 22–23, p. 151.
- (20 min.) Review **Gramática 1,** pp. 146–151.

Wrap-Up
- (5 min.) Present Practices and Perspectives, p. 151. Then remind students to study for **Prueba: Gramática 1.**

OPTIONAL RESOURCES
- (5 min.) See **Comunicación (TE)**, p. 151.

Practice Options
- *Lab Book,* pp. 21–22 ▲ ● ■
- ***Cuaderno de vocabulario y gramática***, pp. 40–42 ▲ ◆ ●
- ***Cuaderno de actividades***, pp. 31–33 ▲ ● ■
- *Activities for Communication,* pp. 13–14, 61–62 ▲ ■
- *Teaching Transparencies:* Bell Work 4.5; ***Vocabulario y gramática*** Answers, pp. 40–42 ▲ ◆ ●
- *Video Guide,* pp. 34–35 ▲ ● ■
- *Grammar Tutor for Students of Spanish,* pp. 21–22, 171–172 ◆ ●
- *TPR Storytelling Book,* pp. 18–19 ▲ ●
- *Interactive Tutor* (Disc 1) or *DVD Tutor* (Disc 1) ▲ ● ■
- Online practice, Chapter 4 (go.hrw.com, Keyword: EXP1A CH4) ▲ ● ■

▲ = Advanced Learners   ◆ = Slower Pace Learners   ● = Special Learning Needs   ■ = Heritage Speakers

Holt Spanish 1A

Lesson Planner

CAPÍTULO **4**

La vida escolar

DAY 11 50-MINUTE LESSON PLAN

NATIONAL STANDARDS

Gramática en acción 1

Communication 1.1: Student engages in oral and written exchanges of learned material to socialize and to provide and obtain information.

Communication 1.2: Student demonstrates understanding of simple, clearly spoken, and written language such as simple stories, high-frequency commands, and brief instructions when dealing with familiar topics.

Communication 1.3: Student presents information using familiar words, phrases, and sentences to listeners and readers.

Connections 3.2: Student uses resources (that may include technology) in the language and cultures being studied to gain access to information.

Cultura

Cultures 2.1: Student demonstrates an understanding of the practices (what people do) and how they are related to the perspectives (how people perceive things) of the cultures studied.

Comparisons 4.2: Student demonstrates an understanding of the concept of culture through comparisons of the student's own culture and the cultures studied.

CORE INSTRUCTION

Warm-Up

- (5 min.) Ask students the following questions: **¿A qué hora vienes al colegio? / ¿Tienes una prueba hoy? / ¿Tienes un lápiz para la prueba? /¿Tienes mucha tarea esta semana?**

Gramática en acción 1

- (5 min.) Review **Gramática 1,** pp. 146–151.

Assessment

- (20 min.) Give **Prueba: Gramática 1.**

Cultura

- (15 min.) Present **Cultura,** pp. 152–153, using Teaching **Cultura,** p. 152, #s 1–2.

Wrap-Up

- (5 min.) See Map Activities, p. 152.

OPTIONAL RESOURCES

- (15 min.) See Special Learning Needs, p. 153. ●
- You can find alternative quizzes in the Assessment Options listed below.

Practice Options

- *Lab Book,* pp. 21–22, 51 ▲ ● ■
- *Cuaderno de vocabulario y gramática,* pp. 40–42 ▲ ◆ ●
- *Cuaderno de actividades,* pp. 31–33, 34 ▲ ● ■
- *Cuaderno para hispanohablantes,* p. 44
- *Activities for Communication,* pp. 13–14, 61–62 ▲ ■
- *Teaching Transparencies:* **Vocabulario y gramática** Answers, pp. 40–42 ▲ ● ■
- *Video Guide,* pp. 34–35, 37 ▲ ● ■
- *Grammar Tutor for Students of Spanish,* pp. 21–22, 171–172 ◆ ●

- *TPR Storytelling Book,* pp. 18–19 ▲ ●
- *Interactive Tutor* (Disc 1) or *DVD Tutor* (Disc 1) ▲ ● ■
- Online practice, Chapter 4 (go.hrw.com, Keyword: EXP1A CH4) ▲ ● ■

Assessment Options

- *Assessment Program:* **Prueba: Gramática 1,** pp. 63–64 ▲ ● ■
- *Assessment Program:* **Prueba: Aplicación 1,** pp. 65–66 ▲ ● ■
- Audio CD 4, Tr. 19
- Test Generator ▲ ● ■

▲ = Advanced Learners   ◆ = Slower Pace Learners   ● = Special Learning Needs   ■ = Heritage Speakers

La vida escolar

NATIONAL STANDARDS

Cultura

Communication 1.2: Student demonstrates understanding of simple, clearly spoken, and written language such as simple stories, high-frequency commands, and brief instructions when dealing with familiar topics.

Comparisons 4.1: Student demonstrates an understanding of the nature of language through comparisons of the student's own language and the language studied.

Communities 5.1: Student uses the language both within and beyond the school setting through activities such as participating in cultural events and using technology to communicate.

Vocabulario en acción 2

Communication 1.2: Student demonstrates understanding of simple, clearly spoken, and written language such as simple stories, high-frequency commands, and brief instructions when dealing with familiar topics.

CORE INSTRUCTION

Warm-Up
- (5 min.) Present Language Note, p. 153.

Cultura
- (10 min.) Show **VideoCultura,** Ch. 4.
- (10 min.) See Teaching **Cultura,** #3, p. 152.
- (5 min.) Present and assign **Comunidad,** p. 153.

Vocabulario en acción 2
- (10 min.) Present **Vocabulario,** pp. 154–155, using Teaching **Vocabulario 2,** #s 1–2, p. 154.

Wrap-Up
- (10 min.) Have students do the activity described in Advanced Learners, p. 153. ▲

OPTIONAL RESOURCES
- (5 min.) See Common Error Alert, p. 155.
- (5 min.) See Language Note, p. 155.

Practice Options
- *Lab Book,* pp. 23–24, 51, 52 ▲ ● ■
- *Cuaderno de actividades,* p. 34 ▲ ● ■
- *Cuaderno de vocabulario y gramática,* pp. 43–45 ▲ ◆ ●
- *Cuaderno para hispanohablantes,* p. 44
- *Teaching Transparencies:* **Vocabulario** 4.3, 4.4; *Vocabulario y gramática* Answers, pp. 43–45 ▲ ◆ ●
- *Video Guide,* pp. 34–35, 37, 38 ▲ ● ■
- *Interactive Tutor* (Disc 1) or *DVD Tutor* (Disc 1) ▲ ● ■
- Online practice, Chapter 4 (go.hrw.com, Keyword: EXP1A CH4) ▲ ● ■

▲ = Advanced Learners   ◆ = Slower Pace Learners   ● = Special Learning Needs   ■ = Heritage Speakers

La vida escolar

DAY 13 50-MINUTE LESSON PLAN

NATIONAL STANDARDS

Vocabulario en acción 2

Communication 1.1: Student engages in oral and written exchanges of learned material to socialize and to provide and obtain information.

Communication 1.2: Student demonstrates under-standing of simple, clearly spoken, and written language such as simple stories, high-frequency commands, and brief instructions when dealing with familiar topics.

Communication 1.3: Student presents information using familiar words, phrases, and sentences to listeners and readers.

CORE INSTRUCTION

Warm-Up

• (10 min.) Have students do the activity described in Advanced Learners, p. 155. ▲

Vocabulario en acción 2

• (10 min.) Show **ExpresaVisión,** Ch. 4.
• (5 min.) Review **Vocabulario 2,** pp. 154–155.
• (10 min.) See Teaching **Vocabulario,** #s 3–4, p. 154.
• (10 min.) Present other expressions from **¡Exprésate!,** p. 155.

Wrap-Up

• (5 min.) Have students work with a partner. They should ask each other in Spanish what their plans are for the upcoming weekend.

OPTIONAL RESOURCES

• (15 min.) See TPR, p. 155. ●
• (10 min.) See Special Learning Needs, p. 155. ●

Practice Options

• *Lab Book*, pp. 23–24, 52 ▲ ● ■
• *Cuaderno de vocabulario y gramática*, pp. 43–45 ▲ ◆ ●
• *Teaching Transparencies:* **Vocabulario** 4.3, 4.4; *Vocabulario y gramática* Answers, pp. 43–45 ▲ ◆ ●
• *Video Guide*, pp. 34–35, 38 ▲ ● ■
• *Interactive Tutor* (Disc 1) or *DVD Tutor* (Disc 1) ▲ ● ■
• Online practice, Chapter 4 (go.hrw.com, Keyword: EXP1A CH4) ▲ ● ■

▲ = Advanced Learners   ◆ = Slower Pace Learners   ● = Special Learning Needs   ■ = Heritage Speakers

Holt Spanish 1A

Lesson Planner

La vida escolar

DAY 14 50-MINUTE LESSON PLAN

NATIONAL STANDARDS

Vocabulario en acción 2

Communication 1.1: Student engages in oral and written exchanges of learned material to socialize and to provide and obtain information.

Communication 1.2: Student demonstrates understanding of simple, clearly spoken, and written language such as simple stories, high-frequency commands, and brief instructions when dealing with familiar topics.

Communication 1.3: Student presents information using familiar words, phrases, and sentences to listeners and readers.

Cultures 2.1: Student demonstrates an understanding of the practices (what people do) and how they are related to the perspectives (how people perceive things) of the cultures studied.

Comparisons 4.2: Student demonstrates an understanding of the concept of culture through comparisons of the student's own culture and the cultures studied.

CORE INSTRUCTION

Warm-Up

- (5 min.) Ask students the following question: **¿Qué vas a hacer este fin de semana?**

Vocabulario en acción 2

- (10 min.) Review **Vocabulario 2** and **¡Exprésate!,** pp. 154–155.
- (10 min.) Play Audio CD 4, Tr. 8, for Activity 24, p. 156. ●
- (10 min.) Have students do Activities 25–26, p. 156.
- (10 min.) Present **Nota cultural,** p. 156.

Wrap-Up

- (5 min.) Have students write out five of the sentences required for Activity 26, p. 156.

OPTIONAL RESOURCES

- (15 min.) See **Comunicación** (TE), p. 156.
- (20 min.) See Game, p. 156. ●
- (5 min.) See Advanced Learners, p. 157. ▲

Practice Options

- *Lab Book*, pp. 23–24, 52 ▲ ● ■
- *Cuaderno de vocabulario y gramática*, pp. 43–45 ▲ ◆ ●
- *Teaching Transparencies:* **Vocabulario** 4.3, 4.4; *Vocabulario y gramática* Answers, pp. 43–45 ▲ ◆ ●
- *Video Guide*, pp. 34–35, 38 ▲ ● ■
- *Interactive Tutor* (Disc 1) or *DVD Tutor* (Disc 1) ▲ ● ■
- Online practice, Chapter 4 (go.hrw.com, Keyword: EXP1A CH4) ▲ ● ■

▲ = Advanced Learners   ◆ = Slower Pace Learners   ● = Special Learning Needs   ■ = Heritage Speakers

(104)

La vida escolar

DAY 15 50-MINUTE LESSON PLAN

NATIONAL STANDARDS

Vocabulario en acción 2
Communication 1.1: Student engages in oral and written exchanges of learned material to socialize and to provide and obtain information.

Communication 1.2: Student demonstrates understanding of simple, clearly spoken, and written language such as simple stories, high-frequency commands, and brief instructions when dealing with familiar topics.

Communication 1.3: Student presents information using familiar words, phrases, and sentences to listeners and readers.

CORE INSTRUCTION

Warm-Up
- (5 min.) Present Common Error Alert, p. 157.

Vocabulario en acción 2
- (15 min.) Have students do Activities 27–28, p. 157.
- (10 min.) Present **¡Exprésate!,** p. 158, using Teaching **¡Exprésate!,** p. 158.
- (10 min.) Play Audio CD 4, Tr. 9, for Activity 29, p. 158. ●
- (5 min.) Have students do Activity 30, p. 158.

Wrap-Up
- (5 min.) Have students read the conversation in Activity 30 aloud with a partner.

OPTIONAL RESOURCES
- (10 min.) See Comparing and Contrasting, p. 157.
- (10 min.) See **Comunicación** (TE), p. 157.
- (25 min.) See Multiple Intelligences, p. 157. ●
- (5 min.) See Language Note, p. 159.
- (5 min.) See Heritage Speakers, p. 159. ■

Practice Options
- *Lab Book*, pp. 23–24, 52 ▲ ● ■
- *Cuaderno de vocabulario y gramática*, pp. 43–45 ▲ ◆ ●
- *Teaching Transparencies:* **Vocabulario** 4.3, 4.4; *Vocabulario y gramática* Answers, pp. 43–45 ▲ ◆ ●
- *Video Guide*, pp. 34–35, 38 ▲ ● ■
- *Interactive Tutor* (Disc 1) or *DVD Tutor* (Disc 1) ▲ ● ■
- Online practice, Chapter 4 (go.hrw.com, Keyword: EXP1A CH4) ▲ ● ■

▲ = Advanced Learners   ◆ = Slower Pace Learners   ● = Special Learning Needs   ■ = Heritage Speakers

¡Empecemos!

DAY 16 50-MINUTE LESSON PLAN

NATIONAL STANDARDS

Vocabulario en acción 2

Communication 1.1: Student engages in oral and written exchanges of learned material to socialize and to provide and obtain information.

Communication 1.2: Student demonstrates understanding of simple, clearly spoken, and written language such as simple stories, high-frequency commands, and brief instructions when dealing with familiar topics.

Communication 1.3: Student presents information using familiar words, phrases, and sentences to listeners and readers.

CORE INSTRUCTION

Warm-Up

- (5 min.) Have students do Bell Work 4.6, p. 160.

Vocabulario en acción 2

- (10 min.) Review ¡Exprésate!, p. 158.
- (20 min.) Have students do Activities 31–33, p. 159.
- (10 min.) Review **Vocabulario 2,** pp. 154–159.

Wrap-Up

- (5 min.) Assign Advanced Learners, p. 159, as homework. Then remind students to study for **Prueba: Vocabulario 2.** ▲

OPTIONAL RESOURCES

- (20 min.) See **Comunicación** (TE), p. 159.
- (60 min.) See Multiple Intelligences, p. 159. ●

Practice Options

- *Lab Book,* pp. 23–24, 52 ▲ ● ■
- *Cuaderno de vocabulario y gramática,* pp. 43–45 ▲ ◆ ●
- *Teaching Transparencies:* Bell Work 4.6; **Vocabulario** 4.3, 4.4; *Vocabulario y gramática* Answers, pp. 43–45 ▲ ◆ ●
- *Video Guide,* pp. 34–35, 38 ▲ ● ■
- *Interactive Tutor* (Disc 1) or *DVD Tutor* (Disc 1) ▲ ● ■
- Online practice, Chapter 4 (go.hrw.com, Keyword: EXP1A CH4) ▲ ● ■

▲ = Advanced Learners ◆ = Slower Pace Learners ● = Special Learning Needs ■ = Heritage Speakers

CAPÍTULO

4

La vida escolar

DAY 17 50-MINUTE LESSON PLAN

NATIONAL STANDARDS

Vocabulario en acción 2

Communication 1.1: Student engages in oral and written exchanges of learned material to socialize and to provide and obtain information.

Communication 1.2: Student demonstrates understanding of simple, clearly spoken, and written language such as simple stories, high-frequency commands, and brief instructions when dealing with familiar topics.

Communication 1.3: Student presents information using familiar words, phrases, and sentences to listeners and readers.

Gramática en acción 2

Communication 1.1: Student engages in oral and written exchanges of learned material to socialize and to provide and obtain information.

Communication 1.2: Student demonstrates understanding of simple, clearly spoken, and written language such as simple stories, high-frequency commands, and brief instructions when dealing with familiar topics.

CORE INSTRUCTION

Warm-Up

• (5 min.) Ask students the following question: **¿A qué hora sales del colegio hoy?**

Vocabulario en acción 2

• (5 min.) Review **Vocabulario 2,** pp. 154–159.

Assessment

• (20 min.) Give **Prueba: Vocabulario 2.**

Gramática en acción 2

• (15 min.) Present **Gramática: ir a** *with infinitive*, p. 160, using Teaching **Gramática,** p. 160.

Wrap-Up

• (5 min.) Have students ask each other the following question: **¿Qué vas a hacer esta noche?**

OPTIONAL RESOURCES

• You can find alternative quizzes in the Assessment Options listed below.

Practice Options

• *Lab Book*, pp. 23–24, 52 ▲ ● ■
• ***Cuaderno de vocabulario y gramática***, pp. 43–45, 46–48 ▲ ◆ ●
• ***Cuaderno de actividades***, pp. 35–37 ▲ ● ■
• *Activities for Communication*, pp. 15–16, 61–62 ▲ ■
• *Teaching Transparencies:* **Vocabulario** 4.3, 4.4; ***Vocabulario y gramática***
  Answers, pp. 43–45, 46–48 ▲ ◆ ●
• *TPR Storytelling Book*, pp. 20–21 ▲ ●
• *Video Guide*, pp. 34–35, 38 ▲ ● ■
• *Grammar Tutor for Students of Spanish*, pp. 23–26, 171–172 ◆ ●
• *Interactive Tutor* (Disc 1) or *DVD Tutor* (Disc 1) ▲ ● ■
• Online practice, Chapter 4 (go.hrw.com, Keyword: EXP1A CH4) ▲ ● ■

Assessment Options

• *Assessment Program*: **Prueba: Vocabulario 2**, pp. 67–68 ▲ ● ■
• Test Generator ▲ ● ■

▲ = Advanced Learners   ◆ = Slower Pace Learners   ● = Special Learning Needs   ■ = Heritage Speakers

107

La vida escolar

DAY 18 50-MINUTE LESSON PLAN

NATIONAL STANDARDS

Gramática en acción 2

Communication 1.1: Student engages in oral and written exchanges of learned material to socialize and to provide and obtain information.

Communication 1.2: Student demonstrates understanding of simple, clearly spoken, and written language such as simple stories, high-frequency commands, and brief instructions when dealing with familiar topics.

Communication 1.3: Student presents information using familiar words, phrases, and sentences to listeners and readers.

CORE INSTRUCTION

Warm-Up

• (5 min.) Ask students **¿Qué haces los sábados?**

Gramática en acción 2

• (10 min.) Show **GramaVisión** *(ir a with infinitives), Video Program* (Videocassette 2) or *DVD Tutor* (Disc 1).

• (5 min.) Review **ir a** with an infinitive, p. 160.

• (10 min.) Play Audio CD 4, Tr. 10, for Activity 34, p. 160. ●

• (15 min.) Have students do Activities 35–37, pp. 160–161.

Wrap-Up

• (5 min.) Have students read aloud their responses for Activity 37, p. 161.

OPTIONAL RESOURCES

• (10 min.) See Slower Pace Learners, p. 161. ◆

• (15 min.) See **Comunicación (TE)**, p. 161.

Practice Options

• *Lab Book*, pp. 23–24 ▲ ● ■
• *Cuaderno de vocabulario y gramática*, pp. 46–48 ▲ ◆ ●
• *Cuaderno de actividades*, pp. 35–37 ▲ ● ■
• *Activities for Communication*, pp. 15–16, 61–62 ▲ ■
• *Teaching Transparencies: Vocabulario y gramática* Answers, pp. 46–48 ▲ ◆ ●
• *TPR Storytelling Book*, pp. 20–21 ▲ ●
• *Video Guide*, pp. 34–35 ▲ ● ■
• *Grammar Tutor for Students of Spanish*, pp. 23–26, 171–172 ◆ ●
• *Interactive Tutor* (Disc 1) or *DVD Tutor* (Disc 1) ▲ ● ■
• Online practice, Chapter 4 (go.hrw.com, Keyword: EXP1A CH4) ▲ ● ■

▲ = Advanced Learners   ◆ = Slower Pace Learners   ● = Special Learning Needs   ■ = Heritage Speakers

CAPÍTULO

4

La vida escolar

DAY 19 50-MINUTE LESSON PLAN

NATIONAL STANDARDS

Gramática en acción 2

Communication 1.1: Student engages in oral and written exchanges of learned material to socialize and to provide and obtain information.

Communication 1.2: Student demonstrates understanding of simple, clearly spoken, and written language such as simple stories, high-frequency commands, and brief instructions when dealing with familiar topics.

CORE INSTRUCTION

Warm-Up

- (5 min.) Have students do Bell Work 4.7, p. 162.

Gramática en acción 2

- (10 min.) Have students do Activity 38, p. 161.
- (25 min.) Present **Gramática: -er** *and* **-ir** *verbs; tag questions,* p. 162, using Teaching **Gramática,** p. 162.
- (5 min.) Have students do Activity 39, p. 162.

Wrap-Up

- (5 min.) Have students write out the present-tense conjugations of **beber** and **asistir.**

OPTIONAL RESOURCES

- (10 min.) See Multiple Intelligences, p. 161. ●
- (10 min.) See Special Learning Needs, p. 163. ●

Practice Options

- *Lab Book,* pp. 23–24 ▲ ● ■
- *Cuaderno de vocabulario y gramática,* pp. 46–48 ▲ ◆ ●
- *Cuaderno de actividades,* pp. 35–37 ▲ ● ■
- *Activities for Communication,* pp. 15–16, 61–62 ▲ ■
- *Teaching Transparencies:* Bell Work 4.7; *Vocabulario y gramática* Answers, pp. 46–48 ▲ ◆ ●
- *TPR Storytelling Book,* pp. 20–21 ▲ ●
- *Video Guide,* pp. 34–35 ▲ ● ■
- *Grammar Tutor for Students of Spanish,* pp. 23–26, 171–172 ◆ ●
- *Interactive Tutor* (Disc 1) or *DVD Tutor* (Disc 1) ▲ ● ■
- Online practice, Chapter 4 (go.hrw.com, Keyword: EXP1A CH4) ▲ ● ■

▲ = Advanced Learners ◆ = Slower Pace Learners ● = Special Learning Needs ■ = Heritage Speakers

Holt Spanish 1A

Lesson Planner

La vida escolar

DAY 20 50-MINUTE LESSON PLAN

NATIONAL STANDARDS

Gramática en acción 2

Communication 1.2: Student demonstrates understanding of simple, clearly spoken, and written language such as simple stories, high-frequency commands, and brief instructions when dealing with familiar topics.

Communication 1.3: Student presents information using familiar words, phrases, and sentences to listeners and readers.

Cultures 2.1: Student demonstrates an understanding of the practices (what people do) and how they are related to the perspectives (how people perceive things) of the cultures studied.

Comparisons 4.2: Student demonstrates an understanding of the concept of culture through comparisons of the student's own culture and the cultures studied.

CORE INSTRUCTION

Warm-Up

- (5 min.) Have students tell you the conjugations of **escribir** and **leer** as you write them on the board.

Gramática en acción 2

- (10 min.) Show **GramaVisión** -er *and* -ir *verbs; tag questions), Video Program* (Videocassette 2) or *DVD Tutor* (Disc 1).
- (10 min.) Review **-er** and **-ir** verbs and tag questions, p. 162.
- (10 min.) Have students do Activities 40–41, p. 163.
- (5 min.) Present **Nota cultural,** p. 162.

Wrap-Up

- (10 min.) Have students do the activity described in Advanced Learners, p. 163. ▲

OPTIONAL RESOURCES

- (5 min.) See Teacher to Teacher, p. 163.

Practice Options

- *Lab Book*, pp. 23–24 ▲ ● ■
- *Cuaderno de vocabulario y gramática*, pp. 46–48 ▲ ◆ ●
- *Cuaderno de actividades*, pp. 35–37 ▲ ● ■
- *Activities for Communication*, pp. 15–16, 61–62 ▲ ■
- *Teaching Transparencies: Vocabulario y gramática* Answers, pp. 46–48 ▲ ◆ ●
- *TPR Storytelling Book*, pp. 20–21 ▲ ●
- *Video Guide*, pp. 34–35 ▲ ● ■
- *Grammar Tutor for Students of Spanish*, pp. 23–26, 171–172 ▲ ●
- *Interactive Tutor* (Disc 1) or *DVD Tutor* (Disc 1) ▲ ● ■
- Online practice, Chapter 4 (go.hrw.com, Keyword: EXP1A CH4) ▲ ● ■

▲ = Advanced Learners   ◆ = Slower Pace Learners   ● = Special Learning Needs   ■ = Heritage Speakers

Holt Spanish 1A

Lesson Planner

CAPÍTULO
4

La vida escolar

DAY 21 50-MINUTE LESSON PLAN

NATIONAL STANDARDS

Gramática en acción 2

Communication 1.1: Student engages in oral and written exchanges of learned material to socialize and to provide and obtain information.

Communication 1.2: Student demonstrates understanding of simple, clearly spoken, and written language such as simple stories, high-frequency commands, and brief instructions when dealing with familiar topics.

Communication 1.3: Student presents information using familiar words, phrases, and sentences to listeners and readers.

CORE INSTRUCTION

Warm-Up

- (5 min.) Have students do Bell Work 4.8, p. 164.

Gramática en acción 2

- (10 min.) Have students do Activity 42, p. 163.
- (20 min.) Present **Gramática:** *some* **–er/-ir** *verbs with irregular* **yo** *forms*, p. 164, using Teaching **Gramática**, p. 164.
- (5 min.) Have students do Activity 43, p. 164.

Wrap-Up

- (10 min.) See Multiple Intelligences, p. 165. ●

OPTIONAL RESOURCES

- (5 min.) See **Comunicación** (TE), p. 163.

Practice Options

- *Lab Book*, pp. 23–24 ▲ ● ■
- *Cuaderno de vocabulario y gramática*, pp. 46–48 ▲ ◆ ●
- *Cuaderno de actividades*, pp. 35–37 ▲ ● ■
- *Activities for Communication*, pp. 15–16, 61–62 ▲ ■
- *Teaching Transparencies:* Bell Work 4.8; *Vocabulario y gramática* Answers, pp. 46–48 ▲ ◆ ●
- *TPR Storytelling Book*, pp. 20–21 ▲ ●
- *Video Guide*, pp. 34–35 ▲ ● ■
- *Grammar Tutor for Students of Spanish*, pp. 23–26, 171–172 ◆ ●
- *Interactive Tutor* (Disc 1) or *DVD Tutor* (Disc 1) ▲ ● ■
- Online practice, Chapter 4 (go.hrw.com, Keyword: EXP1A CH4) ▲ ● ■

▲ = Advanced Learners   ◆ = Slower Pace Learners   ● = Special Learning Needs   ■ = Heritage Speakers

Holt Spanish 1A

Lesson Planner

CAPÍTULO
4

La vida escolar

DAY 22 50-MINUTE LESSON PLAN

NATIONAL STANDARDS

Gramática en acción 2

Communication 1.1: Student engages in oral and written exchanges of learned material to socialize and to provide and obtain information.

Communication 1.2: Student demonstrates understanding of simple, clearly spoken, and written language such as simple stories, high-frequency commands, and brief instructions when dealing with familiar topics.

Communication 1.3: Student presents information using familiar words, phrases, and sentences to listeners and readers.

CORE INSTRUCTION

Warm-Up

- (5 min.) Have students write out the present-tense conjugations of **saber, ver,** and **hacer.**

Gramática en acción 2

- (10 min.) Show **GramaVisión** (*some* **–er/-ir** *verbs with irregular* **yo** *forms*), *Video Program* (Videocassette 2) or *DVD Tutor* (Disc 1).
- (20 min.) Have students do Activities 44–46, p. 165.
- (10 min.) Review **Gramática 2,** pp. 160–165.

Wrap-Up

- (5 min.) Read each part (a, b, and c) of the description in AP Language Examination, p. 165, out of order while students choose the picture in Activity 46 that goes with each. Remind students to study for **Prueba: Gramática 2.**

OPTIONAL RESOURCES

- (10 min.) See Slower Pace Learners, p. 165. ◆
- (20 min.) See **Comunicación** (TE), p. 165.

Practice Options

- *Lab Book,* pp. 23–24 ▲ ● ■
- ***Cuaderno de vocabulario y gramática,*** pp. 46–48 ▲ ◆ ●
- ***Cuaderno de actividades,*** pp. 35–37 ▲ ● ■
- *Activities for Communication,* pp. 15–16, 61–62 ▲ ■
- *Teaching Transparencies:* ***Vocabulario y gramática*** Answers, pp. 46–48 ▲ ◆ ●
- *Video Guide,* pp. 34–35 ▲ ● ■
- *Grammar Tutor for Students of Spanish,* pp. 23–26, 171–172 ◆ ●
- *TPR Storytelling Book,* pp. 20–21 ▲ ●
- *Interactive Tutor* (Disc 1) or *DVD Tutor* (Disc 1) ▲ ● ■
- Online practice, Chapter 4 (go.hrw.com, Keyword: EXP1A CH4) ▲ ● ■

▲ = Advanced Learners   ◆ = Slower Pace Learners   ● = Special Learning Needs   ■ = Heritage Speakers

CAPÍTULO
4

La vida escolar

DAY 23 50-MINUTE LESSON PLAN

NATIONAL STANDARDS

Gramática en acción 2

Communication 1.1: Student engages in oral and written exchanges of learned material to socialize and to provide and obtain information.

Communication 1.2: Student demonstrates understanding of simple, clearly spoken, and written language such as simple stories, high-frequency commands, and brief instructions when dealing with familiar topics.

Communication 1.3: Student presents information using familiar words, phrases, and sentences to listeners and readers.

Conexiones culturales

Cultures 2.1: Student demonstrates an understanding of the practices (what people do) and how they are related to the perspectives (how people perceive things) of the cultures studied.

Cultures 2.2: Student demonstrates an understanding of the products (what people create) and how they are related to the perspectives (how people perceive things) of the cultures studied.

CORE INSTRUCTION

Warm-Up

• (5 min.) Ask students the following questions: **Tenemos una prueba hoy, ¿no? / ¿Qué vas a hacer hoy después de clases?**

Gramática en acción 2

• (5 min.) Review **Gramática 2,** pp. 160–165.

Assessment

• (20 min.) Give **Prueba: Gramática 2.**

Conexiones culturales

• (15 min.) Present **Conexiones culturales,** pp. 166–167, using Teaching **Conexiones culturales,** #s 1–2, p. 166.

Wrap-Up

• (5 min.) Present the information from History Link, p. 167.

OPTIONAL RESOURCES

• (5 min.) See Advanced Learners, p. 167. ▲
• (20 min.) See Multiple Intelligences, p. 167. ●
• You can find alternative quizzes in the Assessment Options listed below.

Practice Options

• *Lab Book*, pp. 23–24 ▲ ● ■
• ***Cuaderno de vocabulario y gramática*,** pp. 46–48 ▲ ♦ ●
• ***Cuaderno de actividades*,** pp. 35–37 ▲ ● ■
• *Activities for Communication*, pp. 15–16, 61–62 ▲ ■
• *Teaching Transparencies:* **Vocabulario y gramática** Answers, pp. 46–48 ▲ ♦ ●
• *TPR Storytelling Book*, pp. 20–21
• *Video Guide*, pp. 34–35 ▲ ● ■
• *Grammar Tutor for Students of Spanish*, pp. 23–26, 171–172 ♦ ●

• *Interactive Tutor* (Disc 1) or *DVD Tutor* (Disc 1) ▲ ● ■
• Online practice, Chapter 4 (go.hrw.com, Keyword: EXP1A CH4) ▲ ● ■

Assessment Options

• *Assessment Program*: **Prueba: Gramática 2**, pp. 69–70 ▲ ● ■
• *Assessment Program*: **Prueba: Aplicación 2**, pp. 71–72 ▲ ● ■
• Audio CD 4, Tr. 19 ●
• Test Generator ▲ ● ■

▲ = Advanced Learners ♦ = Slower Pace Learners ● = Special Learning Needs ■ = Heritage Speakers

La vida escolar

DAY 24 50-MINUTE LESSON PLAN

NATIONAL STANDARDS

Conexiones culturales

Cultures 2.1: Student demonstrates an understanding of the practices (what people do) and how they are related to the perspectives (how people perceive things) of the cultures studied.

Cultures 2.2: Student demonstrates an understanding of the products (what people create) and how they are related to the perspectives (how people perceive things) of the cultures studied.

Connections 3.1: Student uses the language to obtain, reinforce, or expand knowledge of other subject areas.

Novela en video

Communication 1.2: Student demonstrates understanding of simple, clearly spoken, and written language such as simple stories, high-frequency commands, and brief instructions when dealing with familiar topics.

CORE INSTRUCTION

Warm-Up
- (10 min.) Have students do the activity described in Math Link, p. 167.

Conexiones culturales
- (5 min.) Have students do Activity 2, p. 166.
- (15 min.) See Teaching **Conexiones,** #s 4–6, p. 166.

Novela en video
- (15 min.) See Teaching **Novela en video,** #s 1–2, p. 168.

Wrap-Up
- (5 min.) Present Gestures, p. 169.

OPTIONAL RESOURCES
- (5 min.) See Visual Learners, p. 168. ●
- (5 min.) See Comparing and Contrasting, p. 169.
- (5 min.) See Thinking Critically, p. 170.

Practice Options
- *Lab Book*, p. 53 ▲ ● ■
- *Video Guide*, pp. 34–35, 39 ▲ ● ■
- *Interactive Tutor* (Disc 1) or *DVD Tutor* (Disc 1) ▲ ● ■
- Online practice, Chapter 4 (go.hrw.com, Keyword: EXP1A CH4) ▲ ● ■

▲ = Advanced Learners   ◆ = Slower Pace Learners   ● = Special Learning Needs   ■ = Heritage Speakers

CAPÍTULO

4

La vida escolar

DAY 25 50-MINUTE LESSON PLAN

NATIONAL STANDARDS

Novela en video

Communication 1.2: Student demonstrates understanding of simple, clearly spoken, and written language such as simple stories, high-frequency commands, and brief instructions when dealing with familiar topics.

Connections 3.2: Student uses resources (that may include technology) in the language and cultures being studied to gain access to information.

Leamos y escribamos

Communication 1.1: Student engages in oral and written exchanges of learned material to socialize and to provide and obtain information.

Communication 1.2: Student demonstrates understanding of simple, clearly spoken, and written language such as simple stories, high-frequency commands, and brief instructions when dealing with familiar topics.

CORE INSTRUCTION

Warm-Up

- (5 min.) Ask students to say aloud in English what they recall from the **Novela en video.**

Novela en video

- (25 min.) See Teaching **Novela en video,** #s 3–4, p. 168.

Leamos y escribamos

- (10 min.) See Teaching **Leamos,** #s 1–3, p. 172.
- (5 min.) Play Audio CD 4, Tr. 11, for **Pepito, el niño precoz.** ●

Wrap-Up

- (5 min.) Have students work with a partner to describe the two cartoons on p. 172 in Spanish.

OPTIONAL RESOURCES

- (15 min.) See **Comunicación** (TE), p. 171.
- (5 min.) See Slower Pace Learners, p. 171. ◆
- (15 min.) See Applying the Strategies, p. 172.
- (15 min.) See Special Learning Needs, p. 173. ●

Practice Options

- *Lab Book*, pp. 53 ▲ ● ■
- *Cuaderno de actividades*, p. 38 ▲ ● ■
- *Student Edition*, **Literatura y variedades,** pp. 234–235 ▲ ● ■
- *Reading Strategies and Skills Handbook*, pp. xi–xii, 69, 34–37 ▲ ● ■
- *¡Lee conmigo!* Level 1 Reader ▲ ■
- *Video Guide*, pp. 34–35, 39 ▲ ● ■
- *Interactive Tutor* (Disc 1) or *DVD Tutor* (Disc 1) ▲ ● ■
- Online practice, Chapter 4 (go.hrw.com, Keyword: EXP1A CH4) ▲ ● ■

▲ = Advanced Learners ◆ = Slower Pace Learners ● = Special Learning Needs ■ = Heritage Speakers

Holt Spanish 1A

Lesson Planner

La vida escolar

DAY 26 50-MINUTE LESSON PLAN

NATIONAL STANDARDS

Leamos y escribamos

Communication 1.2: Student demonstrates understanding of simple, clearly spoken, and written language such as simple stories, high-frequency commands, and brief instructions when dealing with familiar topics.

Communication 1.3: Student presents information using familiar words, phrases, and sentences to listeners and readers.

CORE INSTRUCTION

Warm-Up

- (5 min.) Ask students to describe the three characters in **Pepito, el niño precoz.**

Leamos y escribamos

- (10 min.) Have students read **Leamos** again, p. 172.
- (10 min.) See Teaching **Leamos,** #4, p. 172.
- (20 min.) Present **Taller del escritor,** p. 173, using Teaching **Escribamos,** #s 1–4, p. 172.

Wrap-Up

- (5 min.) Show students the rubric you will use to grade the writing assignment. See Writing Assessment, p. 173.

OPTIONAL RESOURCES

- (5 min.) See Advanced Learners, p. 173. ▲

Practice Options
- *Cuaderno de actividades*, p. 38 ▲ ● ■
- *Student Edition,* **Literatura y variedades,** pp. 234–235 ▲ ● ■
- *Reading Strategies and Skills Handbook,* pp. xi–xii, 69, 34–37 ▲ ● ■
- *¡Lee conmigo!* Level 1 Reader ▲ ■
- *Interactive Tutor* (Disc 1) or *DVD Tutor* (Disc 1) ▲ ● ■
- Online practice, Chapter 4 (go.hrw.com, Keyword: EXP1A CH4) ▲ ● ■

Assessment Options
- *Assessment Program,* **Prueba: Lectura,** pp. 73, 79 ▲ ● ■

▲ = Advanced Learners   ◆ = Slower Pace Learners   ● = Special Learning Needs   ■ = Heritage Speakers

Holt Spanish 1A

Lesson Planner

La vida escolar

DAY 27 50-MINUTE LESSON PLAN

NATIONAL STANDARDS

Leamos y escribamos

Communication 1.1: Student engages in oral and written exchanges of learned material to socialize and to provide and obtain information.

Communication 1.3: Student presents information using familiar words, phrases, and sentences to listeners and readers.

Repaso

Communication 1.1: Student engages in oral and written exchanges of learned material to socialize and to provide and obtain information.

Communication 1.2: Student demonstrates understanding of simple, clearly spoken, and written language such as simple stories, high-frequency commands, and brief instructions when dealing with familiar topics.

Communication 1.3: Student presents information using familiar words, phrases, and sentences to listeners and readers.

CORE INSTRUCTION

Warm-Up
- (5 min.) Give students a few minutes to practice the dialogs described in Teaching **Escribamos** #5, p. 172.

Leamos y escribamos
- (15 min.) Have students act out the dialogs described in Teaching **Escribamos,** #5, p. 172.

Repaso
- (25 min.) Have students do Activities 1–3, p. 174.

Wrap-Up
- (5 min.) Present to students the Fold-N-Learn activity suggestion on p. 174. Suggest that they use the Fold-N-Learn activity as part of their review for the Chapter Test. ●

OPTIONAL RESOURCES
- (25 min.) See Reteaching, p. 174.
- (5 min.) See Test-Taking Strategy, p. 174.

Practice Options
- *Lab Book,* pp. 23–24, 54 ▲ ● ■
- *Activities for Communication,* pp. 46, 61–62 ▲ ■
- *Teaching Transparencies:* Situation; Picture Sequences ▲ ● ■
- *Video Guide,* pp. 34–35, 40 ▲ ● ■
- *TPR Storytelling Book,* pp. 22–23 ▲ ●
- *Interactive Tutor* (Disc 1) or *DVD Tutor* (Disc 1) ▲ ● ■
- Online practice, Chapter 4 (go.hrw.com, Keyword: EXP1A CH4) ▲ ● ■

Assessment Options
- *Assessment Program,* **Prueba: Escritura,** p. 74 ▲ ● ■

▲ = Advanced Learners   ◆ = Slower Pace Learners   ● = Special Learning Needs   ■ = Heritage Speakers

La vida escolar

DAY 28 50-MINUTE LESSON PLAN

NATIONAL STANDARDS

Repaso

Communication 1.1: Student engages in oral and written exchanges of learned material to socialize and to provide and obtain information.

Communication 1.2: Student demonstrates understanding of simple, clearly spoken, and written language such as simple stories, high-frequency commands, and brief instructions when dealing with familiar topics.

Communication 1.3: Student presents information using familiar words, phrases, and sentences to listeners and readers.

Comparisons 4.2: Student demonstrates an understanding of the concept of culture through comparisons of the student's own culture and the cultures studied.

CORE INSTRUCTION

Warm-Up
- (5 min.) Have students read out their answers to Activities 1 and 3, p. 174.

Repaso
- (10 min.) Have students do Activities 4–5, p. 175.
- (10 min.) Play Audio CD 4, Tr. 13, for Activity 6, p. 175. ●
- (10 min.) Have students do Activity 7, p. 175.
- (10 min.) Play Audio CD 4, Tr. 14, 15, 16, for **Letra y sonido,** p. 176. ●

Wrap-Up
- (5 min.) Read the picture sequence in AP Language Examination, p. 175, aloud to the class while students look at the pictures for Activity 7.

OPTIONAL RESOURCES
- (15 min.) See **Más práctica,** p. 174.
- (20 min.) See Game, p. 177. ●

Practice Options
- *Lab Book,* pp. 23–24, 54 ▲ ● ■
- *Activities for Communication,* pp. 46, 61–62 ▲ ■
- *Teaching Transparencies:* Situation; Picture Sequences, ▲ ● ■
- *Video Guide,* pp. 34–35, 40 ▲ ● ■
- *TPR Storytelling Book,* pp. 22–23 ▲ ●
- *Interactive Tutor* (Disc 1) or *DVD Tutor* (Disc 1) ▲ ● ■
- Online practice, Chapter 4 (go.hrw.com, Keyword: EXP1A CH4) ▲ ● ■

▲ = Advanced Learners   ◆ = Slower Pace Learners   ● = Special Learning Needs   ■ = Heritage Speakers

La vida escolar

DAY 29 50-MINUTE LESSON PLAN

NATIONAL STANDARDS

Integración

Communication 1.1: Student engages in oral and written exchanges of learned material to socialize and to provide and obtain information.

Communication 1.2: Student demonstrates understanding of simple, clearly spoken, and written language such as simple stories, high-frequency commands, and brief instructions when dealing with familiar topics.

Communication 1.3: Student presents information using familiar words, phrases, and sentences to listeners and readers.

CORE INSTRUCTION

Warm-Up

- (5 min.) Have students make up a sentence in Spanish to describe each picture that accompanies Activity 1, p. 178.

Integración

- (10 min.) Play Audio CD 4, Tr. 17, for Activity 1, p. 178. ●
- (25 min.) Have students do Activities 2–4, pp. 178–179.

Wrap-Up

- (10 min.) Present Fine Art Connection: Introduction and Analyzing, p. 179. Then remind students to study for the Chapter Test.

OPTIONAL RESOURCES

- (15 min.) See **Más práctica,** p. 178.
- (10 min.) See Culture Project, p. 178.

Practice Options

- *Lab Book*, pp. 23–24 ▲ ● ■
- *Cuaderno de actividades*, p. 39–40, 58–59 ▲ ● ■
- *Teaching Transparencies:* Fine Art, Chapter 4 ▲ ● ■
- Online practice, Chapter 4 (go.hrw.com, Keyword: EXP1A CH4) ▲ ● ■

▲ = Advanced Learners   ◆ = Slower Pace Learners   ● = Special Learning Needs   ■ = Heritage Speakers

Holt Spanish 1A

Lesson Planner

La vida escolar

DAY 30 50-MINUTE LESSON PLAN

CORE INSTRUCTION

Assessment
- (50 min.) Give the Chapter 4 Test.

OPTIONAL RESOURCES
- You may also choose from the other modes of assessment listed in the Assessment Options box below

---

Practice Options
- *Interactive Tutor* (Disc 1) or *DVD Tutor* (Disc 1) ▲ ● ■
- Online practice, Chapter 4 (go.hrw.com, Keyword: EXP1A CH4) ▲ ● ■

Assessment Options
- *Assessment Program:* **Examen: Capítulo 4,** pp. 157–167 ▲ ● ■
- *Assessment Program:* **Examen oral: Capítulo 4,** p. 168 ▲ ● ■
- *Assessment Program:* Alternative Assessment, pp. 215, 221, 228 ▲ ● ■
- Audio CD 4, Tr. 21–22 ●
- Test Generator ▲ ● ■

▲ = Advanced Learners ◆ = Slower Pace Learners ● = Special Learning Needs ■ = Heritage Speakers

CAPÍTULO
5

En casa con la familia

DAY 1 50-MINUTE LESSON PLAN

NATIONAL STANDARDS

Chapter Opener

Communication 1.2: Student demonstrates understanding of simple, clearly spoken, and written language such as simple stories, high-frequency commands, and brief instructions when dealing with familiar topics.

Comparisons 4.1: Student demonstrates an understanding of the nature of language through comparisons of the student's own language and the language studied.

Vocabulario en acción 1

Communication 1.1: Student engages in oral and written exchanges of learned material to socialize and to provide and obtain information.

Before starting **Capítulo 5,** you may wish to teach **Geocultura: Chile,** pp. 180–183. For teaching suggestions, see pp. xv–xvi of this *Lesson Planner.*

CORE INSTRUCTION

Warm-Up
- (5 min.) See Learning and Pacing Tips, p. 185.

Chapter Opener
- (5 min.) Present information from Using the Photo and **Más vocabulario,** p. 184.
- (5 min.) Present **Objetivos,** p. 184.

Vocabulario en acción 1
- (25 min.) Present **Vocabulario,** pp. 186–187, using Teaching **Vocabulario,** p. 186.
- (5 min.) Present **¡Exprésate!,** p. 187.

Wrap-Up
- (5 min.) Present Language to Language and **También se puede decir… ,** p. 187.

OPTIONAL RESOURCES
- (20 min.) See Special Learning Needs, p. 187. ●

Practice Options
- *Lab Book,* pp. 5, 25–26, 55, 56 ▲ ● ■
- *Cuaderno de vocabulario y gramática,* pp. 49–51 ▲ ◆ ●
- *Cuaderno para hispanohablantes,* pp. 45–53, 54 ■
- *Teaching Transparencies:* Map 3; **Vocabulario** 5.1, 5.2; Situation; *Cuaderno de vocabulario y gramática* Answers, pp. 49–51 ▲ ◆ ●
- *Video Guide,* pp. 41, 42, 44–45, 46 ▲ ● ■
- *Interactive Tutor* (Disc 1) or *DVD Tutor* (Disc 1) ▲ ● ■
- Online practice, Chapter 5 (go.hrw.com, Keyword: EXP1A CH5) ▲ ● ■

▲ = Advanced Learners   ◆ = Slower Pace Learners   ● = Special Learning Needs   ■ = Heritage Speakers

(121)

En casa con la familia

DAY 2 50-MINUTE LESSON PLAN

NATIONAL STANDARDS

Vocabulario en acción 1

Communication 1.1: Student engages in oral and written exchanges of learned material to socialize and to provide and obtain information.

Communication 1.2: Student demonstrates understanding of simple, clearly spoken, and written language such as simple stories, high-frequency commands, and brief instructions when dealing with familiar topics.

Comparisons 4.2: Student demonstrates an understanding of the concept of culture through comparisons of the student's own culture and the cultures studied.

CORE INSTRUCTION

Warm-Up

- (5 min.) Have students do Bell Work 5.1, p. 186.

Vocabulario en acción 1

- (10 min.) Show **ExpresaVisión**, Ch. 5.
- (15 min.) Review **Vocabulario 1** and **¡Exprésate!,** pp. 186–187.
- (5 min.) Present **Nota cultural,** p. 188.
- (10 min.) Play Audio CD 5, Tr. 1, for Activity 1, p. 188. ●

Wrap-Up

- (5 min.) Present the Fold-N-Learn activity suggestion, p. 188.

OPTIONAL RESOURCES

- (15 min.) See Advanced Learners, p. 187. ▲
- (10 min.) See TPR, p. 187. ●
- (15 min.) See Practices and Perspectives, p. 188.
- (5 min.) See Slower Pace Learners, p. 189. ◆

Practice Options

- *Lab Book*, pp. 25–26, 56 ▲ ● ■
- *Cuaderno de vocabulario y gramática*, pp. 49–51 ▲ ◆ ●
- *Teaching Transparencies:* Bell Work, 5.1; **Vocabulario** 5.1, 5.2; *Cuaderno de vocabulario y gramática* Answers, pp. 49–51▲ ◆ ●
- *Video Guide*, pp. 44–45, 46 ▲ ● ■
- *Interactive Tutor* (Disc 1) or *DVD Tutor* (Disc 1) ▲ ● ■
- Online practice, Chapter 5 (go.hrw.com, Keyword: EXP1A CH5) ▲ ● ■

▲ = Advanced Learners   ◆ = Slower Pace Learners   ● = Special Learning Needs   ■ = Heritage Speakers

¡Empecemos!

DAY 3 50-MINUTE LESSON PLAN

NATIONAL STANDARDS

Vocabulario en acción 1

Communication 1.1: Student engages in oral and written exchanges of learned material to socialize and to provide and obtain information.

Communication 1.2: Student demonstrates understanding of simple, clearly spoken, and written language such as simple stories, high-frequency commands, and brief instructions when dealing with familiar topics.

Comparisons 4.1: Student demonstrates an understanding of the nature of language through comparisons of the student's own language and the language studied.

CORE INSTRUCTION

Warm-Up
- (5 min.) Present Language Note, p. 190.

Vocabulario en acción 1
- (5 min.) Have students do Bell Work 5.2, p. 192.
- (35 min.) Have students do Activities 2–6, pp. 188–190.

Wrap-Up
- (5 min.) Present Circumlocution, p. 190.

OPTIONAL RESOURCES
- (25 min.) See **Más práctica,** p. 188.
- (20 min.) See **Comunicación** (TE), p. 189.
- (15 min.) See Multiple Intelligences, p. 189. ●

Practice Options
- *Lab Book*, pp. 25–26, 56 ▲ ● ■
- *Cuaderno de vocabulario y gramática*, pp. 49–51 ▲ ◆ ●
- *Teaching Transparencies:* Bell Work, 5.2; **Vocabulario** 5.1, 5.2; *Cuaderno de vocabulario y gramática* Answers, pp. 49–51 ▲ ◆ ●
- *Video Guide*, pp. 44–45, 46 ▲ ● ■
- *Interactive Tutor* (Disc 1) or *DVD Tutor* (Disc 1) ▲ ● ■
- Online practice, Chapter 5 (go.hrw.com, Keyword: EXP1A CH5) ▲ ● ■

▲ = Advanced Learners   ◆ = Slower Pace Learners   ● = Special Learning Needs   ■ = Heritage Speakers

En casa con la familia

DAY 4 50-MINUTE LESSON PLAN

NATIONAL STANDARDS

Vocabulario en acción 1

Communication 1.1: Student engages in oral and written exchanges of learned material to socialize and to provide and obtain information.

Communication 1.2: Student demonstrates understanding of simple, clearly spoken, and written language such as simple stories, high-frequency commands, and brief instructions when dealing with familiar topics.

Communication 1.3: Student presents information using familiar words, phrases, and sentences to listeners and readers.

Cultures 2.1: Student demonstrates an understanding of the practices (what people do) and how they are related to the perspectives (how people perceive things) of the cultures studied.

CORE INSTRUCTION

Warm-Up
- (5 min.) See Practices and Perspectives, p. 191.

Vocabulario en acción 1
- (40 min.) Have students do Activities 7–10, pp. 190–191.

Wrap-Up
- (5 min.) Have students tell a partner in Spanish about one of the family members they described for Activity 8, p. 191. Then remind the class to study for **Prueba: Vocabulario 1.**

OPTIONAL RESOURCES
- (10 min.) See Heritage Speakers, p. 190. ■
- (30 min.) See Teacher to Teacher, p. 190.
- (5 min.) See Heritage Speakers, p. 191. ■
- (10 min.) See Slower Pace Learners, p. 191. ◆
- (15 min.) See Special Learning Needs, p. 191. ●
- (20 min.) See **Comunicación (TE),** p. 191.

Practice Options
- *Lab Book*, pp. 25–26, 56 ▲ ● ■
- *Cuaderno de vocabulario y gramática*, pp. 49–51 ▲ ◆ ●
- *Teaching Transparencies:* **Vocabulario** 5.1, 5.2; *Cuaderno de vocabulario y gramática* Answers, pp. 49–51 ▲ ◆ ●
- *Video Guide*, pp. 44–45, 46 ▲ ● ■
- *Interactive Tutor* (Disc 1) or *DVD Tutor* (Disc 1) ▲ ● ■
- Online practice, Chapter 5 (go.hrw.com, Keyword: EXP1A CH5) ▲ ● ■

▲ = Advanced Learners   ◆ = Slower Pace Learners   ● = Special Learning Needs   ■ = Heritage Speakers

CAPÍTULO
5

En casa con la familia

DAY 5 50-MINUTE LESSON PLAN

NATIONAL STANDARDS

Vocabulario en acción 1

Communication 1.1: Student engages in oral and written exchanges of learned material to socialize and to provide and obtain information.

Communication 1.2: Student demonstrates understanding of simple, clearly spoken, and written language such as simple stories, high-frequency commands, and brief instructions when dealing with familiar topics.

Communication 1.3: Student presents information using familiar words, phrases, and sentences to listeners and readers.

CORE INSTRUCTION

Warm-Up

• (10 min.) Have students do Activity 10, p. 191, again with a different partner.

Vocabulario en acción 1

• (15 min.) Review **Vocabulario 1,** pp. 186–191.

Assessment

• (20 min.) Give **Prueba: Vocabulario 1.**

Wrap-Up

• (5 min.) Have the class ask one student who doesn't mind questions about his or her family in Spanish. Tell everyone that they should try to remember as much information about the student's family as they can to answer questions during the next class meeting.

OPTIONAL RESOURCES

• You can find alternative quizzes in the Assessment Options listed below.

Practice Options

• *Lab Book,* pp. 25–26, 56 ▲ ● ■
• *Cuaderno de vocabulario y gramática*, pp. 49–51 ▲ ◆ ●
• *Teaching Transparencies:* **Vocabulario** 5.1, 5.2; *Vocabulario y gramática* Answers, pp. 49–51 ▲ ◆ ●
• *Video Guide*, pp. 44–45, 46 ▲ ● ■
• *Interactive Tutor* (Disc 1) or *DVD Tutor* (Disc 1) ▲ ● ■
• Online practice, Chapter 5 (go.hrw.com, Keyword: EXP1A CH5) ▲ ● ■

Assessment Options

• *Assessment Program:* **Prueba: Vocabulario 1**, pp. 81–82 ▲ ● ■
• *Test Generator* ▲ ● ■

▲ = Advanced Learners   ◆ = Slower Pace Learners   ● = Special Learning Needs   ■ = Heritage Speakers

Lesson Planner

En casa con la familia

DAY 6 50-MINUTE LESSON PLAN

NATIONAL STANDARDS

Gramática en acción 1

Communication 1.1: Student engages in oral and written exchanges of learned material to socialize and to provide and obtain information.

Communication 1.2: Student demonstrates understanding of simple, clearly spoken, and written language such as simple stories, high-frequency commands, and brief instructions when dealing with familiar topics.

Communication 1.3: Student presents information using familiar words, phrases, and sentences to listeners and readers.

CORE INSTRUCTION

Warm-Up

- (5 min.) Ask students to recall information from the Wrap-Up activity done during the last class. Elicit answers from them with questions such as: **¿Cómo es la familia de… ? / ¿Cuántos hermanos tiene?**

Gramática en acción 1

- (15 min.) Present **Gramática:** *Possessive adjectives,* p. 192, using Teaching **Gramática,** p. 192.
- (5 min.) Have students do Activity 11, p. 192.
- (10 min.) Present **Nota cultural,** p. 193.
- (10 min.) Play Audio CD 5, Tr. 2, for Activity 12, p. 193. ●

Wrap-Up

- (5 min.) Have students check Activity 11, p. 192, with a partner.

OPTIONAL RESOURCES

- (10 min.) See **GramaVisión,** *(possessive adjectives), Video Program* (Videocassette 3) or *DVD Tutor* (Disc 1).
- (5 min.) See Common Error Alert, p. 193.
- (5 min.) See Practices and Perspectives, p. 193.
- (5 min.) See Slower Pace Learners, p. 193. ◆

Practice Options

- *Lab Book,* pp. 25–26, 56 ▲ ● ■
- ***Cuaderno de vocabulario y gramática,*** pp. 52–54 ▲ ◆ ●
- ***Cuaderno de actividades,*** pp. 41–43 ▲ ● ■
- *Grammar Tutor for Students of Spanish,* pp. 27–28, 172–173
- *Activities for Communication,* pp. 17–18, 63–64 ▲ ■
- *Teaching Transparencies:* ***Vocabulario y gramática*** Answers, pp. 52–54 ▲ ◆ ●
- *Video Guide,* pp. 44–45 ▲ ● ■
- *Interactive Tutor* (Disc 1) or *DVD Tutor* (Disc 1) ▲ ● ■
- Online practice, Chapter 5 (go.hrw.com, Keyword: EXP1A CH5) ▲ ● ■

▲ = Advanced Learners   ◆ = Slower Pace Learners   ● = Special Learning Needs   ■ = Heritage Speakers

CAPÍTULO

5

En casa con la familia

DAY 7 50-MINUTE LESSON PLAN

NATIONAL STANDARDS

Gramática en acción 1

Communication 1.1: Student engages in oral and written exchanges of learned material to socialize and to provide and obtain information.

Communication 1.2: Student demonstrates understanding of simple, clearly spoken, and written language such as simple stories, high-frequency commands, and brief instructions when dealing with familiar topics.

Communication 1.3: Student presents information using familiar words, phrases, and sentences to listeners and readers.

CORE INSTRUCTION

Warm-Up
- (5 min.) Have students do Bell Work 5.3, p. 194.

Gramática en acción 1
- (5 min.) Review possessive adjectives, p. 192.
- (15 min.) Have students do Activities 13–14, p. 193.
- (20 min.) Present **Gramática:** *Stem–changing verbs:* **o–>ue,** p. 194, using Teaching **Gramática,** p. 194.

Wrap-Up
- (5 min.) Have students write three sentences using the new stem–changing verbs.

OPTIONAL RESOURCES
- (20 min.) See **Comunicación** (TE), p. 193.
- (5 min.) See Special Learning Needs, p. 193. ●

Practice Options
- *Lab Book*, pp. 25–26 ▲ ● ■
- ***Cuaderno de vocabulario y gramática***, pp. 52–54 ▲ ◆ ●
- *Activities for Communication*, pp. 17–18, 63–64 ▲ ■
- ***Cuaderno de actividades***, pp. 41–43 ■
- *Teaching Transparencies:* Bell Work, 5.3; ***Vocabulario y gramática*** Answers, pp. 52–54 ▲ ◆ ●
- *Video Guide*, pp. 44–45 ▲ ● ■
- *Grammar Tutor for Students of Spanish*, pp. 27–28, 172–173 ◆ ●
- *Interactive Tutor* (Disc 1) or *DVD Tutor* (Disc 1) ▲ ● ■
- Online practice, Chapter 5 (go.hrw.com, Keyword: EXP1A CH5) ▲ ● ■

▲ = Advanced Learners   ◆ = Slower Pace Learners   ● = Special Learning Needs   ■ = Heritage Speakers

(127)

En casa con la familia

DAY 8 50-MINUTE LESSON PLAN

NATIONAL STANDARDS

Gramática en acción 1

Communication 1.1: Student engages in oral and written exchanges of learned material to socialize and to provide and obtain information.

Communication 1.2: Student demonstrates understanding of simple, clearly spoken, and written language such as simple stories, high-frequency commands, and brief instructions when dealing with familiar topics.

Communication 1.3: Student presents information using familiar words, phrases, and sentences to listeners and readers.

Comparisons 4.2: Student demonstrates an understanding of the concept of culture through comparisons of the student's own culture and the cultures studied.

CORE INSTRUCTION

Warm-Up
- (5 min.) Have students do Bell Work 5.4, p. 196.

Gramática en acción 1
- (10 min.) Show **GramaVisión**(*stem-changing verbs:* **o–>ue**), *Video Program* (Videocassette 3) or *DVD Tutor* (Disc 1).
- (5 min.) Review stem-changing verbs: **o–>ue,** p. 194.
- (15 min.) Have students do Activities 15–17, pp. 194–195.
- (10 min.) Present **Nota cultural,** p. 195.

Wrap-Up
- (5 min.) Present Family Link, p. 195, and assign it as homework.

OPTIONAL RESOURCES
- (15 min.) See Advanced Learners, p. 195. ▲
- (5 min.) See Special Learning Needs, p. 195. ●
- (20 min.) See **Comunicación** (TE), p. 195.

Practice Options
- *Lab Book*, pp. 25–26 ▲ ● ■
- ***Cuaderno de vocabulario y gramática***, pp. 52–54 ▲ ◆ ●
- *Activities for Communication*, pp. 17–18, 63–64 ▲ ■
- ***Cuaderno de actividades***, pp. 41–43 ■
- *Teaching Transparencies:* Bell Work, 5.4; ***Vocabulario y gramática*** Answers, pp. 52–54 ▲ ◆ ●
- *Video Guide*, pp. 44–45 ▲ ● ■
- *Grammar Tutor for Students of Spanish*, pp. 27–28, 172–173 ◆ ●
- *Interactive Tutor* (Disc 1) or *DVD Tutor* (Disc 1) ▲ ● ■
- Online practice, Chapter 5 (go.hrw.com, Keyword: EXP1A CH5) ▲ ● ■

▲ = Advanced Learners   ◆ = Slower Pace Learners   ● = Special Learning Needs   ■ = Heritage Speakers

Holt Spanish 1A

Lesson Planner

CAPÍTULO

5

En casa con la familia

DAY 9 50-MINUTE LESSON PLAN

NATIONAL STANDARDS

Communication 1.1: Student engages in oral and written exchanges of learned material to socialize and to provide and obtain information.

Communication 1.2: Student demonstrates understanding of simple, clearly spoken, and written language such as simple stories, high-frequency commands, and brief instructions when dealing with familiar topics.

CORE INSTRUCTION

Warm-Up
- (5 min.) Present Common Error Alert, p. 197.

Gramática en acción 1
- (10 min.) Show **GramaVisión** (*stem-changing verbs:* **e–>ie**), *Video Program* (Videocassette 3) or *DVD Tutor* (Disc 1).
- (15 min.) Present **Gramática:** *Stem-changing verbs:* **e–>ie**, using Teaching **Gramática**, p. 196.
- (15 min.) Have students do Activities 18–19, pp. 196–197.

Wrap-Up
- (5 min.) Have students ask a partner at what time he or she eats lunch, and at what time his or her classes begin.

OPTIONAL RESOURCES
- (10 min.) See Slower Pace Learners, p. 197. ◆

Practice Options
- *Lab Book*, pp. 25–26 ▲ ● ■
- *Cuaderno de vocabulario y gramática*, pp. 52–54 ▲ ◆ ●
- *Cuaderno de actividades*, pp. 41–43
- *Activities for Communication*, pp. 17–18, 63–64 ▲ ■
- *Teaching Transparencies:* **Vocabulario y gramática** Answers, pp. 52–54 ▲ ◆ ●
- *Grammar Tutor for Students of Spanish*, pp. 27–28, 172–173 ◆ ●
- *Video Guide*, pp. 44–45 ▲ ● ■
- *Interactive Tutor* (Disc 1) or *DVD Tutor* (Disc 1) ▲ ● ■
- Online practice, Chapter 5 (go.hrw.com, Keyword: EXP1A CH5) ▲ ● ■

▲ = Advanced Learners   ◆ = Slower Pace Learners   ● = Special Learning Needs   ■ = Heritage Speakers

Holt Spanish 1A

Lesson Planner

En casa con la familia

DAY 10 50-MINUTE LESSON PLAN

NATIONAL STANDARDS

Gramática en acción 1

Communication 1.1: Student engages in oral and written exchanges of learned material to socialize and to provide and obtain information.

Communication 1.2: Student demonstrates understanding of simple, clearly spoken, and written language such as simple stories, high-frequency commands, and brief instructions when dealing with familiar topics.

Communication 1.3: Student presents information using familiar words, phrases, and sentences to listeners and readers.

CORE INSTRUCTION

Warm-Up
- (5 min.) Have students do Bell Work 5.5, p. 200.

Gramática en acción 1
- (20 min.) Have students do Activity 20, p. 197.
- (20 min.) Review **Gramática 1,** pp. 192–197.

Wrap-Up
- (5 min.) Review the present-tense conjugation of **merendar.** Remind students to study for **Prueba: Gramática 1.**

OPTIONAL RESOURCES
- (10 min.) See Multiple Intelligences, p. 197. ●
- (25 min.) See **Comunicación** (TE), p. 197.

Practice Options
- *Lab Book,* pp. 25–26 ▲ ● ■
- *Cuaderno de vocabulario y gramática*, pp. 52–54 ▲ ◆ ●
- *Cuaderno de actividades*, pp. 41–43 ▲ ● ■
- *Activities for Communication,* pp. 17–18, 63–64 ▲ ■
- *Teaching Transparencies:* Bell Work, 5.5; *Vocabulario y gramática* Answers, pp. 52–54 ▲ ◆ ●
- *Grammar Tutor for Students of Spanish,* pp. 27–28, 172–173 ◆ ●
- *Video Guide,* pp. 44–45 ▲ ● ■
- *Interactive Tutor* (Disc 1) or *DVD Tutor* (Disc 1) ▲ ● ■
- Online practice, Chapter 5 (go.hrw.com, Keyword: EXP1A CH5) ▲ ● ■

▲ = Advanced Learners   ◆ = Slower Pace Learners   ● = Special Learning Needs   ■ = Heritage Speakers

Teacher's Name _____ Class _____ Date _____

En casa con la familia

DAY 11 50-MINUTE LESSON PLAN

NATIONAL STANDARDS

Gramática en acción

Communication 1.1: Student engages in oral and written exchanges of learned material to socialize and to provide and obtain information.

Cultura

Communication 1.2: Student demonstrates understanding of simple, clearly spoken, and written language such as simple stories, high-frequency commands, and brief instructions when dealing with familiar topics.

Comparisons 4.2: Student demonstrates an understanding of the concept of culture through comparisons of the student's own culture and the cultures studied.

CORE INSTRUCTION

Warm-Up
• (5 min.) Ask students **¿A qué hora empieza la clase de español?** and **¿A qué hora empiezas a hacer tu tarea?**

Assessment
• (20 min.) Give **Prueba: Gramática 1.**

Cultura
• (20 min.) Present **Cultura,** pp. 198–199, using Teaching **Cultura,** p. 198.

Wrap-Up
• (5 min.) See Map Activities, p. 198.

OPTIONAL RESOURCES
• (5 min.) See Interdisciplinary Link, p. 199.
• (15 min.) See Advanced Learners, p. 199. ▲
• You can find alternative quizzes in the Assessment Options listed below.

Practice Options
• *Lab Book*, pp. 57 ▲ ● ■
• *Cuaderno de actividades*, pp. 41–43, 44 ▲ ● ■
• *Video Guide*, pp. 44–45, 121–127 ▲ ● ■
• *Cuaderno para hispanohablantes*, p. 56 ■
• *Interactive Tutor* (Disc 1) or *DVD Tutor* (Disc 1) ▲ ● ■
• Online practice, Chapter 5 (go.hrw.com, Keyword: EXP1A CH5) ▲ ● ■

Assessment Options
• *Assessment Program:* **Prueba: Gramática 1**, pp. 83–84 ▲ ● ■
• *Assessment Program:* **Prueba: Aplicación 1**, pp. 85–86 ▲ ● ■
• Audio CD 5, Tr. 16 ●
• Test Generator ▲ ● ■

▲ = Advanced Learners   ◆ = Slower Pace Learners   ● = Special Learning Needs   ■ = Heritage Speakers

(131)

CAPÍTULO

5

En casa con la familia

DAY 12 50-MINUTE LESSON PLAN

NATIONAL STANDARDS

Cultura

Communication 1.1: Student engages in oral and written exchanges of learned material to socialize and to provide and obtain information.

Connections 3.2: Student uses resources (that may include technology) in the language and cultures being studied to gain access to information.

Connections 3.1: Student uses the language to obtain, reinforce, or expand knowledge of other subject areas.

CORE INSTRUCTION

Warm-Up
- (5 min.) Have students do the activity described in Multiple Intelligences, p. 199. ●

Cultura
- (10 min.) Discuss and assign **Comunidad,** p. 199.

Vocabulario en acción 2
- (20 min.) Present **Vocabulario,** pp. 200–201, using Teaching **Vocabulario,** p. 200.
- (10 min.) Present **¡Exprésate!,** p. 201.

Wrap-Up
- (5 min.) Have students ask a partner **¿Cuál es tu dirección?** and **¿Cómo es tu casa?**

OPTIONAL RESOURCES
- (10 min.) See Slower Pace Learners, p. 201. ◆
- (60 min.) See Multiple Intelligences, p. 201. ●
- (15 min.) Family Link, p. 199

Practice Options
- *Lab Book,* pp. 27–28, 58 ▲ ● ■
- *Cuaderno de vocabulario y gramática,* pp. 55–57 ▲ ◆ ●
- *Teaching Transparencies:* **Vocabulario** 5.3, 5.4; *Cuaderno de vocabulario y gramática,* Answers, pp. 55–57 ▲ ● ■
- *Video Guide,* pp. 44–45, 47, 48 ▲ ● ■
- *Interactive Tutor* (Disc 1) or *DVD Tutor* (Disc 1) ▲ ● ■
- Online practice, Chapter 5 (go.hrw.com, Keyword: EXP1A CH5) ▲ ● ■

▲ = Advanced Learners ◆ = Slower Pace Learners ● = Special Learning Needs ■ = Heritage Speakers

(132)

En casa con la familia

DAY 13 50-MINUTE LESSON PLAN

NATIONAL STANDARDS

Vocabulario en acción 2

Communication 1.1: Student engages in oral and written exchanges of learned material to socialize and to provide and obtain information.

Communication 1.2: Student demonstrates understanding of simple, clearly spoken, and written language such as simple stories, high-frequency commands, and brief instructions when dealing with familiar topics.

Communication 1.3: Student presents information using familiar words, phrases, and sentences to listeners and readers.

CORE INSTRUCTION

Warm-Up

- (5 min.) Present **También se puede decir...**, p. 201.

Vocabulario en acción 2

- (10 min.) Show **ExpresaVisión,** Ch. 5.
- (15 min.) Review **Vocabulario 2** and **¡Exprésate!,** pp. 200–205.
- (15 min.) Have students do Activities 21–22, p. 202.

Wrap-Up

- (10 min.) Have students do the activity described in **Más práctica,** p. 202.

OPTIONAL RESOURCES

- (50 min.) See TPR, p. 201. ●
- (10 min.) See Comparisons, p. 202.
- (25 min.) See Game, p. 202. ●
- (15 min.) See Slower Pace Learners, p. 203. ◆

Practice Options

- *Lab Book,* pp. 27–28, 58 ▲ ● ■
- *Cuaderno de vocabulario y gramática*, pp. 55–57 ▲ ◆ ●
- *Teaching Transparencies:* **Vocabulario** 5.3, 5.4; *Cuaderno de vocabulario y gramática*, Answers, pp. 55–57 ▲ ● ■
- *Video Guide,* pp. 44–45, 48 ▲ ● ■
- *Interactive Tutor* (Disc 1) or *DVD Tutor* (Disc 1) ▲ ● ■
- Online practice, Chapter 5 (go.hrw.com, Keyword: EXP1A CH5) ▲ ● ■

▲ = Advanced Learners   ◆ = Slower Pace Learners   ● = Special Learning Needs   ■ = Heritage Speakers

Holt Spanish 1A

Lesson Planner

En casa con la familia

DAY 14 50-MINUTE LESSON PLAN

NATIONAL STANDARDS

Vocabulario en acción 2

Communication 1.1: Student engages in oral and written exchanges of learned material to socialize and to provide and obtain information.

Communication 1.2: Student demonstrates understanding of simple, clearly spoken, and written language such as simple stories, high-frequency commands, and brief instructions when dealing with familiar topics.

Communication 1.3: Student presents information using familiar words, phrases, and sentences to listeners and readers.

CORE INSTRUCTION

Warm-Up
- (5 min.) Have students do Bell Work 5.6, p. 206.

Vocabulario en acción 2
- (10 min.) Present **Más vocabulario,** p. 202.
- (15 min.) Have students do Activity 23, p. 203.
- (15 min.) Present **¡Exprésate!,** p. 204, using Teaching **¡Exprésate!,** p. 204.

Wrap-Up
- (5 min.) Ask students to tell a partner in Spanish whether they like or dislike the chores listed in **Más vocabulario,** p. 202.

OPTIONAL RESOURCES
- (5 min.) See Practices and Perspectives, p. 203.
- (20 min.) See **Comunicación** (TE), p. 203.
- (30 min.) See Multiple Intelligences, p. 203. ●

Practice Options
- *Lab Book*, pp. 27–28, 58 ▲ ● ■
- *Cuaderno de vocabulario y gramática*, pp. 55–57 ▲ ◆ ●
- *Teaching Transparencies:* Bell Work, 5.6; **Vocabulario** 5.3, 5.4; *Vocabulario y gramática* Answers, pp. 55–57 ▲ ◆ ●
- *Video Guide*, pp. 44–45, 48 ▲ ● ■
- *Interactive Tutor* (Disc 1) or *DVD Tutor* (Disc 1) ▲ ● ■
- Online practice, Chapter 5 (go.hrw.com, Keyword: EXP1A CH5) ▲ ● ■

▲ = Advanced Learners   ◆ = Slower Pace Learners   ● = Special Learning Needs   ■ = Heritage Speakers

Holt Spanish 1A

Lesson Planner

En casa con la familia

DAY 15 50-MINUTE LESSON PLAN

NATIONAL STANDARDS

Vocabulario en acción 2

Communication 1.1: Student engages in oral and written exchanges of learned material to socialize and to provide and obtain information.

Communication 1.2: Student demonstrates understanding of simple, clearly spoken, and written language such as simple stories, high-frequency commands, and brief instructions when dealing with familiar topics.

Communication 1.3: Student presents information using familiar words, phrases, and sentences to listeners and readers.

Cultures 2.2: Student demonstrates an understanding of the products (what people create) and how they are related to the perspectives (how people perceive things) of the cultures studied.

CORE INSTRUCTION

Warm-Up

- (5 min.) Present Practices and Perspectives, p. 205.

Vocabulario en acción 2

- (5 min.) Review **Más vocabulario** and **¡Exprésate!,** pp. 202, 204.
- (10 min.) Play Audio CD 5, Tr. 6, for Activity 24, p. 204. ●
- (20 min.) Have students do Activities 25–26, p. 204–205.

Wrap-Up

- (10 min.) Have students do the activity described in Advanced Learners, p. 205. ▲

OPTIONAL RESOURCES

- (25 min.) See Multiple Intelligences, p. 205. ●

Practice Options

- *Lab Book*, pp. 27–28, 58 ▲ ● ■
- *Cuaderno de vocabulario y gramática*, pp. 55–57 ▲ ◆ ●
- *Teaching Transparencies:* **Vocabulario** 5.3, 5.4; *Vocabulario y gramática* Answers, pp. 55–57 ▲ ◆ ●
- *Video Guide*, pp. 44–45, 48 ▲ ● ■
- *Interactive Tutor* (Disc 1) or *DVD Tutor* (Disc 1) ▲ ● ■
- Online practice, Chapter 5 (go.hrw.com, Keyword: EXP1A CH5) ▲ ● ■

▲ = Advanced Learners   ◆ = Slower Pace Learners   ● = Special Learning Needs   ■ = Heritage Speakers

Holt Spanish 1A

Lesson Planner

¡Empecemos!

DAY 16 50-MINUTE LESSON PLAN

NATIONAL STANDARDS

Vocabulario en acción 2

Communication 1.1: Student engages in oral and written exchanges of learned material to socialize and to provide and obtain information.

Communication 1.2: Student demonstrates understanding of simple, clearly spoken, and written language such as simple stories, high-frequency commands, and brief instructions when dealing with familiar topics.

Communication 1.3: Student presents information using familiar words, phrases, and sentences to listeners and readers.

CORE INSTRUCTION

Warm-Up
- (5 min.) Have a few students read their paragraphs from Activity 26, p. 205.

Vocabulario en acción 2
- (20 min.) Have students do Activities 27–28, p. 205.
- (15 min.) Review **Vocabulario 2,** pp. 200–205.

Wrap-Up
- (10 min.) Have students work in pairs to check their answers to Activity 27, p. 205.

OPTIONAL RESOURCES
- (15 min.) See **Comunicación (TE),** p. 205.

Practice Options
- *Lab Book*, pp. 27–28, 58 ▲ ● ■
- *Cuaderno de vocabulario y gramática*, pp. 55–57 ▲ ◆ ●
- *Teaching Transparencies:* **Vocabulario** 5.3, 5.4; *Vocabulario y gramática* Answers, pp. 55–57 ▲ ◆ ●
- *Video Guide*, pp. 44–45, 48 ▲ ● ■
- *Interactive Tutor* (Disc 1) or *DVD Tutor* (Disc 1) ▲ ● ■
- Online practice, Chapter 5 (go.hrw.com, Keyword: EXP1A CH5) ▲ ● ■

▲ = Advanced Learners   ◆ = Slower Pace Learners   ● = Special Learning Needs   ■ = Heritage Speakers

En casa con la familia

DAY 17 50-MINUTE LESSON PLAN

NATIONAL STANDARDS

Vocabulario en acción 2

Communication 1.1: Student engages in oral and written exchanges of learned material to socialize and to provide and obtain information.

Communication 1.2: Student demonstrates understanding of simple, clearly spoken, and written language such as simple stories, high-frequency commands, and brief instructions when dealing with familiar topics.

Communication 1.3: Student presents information using familiar words, phrases, and sentences to listeners and readers.

Gramática en acción 2

Communication 1.1: Student engages in oral and written exchanges of learned material to socialize and to provide and obtain information.

Communication 1.2: Student demonstrates understanding of simple, clearly spoken, and written language such as simple stories, high-frequency commands, and brief instructions when dealing with familiar topics.

CORE INSTRUCTION

Warm-Up

• (5 min.) Ask students the following questions: **¿Qué te parece tener que ayudar en casa? / ¿Qué te toca hacer a tí para ayudar en casa?**

Vocabulario en acción 2

• (5 min.) Review **Vocabulario 2,** pp. 200–205.

Assessment

• (20 min.) Give **Prueba: Vocabulario 2.**

Gramática en acción 2

• (15 min.) Present **Gramática: Estar** *with prepositions,* p. 206, using Teaching **Gramática**, p. 206.

Wrap-Up

• (5 min.) Have students do the activity described in **Más práctica,** p. 207.

OPTIONAL RESOURCES

• You can find alternative quizzes in the Assessment Options listed below.

Practice Options

• *Lab Book*, pp. 27–28, 58 ▲ ● ■
• *Cuaderno de vocabulario y gramática*, pp. 55–57, 58–60 ▲ ◆ ●
• *Cuaderno de actividades*, pp. 45–47 ▲ ● ■
• *Activities for Communication*, pp. 19–20, 63–64 ▲ ■
• *Teaching Transparencies: Vocabulario y gramática* Answers, pp. 55–57, 58–60 ▲ ◆ ●
• *Video Guide*, pp. 44–45, 48 ▲ ● ■
• *Grammar Tutor for Students of Spanish*, pp. 29–32, 172–173 ◆ ●
• *Interactive Tutor* (Disc 1) or *DVD Tutor* (Disc 1) ▲ ● ■
• Online practice, Chapter 5 (go.hrw.com, Keyword: EXP1A CH5) ▲ ● ■

Assessment Options

• *Assessment Program:* **Prueba: Vocabulario 2**, pp. 87–88 ▲ ● ■
• *Assessment Program:* Alternative Assessment, pp. 216, 222, 229 ▲ ● ■
• Test Generator ▲ ● ■

▲ = Advanced Learners   ◆ = Slower Pace Learners   ● = Special Learning Needs   ■ = Heritage Speakers

En casa con la familia

DAY 18 50-MINUTE LESSON PLAN

NATIONAL STANDARDS

Gramática en acción 2

Communication 1.1: Student engages in oral and written exchanges of learned material to socialize and to provide and obtain information.

Communication 1.2: Student demonstrates understanding of simple, clearly spoken, and written language such as simple stories, high-frequency commands, and brief instructions when dealing with familiar topics.

Cultures 2.2: Student demonstrates an understanding of the products (what people create) and how they are related to the perspectives (how people perceive things) of the cultures studied.

Comparisons 4.2: Student demonstrates an understanding of the concept of culture through comparisons of the student's own culture and the cultures studied.

CORE INSTRUCTION

Warm-Up

- (5 min.) Ask students questions about where things are located in the classroom. (**¿Dónde está la basura? Está cerca de la puerta, ¿no?**)

Gramática en acción 2

- (10 min.) Present **Nota cultural,** p. 206.
- (10 min.) Show **GramaVisión,** *(estar with prepositions), Video Program* (Videocassette 3) or *DVD Tutor* (Disc 1).
- (10 min.) Review **estar** with prepositions, p. 206.
- (10 min.) Have students do Activities 29–30, pp. 206–207.

Wrap-Up

- (5 min.) Have students tell where they are sitting in relation to their classmates.

OPTIONAL RESOURCES

- (15 min.) See Slower Pace Learners, p. 207. ◆

Practice Options

- *Lab Book,* pp. 27–28, 58 ▲ ● ■
- *Cuaderno de vocabulario y gramática*, pp. 58–60 ▲ ◆ ●
- *Cuaderno de actividades*, pp. 45–47 ▲ ● ■
- *Activities for Communication,* pp. 19–20, 63–64 ▲ ■
- *Teaching Transparencies:* **Vocabulario y gramática** Answers, pp. 58–60 ▲ ◆ ●
- *Video Guide,* pp. 44–45 ▲ ● ■
- *Grammar Tutor for Students of Spanish,* pp. 29–32, 172–173 ◆ ●
- *Interactive Tutor* (Disc 1) or *DVD Tutor* (Disc 1) ▲ ● ■
- Online practice, Chapter 5 (go.hrw.com, Keyword: EXP1A CH5) ▲ ● ■

▲ = Advanced Learners   ◆ = Slower Pace Learners   ● = Special Learning Needs   ■ = Heritage Speakers

Holt Spanish 1A

Lesson Planner

CAPÍTULO

5

En casa con la familia

DAY 19 50-MINUTE LESSON PLAN

NATIONAL STANDARDS

Gramática en acción 2

Communication 1.1: Student engages in oral and written exchanges of learned material to socialize and to provide and obtain information.

Communication 1.2: Student demonstrates understanding of simple, clearly spoken, and written language such as simple stories, high-frequency commands, and brief instructions when dealing with familiar topics.

Communication 1.3: Student presents information using familiar words, phrases, and sentences to listeners and readers.

CORE INSTRUCTION

Warm-Up
- (5 min.) Have students do Bell Work 5.7, p. 208.

Gramática en acción 2
- (15 min.) Have students do Activities 31–32, p. 207.
- (20 min.) Present **Gramática:** *Negation with* **nunca, tampoco, nadie,** *and* **nada,** p. 208, using Teaching **Gramática,** p. 208.

Wrap-Up
- (10 min.) Begin the activity described in **Comunicación (TE),** p. 207.

OPTIONAL RESOURCES
- (5 min.) See Special Learning Needs, p. 207. ●
- (15 min.) See Multiple Intelligences, p. 209. ●

Practice Options
- *Lab Book*, pp. 27–28, 58 ▲ ● ■
- ***Cuaderno de vocabulario y gramática***, pp. 58–60 ▲ ◆ ●
- ***Cuaderno de actividades***, pp. 45–47 ▲ ● ■
- *Activities for Communication*, pp. 19–20, 63–64 ▲ ■
- *Teaching Transparencies:* Bell Work, 5.7; ***Vocabulario y gramática*** Answers, pp. 58–60 ▲ ◆ ●
- *Video Guide*, pp. 44–45 ▲ ● ■
- *Grammar Tutor for Students of Spanish*, pp. 29–32, 172–173 ◆ ●
- *Interactive Tutor* (Disc 1) or *DVD Tutor* (Disc 1) ▲ ● ■
- Online practice, Chapter 5 (go.hrw.com, Keyword: EXP1A CH5) ▲ ● ■

▲ = Advanced Learners   ◆ = Slower Pace Learners   ● = Special Learning Needs   ■ = Heritage Speakers

En casa con la familia

DAY 20 50-MINUTE LESSON PLAN

NATIONAL STANDARDS

Gramática en acción 2

Communication 1.1: Student engages in oral and written exchanges of learned material to socialize and to provide and obtain information.

Communication 1.2: Student demonstrates understanding of simple, clearly spoken, and written language such as simple stories, high-frequency commands, and brief instructions when dealing with familiar topics.

Communication 1.3: Student presents information using familiar words, phrases, and sentences to listeners and readers.

CORE INSTRUCTION

Warm-Up

- (5 min.) Finish **Comunicación (TE)**, p. 207.

Gramática en acción 2

- (10 min.) Show **GramaVisión** (*negation with-nunca, tampoco, nadie, and nada), Video Program* (Videocassette 3) or *DVD Tutor* (Disc 1).
- (5 min.) Review negation with **nunca, tampoco, nadie,** and **nada.**
- (10 min.) Play Audio CD 5, Tr. 7, for Activity 33, p. 208. ●
- (15 min.) Have students to Activities 34–36, p. 209.

Wrap-Up

- (5 min.) Have students do the activity described in **Más práctica,** p. 209.

OPTIONAL RESOURCES

- (5 min.) See Advanced Learners, p. 209. ▲

Practice Options

- *Lab Book,* pp. 27–28 ▲ ● ■
- *Cuaderno de vocabulario y gramática,* pp. 58–60 ▲ ◆ ●
- *Cuaderno de Actividades,* pp. 45–47 ▲ ● ■
- *Activities for Communication,* pp. 19–20, 63–64 ▲ ■
- *Teaching Transparencies: Vocabulario y gramática* Answers, pp. 58–60 ▲ ◆ ●
- *Video Guide,* pp. 44–45 ▲ ● ■
- *Grammar Tutor for Students of Spanish,* pp. 29–32, 172–173 ◆ ●
- *Interactive Tutor* (Disc 1) or *DVD Tutor* (Disc 1) ▲ ● ■
- Online practice, Chapter 5 (go.hrw.com, Keyword: EXP1A CH5) ▲ ● ■

▲ = Advanced Learners   ◆ = Slower Pace Learners   ● = Special Learning Needs   ■ = Heritage Speakers

Holt Spanish 1A

Lesson Planner

En casa con la familia

DAY 21 50-MINUTE LESSON PLAN

NATIONAL STANDARDS

Gramática en acción 2
Communication 1.1: Student engages in oral and written exchanges of learned material to socialize and to provide and obtain information.

Communication 1.2: Student demonstrates understanding of simple, clearly spoken, and written language such as simple stories, high-frequency commands, and brief instructions when dealing with familiar topics.

CORE INSTRUCTION

Warm-Up
• (5 min.) Have students do Bell Work 5.8, p. 210.

Gramática en acción 2
• (20 min.) Present **Gramática: tocar** and **parecer**, p. 210, using Teaching **Gramática**, p. 210.
• (10 min.) Play Audio CD 5, Tr. 8, for Activity 37, p. 210. ●
• (10 min.) Have students do Activity 38, p. 211.

Wrap-Up
• (5 min.) Have students read their answers for Activity 28, p. 205, to a partner.

OPTIONAL RESOURCES
• (5 min.) See Slower Pace Learners, p. 211. ◆
• (15 min.) **Comunicación**, p. 209

Practice Options
• *Lab Book*, pp.27–28 ▲ ● ■
• *Cuaderno de vocabulario y gramática*, pp. 58–60 ▲ ◆ ●
• *Cuaderno de Actividades*, pp. 45–47 ▲ ● ■
• *Activities for Communication*, pp. 19–20, 63–64 ▲ ■
• *Teaching Transparencies:* Bell Work 5.8; *Vocabulario y gramática* Answers, pp. 58–60 ▲ ◆ ●
• *Video Guide*, pp. 44–45 ▲ ● ■
• *Grammar Tutor for Students of Spanish*, pp. 29–32, 172–173 ◆ ●
• *Interactive Tutor* (Disc 1) or *DVD Tutor* (Disc 1) ▲ ● ■
• Online practice, Chapter 5 (go.hrw.com, Keyword: EXP1A CH5) ▲ ● ■

▲ = Advanced Learners   ◆ = Slower Pace Learners   ● = Special Learning Needs   ■ = Heritage Speakers

CAPÍTULO

En casa con la familia

DAY 22 50-MINUTE LESSON PLAN

NATIONAL STANDARDS

Gramática en acción 2

Communication 1.1: Student engages in oral and written exchanges of learned material to socialize and to provide and obtain information.

Communication 1.2: Student demonstrates understanding of simple, clearly spoken, and written language such as simple stories, high-frequency commands, and brief instructions when dealing with familiar topics.

Communication 1.3: Student presents information using familiar words, phrases, and sentences to listeners and readers.

CORE INSTRUCTION

Warm-Up

- (5 min.) List 8–10 chores on the board. Then ask students to tell you in Spanish who in their family **never** does a chore and who **always** does a chore.

Gramática en acción 2

- (10 min.) Show **GramaVisión** (**tocar** *and* **parecer**), *Video Program* (Videocassette 3) or *DVD Tutor* (Disc 1).
- (10 min.) Have students do Activities 39–40, p. 211.
- (20 min.) Review **Gramática 1,** pp. 206–211.

Wrap-Up

- (5 min.) Assign **Comunicación** (TE), p. 211, as homework. Then remind students to study for **Prueba: Gramática 2.**

OPTIONAL RESOURCES

- (5 min.) See Special Learning Needs, p. 211. ●
- (5 min.) See AP Language Examination, p. 211.

Practice Options

- *Lab Book,* pp. 27–28 ▲ ● ■
- *Cuaderno de vocabulario y gramática*, pp. 58–60 ▲ ◆ ●
- *Cuaderno de actividades*, pp. 45–47 ▲ ● ■
- *Activities for Communication*, pp. 19–20, 63–64 ▲ ■
- *Teaching Transparencies: **Vocabulario y gramática*** Answers, pp. 58–60 ▲ ◆ ●
- *Video Guide*, pp. 44–45 ▲ ● ■
- *Grammar Tutor for Students of Spanish*, pp. 29–32, 172–173 ◆ ●
- *Interactive Tutor* (Disc 1) or *DVD Tutor* (Disc 1) ▲ ● ■
- Online practice, Chapter 5 (go.hrw.com, Keyword: EXP1A CH5) ▲ ● ■

▲ = Advanced Learners   ◆ = Slower Pace Learners   ● = Special Learning Needs   ■ = Heritage Speakers

Holt Spanish 1A   Lesson Planner

En casa con la familia

DAY 23 50-MINUTE LESSON PLAN

NATIONAL STANDARDS

Gramática en acción 2

Communication 1.1: Student engages in oral and written exchanges of learned material to socialize and to provide and obtain information.

Communication 1.2: Student demonstrates understanding of simple, clearly spoken, and written language such as simple stories, high-frequency commands, and brief instructions when dealing with familiar topics.

Communication 1.3: Student presents information using familiar words, phrases, and sentences to listeners and readers.

Conexiones Culturales

Communication 1.3: Student presents information using familiar words, phrases, and sentences to listeners and readers.

Cultures 2.2: Student demonstrates an understanding of the products (what people create) and how they are related to the perspectives (how people perceive things) of the cultures studied.

Comparisons 4.2: Student demonstrates an understanding of the concept of culture through comparisons of the student's own culture and the cultures studied.

CORE INSTRUCTION

Warm-Up
- (5 min.) Have a few students present their letter from **Comunicación** (TE), p. 211.

Gramática en acción 2
- (5 min.) Review **Gramática 2,** pp. 206–211.

Assessment
- (20 min.) Give **Prueba: Gramática 2.**

Conexiones culturales
- (15 min.) Present **Conexiones culturales,** p. 212, using Teaching **Conexiones culturales,** #s 1–3, p. 212.

Wrap-Up
- (5 min.) Assign **Más práctica,** p. 212, as homework.

OPTIONAL RESOURCES
- (20 min.) See Special Learning Needs, p. 213. ●
- You can find alternative quizzes in the Assessment Options listed below.
- (5 min.) Teaching **Conexiones culturales**, #4, p. 212

Practice Options
- Online practice, Chapter 5 (go.hrw.com, Keyword: EXP1A CH5) ▲ ● ■

Assessment Options
- *Assessment Program*: **Prueba: Gramática 2,** pp. 89–90 ▲ ● ■
- *Assessment Program*: **Prueba: Aplicación 2,** pp. 89–90 ▲ ● ■ .
- Audio CD 5, Tr. 16 ●
- Test Generator ▲ ● ■

▲ = Advanced Learners   ◆ = Slower Pace Learners   ● = Special Learning Needs   ■ = Heritage Speakers

Holt Spanish 1A

Lesson Planner

CAPÍTULO

En casa con la familia

DAY 24 50-MINUTE LESSON PLAN

NATIONAL STANDARDS

Conexiones culturales

Communication 1.2: Student demonstrates understanding of simple, clearly spoken, and written language such as simple stories, high-frequency commands, and brief instructions when dealing with familiar topics.

Cultures 2.1: Student demonstrates an understanding of the practices (what people do) and how they are related to the perspectives (how people perceive things) of the cultures studied.

Comparisons 4.1: Student demonstrates an understanding of the nature of language through comparisons of the student's own language and the language studied.

Novela en video

Communication 1.2: Student demonstrates understanding of simple, clearly spoken, and written language such as simple stories, high-frequency commands, and brief instructions when dealing with familiar topics.

Connections 3.2: Student uses resources (that may include technology) in the language and cultures being studied to gain access to information.

CORE INSTRUCTION

Warm-Up
- (5 min.) Present Practices and Perspectives: Names, p. 213.

Conexiones culturales
- (20 min.) Present **Conexiones culturales,** p. 213, using Teaching **Conexiones culturales,** #s 5, 7–8, p. 212.

Novela en video
- (15 min.) Present **Novela en video,** pp. 214–215, using Teaching **Novela en video,** #1, p. 214.

Wrap-Up
- (10 min.) Have students do the activity described in Connections, p. 214.

OPTIONAL RESOURCES
- (5 min.) See Variation, p. 213.
- (20 min.) See **Comunicación** (TE), p. 213.
- (15 min.) See Advanced Learners, p. 213. ▲
- (20 min.) Culminating Project, p. 216

Practice Options
- *Video Guide,* pp. 44–45, 49 ▲ ■
- *Lab Book,* p. 59 ▲ ● ■
- Online practice, Chapter 5 (go.hrw.com, Keyword: EXP1A CH5) ▲ ● ■

▲ = Advanced Learners   ◆ = Slower Pace Learners   ● = Special Learning Needs   ■ = Heritage Speakers

Holt Spanish 1A

Lesson Planner

En casa con la familia

DAY 25 50-MINUTE LESSON PLAN

NATIONAL STANDARDS

Novela en video

Communication 1.2: Student demonstrates understanding of simple, clearly spoken, and written language such as simple stories, high-frequency commands, and brief instructions when dealing with familiar topics.

Connections 3.2: Student uses resources (that may include technology) in the language and cultures being studied to gain access to information.

Leamos y escribamos

Communication 1.2: Student demonstrates understanding of simple, clearly spoken, and written language such as simple stories, high-frequency commands, and brief instructions when dealing with familiar topics.

Communication 1.3: Student presents information using familiar words, phrases, and sentences to listeners and readers.

Connections 3.2: Student uses resources (that may include technology) in the language and cultures being studied to gain access to information.

CORE INSTRUCTION

Warm-Up

- (5 min.) Review the charts created for Connections, p. 214.

Novela en video

- (15 min.) Show **Novela en video,** using Teaching **Novela en video,** #s 2–3, p. 214.
- (5 min.) Discuss Gestures, p. 216.

Leamos y escribamos

- (15 min.) Begin presenting **Leamos,** using Teaching **Leamos,** #s 1–3, p. 218.
- (5 min.) Play Audio CD 5, Tr. 9, for Activity A, p. 218. ●

Wrap-Up

- (5 min.) Assign Activities 1–2, p. 217, as homework.

OPTIONAL RESOURCES

- (5 min.) See Career Path, p. 216.
- (30 min.) See **Comunicación** (TE), p. 217.
- (25 min.) See Advanced Learners, p. 217. ▲
- (25 min.) See Multiple Intelligences, p. 217. ●
- (15 min.) See Applying the Strategies, p. 218. ●
- (10 min.) See Special Learning Needs, p. 219. ●

Practice Options

- *Lab Book*, pp. 59 ▲ ● ■
- *Cuaderno de actividades*, p. 48 ▲ ■
- *Video Guide*, pp. 44–45, 49 ▲ ● ■
- *Student Edition*, **Literatura y variedades,** pp. 236–237 ▲ ● ■
- *Reading Strategies and Skills Handbook*, pp. xi–xii, 70, 2–5 ▲ ● ■
- *¡Lee conmigo!* Level 1 Reader
- *Interactive Tutor* (Disc 1) or *DVD Tutor* (Disc 1) ▲ ● ■
- Online practice, Chapter 5 (go.hrw.com, Keyword: EXP1A CH5) ▲ ● ■

▲ = Advanced Learners ◆ = Slower Pace Learners ● = Special Learning Needs ■ = Heritage Speakers

En casa con la familia

DAY 26 50-MINUTE LESSON PLAN

NATIONAL STANDARDS

Leamos y escribamos

Communication 1.1: Student engages in oral and written exchanges of learned material to socialize and to provide and obtain information.

Communication 1.2: Student demonstrates understanding of simple, clearly spoken, and written language such as simple stories, high-frequency commands, and brief instructions when dealing with familiar topics.

Communication 1.3: Student presents information using familiar words, phrases, and sentences to listeners and readers.

CORE INSTRUCTION

Warm-Up

- (5 min.) Ask the class to summarize aloud in English what they read during the last class of **Casas y apartamentos,** p. 218.

Leamos y escribamos

- (5 min.) Have students read **Leamos,** p. 218.
- (10 min.) See Teaching **Leamos,** #4, p. 218.
- (20 min.) Present **Taller del escritor,** p. 219, using Teaching **Escribamos,** p. 218.

Wrap-Up

- (10 min.) Ask students to work with a partner to write a new listing for a house to appear in the **Casas y apartamentos** catalog, p. 218.

OPTIONAL RESOURCES

- (35 min.) See Advanced Learners, p. 219. ▲
- (50 min.) See Process Writing, p. 219.

Practice Options

- *Cuaderno de actividades*, p. 48 ▲ ■
- *Student Edition,* **Literatura y variedades,** pp. 236–237 ▲ ● ■
- *Reading Strategies and Skills Handbook,* pp. 70, 2–5 ▲ ● ■
- *¡Lee conmigo!* Level 1 Reader ▲ ● ■
- *Interactive Tutor* (Disc 1) or *DVD Tutor* (Disc 1) ▲ ● ■
- Online practice, Chapter 5 (go.hrw.com, Keyword: EXP1A CH5) ▲ ● ■

Assessment Options

- *Assessment Program,* **Prueba: Lectura** p. 93, 99 ▲ ● ■
- *Assessment Program,* **Prueba: Escritura** p. 94, 99 ▲ ● ■

▲ = Advanced Learners   ◆ = Slower Pace Learners   ● = Special Learning Needs   ■ = Heritage Speakers

En casa con la familia

DAY 27 50-MINUTE LESSON PLAN

NATIONAL STANDARDS

Leamos y escribamos
Communication 1.1: Student engages in oral and written exchanges of learned material to socialize and to provide and obtain information.

Repaso
Communication 1.2: Student demonstrates understanding of simple, clearly spoken, and written language such as simple stories, high-frequency commands, and brief instructions when dealing with familiar topics.

Communication 1.3: Student presents information using familiar words, phrases, and sentences to listeners and readers.

Cultures 2.1: Student demonstrates an understanding of the practices (what people do) and how they are related to the perspectives (how people perceive things) of the cultures studied.

Cultures 2.2: Student demonstrates an understanding of the products (what people create) and how they are related to the perspectives (how people perceive things) of the cultures studied.

CORE INSTRUCTION

Warm-Up
• (5 min.) Review the Writing Assessment Rubric, p. 219, with students.

Leamos y escribamos
• (5 min.) Have students compare their dream homes from **Taller del escritor,** p. 219.

Repaso
• (35 min.) Have students do Activities 1–5, pp. 220–221.

Wrap-Up
• (5 min.) Present the Fold-N-Learn activity suggestion on p. 220. Suggest that students use the activity as part of their review for the Chapter Test. ●

OPTIONAL RESOURCES
• (30 min.) See Teacher to Teacher, p. 220.

Practice Options
• *Lab Book*, pp. 27–28, 60 ▲ ● ■
• *Activities for Communication*, pp. 47, 63–64 ▲ ■
• *Teaching Transparencies:* Situation, Picture Sequences ▲ ● ■
• *Video Guide*, pp. 44–45, 50 ▲ ● ■
• *Interactive Tutor* (Disc 1) or *DVD Tutor* (Disc 1) ▲ ● ■
• Online practice, Chapter 5 (go.hrw.com, Keyword: EXP1A CH5) ▲ ● ■

▲ = Advanced Learners   ◆ = Slower Pace Learners   ● = Special Learning Needs   ■ = Heritage Speakers

En casa con la familia

DAY 28 50-MINUTE LESSON PLAN

NATIONAL STANDARDS

Repaso

Communication 1.1: Student engages in oral and written exchanges of learned material to socialize and to provide and obtain information.

Communication 1.2: Student demonstrates understanding of simple, clearly spoken, and written language such as simple stories, high-frequency commands, and brief instructions when dealing with familiar topics.

Communication 1.3: Student presents information using familiar words, phrases, and sentences to listeners and readers.

CORE INSTRUCTION

Warm-Up

• (5 min.) Review the answers to Activity 5, p. 221.

Repaso

• (10 min.) Play Audio CD 5, Tr. 11, for Activity 6, p. 221. ●
• (5 min.) Have students do Activity 7, p. 221.
• (10 min.) Play Audio CD 5, Tr. 12, 13, 14, for **Letra y sonido,** p. 222. ●
• (10 min.) Play Game, p. 223.

Wrap-Up

• (10 min.) Review the grammar topics listed on p. 222.

OPTIONAL RESOURCES

• (10 min.) See AP Language Examination, p. 221.
• (20 min.) See Reteaching, p. 222.

Practice Options

• *Lab Book,* pp. 27–28, 60 ▲ ● ■
• *Activities for Communication,* pp. 47, 63–64 ▲ ■
• *Teaching Transparencies:* Situation; Picture Sequences ▲ ● ■
• *Video Guide,* pp. 44–45, 50 ▲ ● ■
• *Interactive Tutor* (Disc 1) or *DVD Tutor* (Disc 1) ▲ ● ■
• Online practice, Chapter 5 (go.hrw.com, Keyword: EXP1A CH5) ▲ ● ■

▲ = Advanced Learners   ◆ = Slower Pace Learners   ● = Special Learning Needs   ■ = Heritage Speakers

CAPÍTULO
5

En casa con la familia

DAY 29 50-MINUTE LESSON PLAN

NATIONAL STANDARDS

Integración
Communication 1.1: Student engages in oral and written exchanges of learned material to socialize and to provide and obtain information.

Communication 1.2: Student demonstrates understanding of simple, clearly spoken, and written language such as simple stories, high-frequency commands, and brief instructions when dealing with familiar topics.

Communication 1.3: Student presents information using familiar words, phrases, and sentences to listeners and readers.

Comparisons 4.2: Student demonstrates an understanding of the concept of culture through comparisons of the student's own culture and the cultures studied.

CORE INSTRUCTION

Warm-Up
- (5 min.) Answer any questions students have from yesterday's **Repaso** activities.

Integración
- (10 min.) Play Audio CD 5, Tr. 15, for Activity 1, p. 224. ●
- (30 min.) Have students do Activities 2–4, pp. 224–225.

Wrap-Up
- (5 min.) Remind students of the Chapter Review resources, pp. 222–223, and present Test-Taking Strategy, p. 221.

OPTIONAL RESOURCES
- (50 min.) See Culture Project, p. 224.
- (35 min.) See Fine Art Connection, p. 225.

Practice Options
- *Lab Book*, pp. 27–28, 60 ▲ ● ■
- *Cuaderno de actividades*, pp. 49–50 ▲ ● ■
- *Teaching Transparencies:* Fine Art, Chapter 5 ▲ ● ■
- *Interactive Tutor* (Disc 1) or *DVD Tutor* (Disc 1) ▲ ● ■
- Online practice, Chapter 5 (go.hrw.com, Keyword: EXP1A CH5) ▲ ● ■

▲ = Advanced Learners   ◆ = Slower Pace Learners   ● = Special Learning Needs   ■ = Heritage Speakers

(149)

En casa con la familia

DAY 30 50-MINUTE LESSON PLAN

CORE INSTRUCTION

Assessment
- (50 min.) Give the Chapter 5 Test.

OPTIONAL RESOURCES
- You may also choose from the other modes of assessment listed in the Assessment Options box below.

Practice Options
- *Interactive Tutor* (Disc 1) or *DVD Tutor* (Disc 1) ▲ ● ■
- Online practice, Chapter 5 (go.hrw.com, Keyword: EXP1A CH5) ▲ ● ■

Assessment Options
- *Assessment Program:* **Prueba: Lectura,** pp. 93–99 ▲ ● ■
- *Assessment Program:* **Prueba: Escritura,** pp. 94, 99 ▲ ● ■
- *Assessment Program:* **Examen: Capítulo 5,** pp. 169–179 ▲ ● ■
- *Assessment Program:* **Examen oral: Capítulo 5,** p. 180 ▲ ● ■
- *Assessment Program:* Alternative Assessment, pp. 217, 222, 229 ▲ ● ■
- *Audio CD 5,* Tr. 17–18, 19–20 ●
- **Examen final: Capítulos 1–5,** pp. 181–191 ▲ ● ■
- *Test Generator* ▲ ● ■

▲ = Advanced Learners   ◆ = Slower Pace Learners   ● = Special Learning Needs   ■ = Heritage Speakers

90-Minute Block Lesson Plans

¡Empecemos!

BLOCK 1 90-MINUTE LESSON PLAN

NATIONAL STANDARDS

Chapter Opener

Communication 1.2: Student demonstrates understanding of simple, clearly spoken, and written language such as simple stories, high-frequency commands, and brief instructions when dealing with familiar topics.

Cultures 2.1: Student demonstrates an understanding of the practices (what people do) and how they are related to the perspectives (how people perceive things) of the cultures studied.

Vocabulario en acción 1

Communication 1.1: Student engages in oral and written exchanges of learned material to socialize and to provide and obtain information.

Communication 1.2: Student demonstrates understanding of simple, clearly spoken, and written language such as simple stories, high-frequency commands, and brief instructions when dealing with familiar topics.

Communication 1.3: Student presents information using familiar words, phrases, and sentences to listeners and readers.

Cultures 2.1: Student demonstrates an understanding of the practices (what people do) and how they are related to the perspectives (how people perceive things) of the cultures studied.

Before starting **Capítulo 1,** you may wish to teach **Geocultura: España,** pp. xxii–3. For teaching suggestions, see pp. xv–xvi of this *Lesson Planner.*

CORE INSTRUCTION

Warm-Up

- (5 min.) See Learning and Pacing Tips, p. 5.

Chapter Opener

- (5 min.) Have students look at the photo on pp. 4–5. Present information from Using the Photo, p. 4.
- (5 min.) Present **Objetivos,** p. 4.

Vocabulario en acción 1

- (10 min.) Show **ExpresaVisión,** Ch. 1, *Video Program* (Videocassette 1) or *DVD Tutor* (Disc 1).
- (15 min.) Present the vocabulary on pp. 6–7, using Teaching **Vocabulario,** p. 6.
- (5 min.) Present **Nota cultural,** p. 7.
- (10 min.) Play Audio CD 1, Tr. 1, for Activity 1, p. 7. ●
- (15 min.) Have students do Activities 2–4, p. 7.
- (15 min.) Present **¡Exprésate!,** p. 8, using Teaching **¡Exprésate!,** p. 8.

Wrap-Up

- (5 min.) Have students do Bell Work 1.1, p. 6, or in *Teaching Transparencies.*

OPTIONAL RESOURCES

- (5 min.) See Common Error Alert, p. 6.
- (5 min.) See TPR, p. 7. ●
- (10 min.) See Special Learning Needs, p. 7. ●
- (15 min.) See **Comunicación** (TE), p. 7.
- (10 min.) See Slower Pace Learners, p. 7. ◆

▲ = Advanced Learners ◆ = Slower Pace Learners ● = Special Learning Needs ■ = Heritage Speakers

BLOCK 1 90-MINUTE LESSON PLAN

Practice Options

- *Lab Book*, pp. 9–10, 32 ▲ ● ■
- ***Cuaderno de vocabulario y gramática***, pp. 1–3 ▲ ◆ ●
- ***Cuaderno para hispanohablantes***, Chapter 1 ■
- *Teaching Transparencies:* Bell Work 1.1; Vocabulary 1.1; ***Cuaderno de vocabulario y gramática*** Answers, pp. 1–3 ▲ ● ■
- *Video program*, Videocassette 1
- *Video Guide*, pp. 4–5, 6 ▲ ● ■
- *Interactive Tutor* (Disc 1) or *DVD Tutor* (Disc 1) ▲ ● ■
- Online practice, Chapter 1 (go.hrw.com, Keyword: EXP1A CH1) ▲ ● ■

¡Empecemos!

BLOCK 2 90-MINUTE LESSON PLAN

NATIONAL STANDARDS

Vocabulario en acción 1

Communication 1.1: Student engages in oral and written exchanges of learned material to socialize and to provide and obtain information.

Communication 1.2: Student demonstrates understanding of simple, clearly spoken, and written language such as simple stories, high-frequency commands, and brief instructions when dealing with familiar topics.

Communication 1.3: Student presents information using familiar words, phrases, and sentences to listeners and readers.

CORE INSTRUCTION

Warm-Up

- (10 min.) Have students do the activity described in **Comunicación (TE)**, p. 9.

Vocabulario en acción 1

-] (10 min.) Show **ExpresaVisión**, Ch. 1, *Video Program* (Videocassette 1) or *DVD Tutor* (Disc 1).
- (10 min.) Play Audio CD 1, Tr. 2, for Activity 5, p. 9. ●
- (15 min.) Have students do Activities 6–8, p. 9.
- (15 min.) Present **¡Exprésate!,** p. 10, using Teaching **¡Exprésate!,** #s 1–2, p. 10.
- (5 min.) Have students do Activity 9, p. 10.
- (10 min.) Present **¡Exprésate!,** p. 11, using Teaching **¡Exprésate!,** #3, p. 10.
- (10 min.) Play Audio CD 1, Tr. 3, for Activity 10, p. 11. ●

Wrap-Up

- (5 min.) Ask students to bring pictures for tomorrow in order to do the activity described in Advanced Learners, p. 11. ▲

OPTIONAL RESOURCES

- (15 min.) See Advanced Learners, p. 9. ▲
- (5 min.) For students with auditory impairments, see Special Learning Needs, p. 9. ●
- (5 min.) See **También se puede decir…**, p. 9.
- (10 min.) See Multiple Intelligences, p. 11. ●

▲ = Advanced Learners   ◆ = Slower Pace Learners   ● = Special Learning Needs   ■ = Heritage Speakers

BLOCK 2 90-MINUTE LESSON PLAN

Practice Options
- *Lab Book*, pp. 9, 32 ▲ ● ■
- ***Cuaderno de vocabulario y gramática***, pp. 1–3 ▲ ◆ ●
- *Teaching Transparencies:* Bell Work 1.1; Vocabulary 1.1; ***Cuaderno de vocabulario y gramática*** Answers, pp. 1–3 ▲ ● ■
- *Video Guide*, pp. 4–5, 6. ▲ ● ■
- *Interactive Tutor* (Disc 1) or *DVD Tutor* (Disc 1) ▲ ● ■
- Online practice, Chapter 1 (go.hrw.com, Keyword: EXP1A CH1) ▲ ● ■

▲ = Advanced Learners   ◆ = Slower Pace Learners   ● = Special Learning Needs   ■ = Heritage Speakers

CAPÍTULO

¡Empecemos!

NATIONAL STANDARDS

Vocabulario en acción 1

Communication 1.1: Student engages in oral and written exchanges of learned material to socialize and to provide and obtain information.

Communication 1.2: Student demonstrates understanding of simple, clearly spoken, and written language such as simple stories, high-frequency commands, and brief instructions when dealing with familiar topics.

Communication 1.3: Student presents information using familiar words, phrases, and sentences to listeners and readers.

Comparisons 4.1: Student demonstrates an understanding of the nature of language through comparisons of the student's own language and the language studied.

Comparisons 4.2: Student demonstrates an understanding of the concept of culture through comparisons of the student's own culture and the cultures studied.

CORE INSTRUCTION

Warm-Up

- (5 min.) Have students complete the first part of the activity described in Advanced Learners, p. 11. ▲

Vocabulario en acción 1

- (5 min.) Have students do Bell Work 1.2, p. 10.
- (15 min.) Review **Más vocabulario** and **¡Exprésate!,** pp. 10–11.
- (15 min.) Have students do Activities 11–12, p. 11.
- (10 min.) Review **Vocabulario 1,** pp. 6–11.

Gramática en acción 1

- (20 min.) Present **Gramática:** *Subjects and verbs in sentences,* p. 12, using Teaching **Gramática,** #s 1–3, p. 12.
- (10 min.) Present **Nota cultural,** p. 12.
- (5 min.) Have students do Activity 13, p. 12.

Wrap-Up

- (5 min.) Have students complete the second part of the activity described in Advanced Learners, p. 11. ▲

OPTIONAL RESOURCES

- (5 min.) See **Comunicación** (TE), p. 11.

▲ = Advanced Learners   ◆ = Slower Pace Learners   ● = Special Learning Needs   ■ = Heritage Speakers

BLOCK 3 90-MINUTE LESSON PLAN

Practice Options

- *Lab Book*, pp. 9–10 ▲ ● ■
- *Cuaderno de vocabulario y gramática*, pp. 4–6 ▲ ◆ ●
- *Cuaderno de actividades*, pp. 1–4. ▲ ● ■
- *Teaching Transparencies:* Bell Work 1.2; *Cuaderno de vocabulario y gramática* Answers, pp. 4–6 ▲ ● ■
- *Video Guide*, pp. 4–5 ▲ ● ■
- *Grammar Tutor for Students of Spanish*, pp. 1–2 ◆ ●
- *Interactive Tutor* (Disc 1) or *DVD Tutor* (Disc 1) ▲ ● ■
- Online practice, Chapter 1 (go.hrw.com, Keyword: EXP1A CH1) ▲ ● ■

▲ = Advanced Learners   ◆ = Slower Pace Learners   ● = Special Learning Needs   ■ = Heritage Speakers

Holt Spanish 1A   Lesson Planner

¡Empecemos!

NATIONAL STANDARDS

Vocabulario en acción 1

Communication 1.1: Student engages in oral and written exchanges of learned material to socialize and to provide and obtain information.

Communication 1.2: Student demonstrates understanding of simple, clearly spoken, and written language such as simple stories, high-frequency commands, and brief instructions when dealing with familiar topics.

Communication 1.3: Student presents information using familiar words, phrases, and sentences to listeners and readers.

CORE INSTRUCTION

Warm-Up

- (5 min.) Have students do Bell Work 1.3, p. 12.

Vocabulario en acción 1

- (15 min.) Review **Vocabulario 1,** pp. 6–11.

Assessment

- (20 min.) Give **Prueba: Vocabulario 1.**

Gramática en acción 1

- (10 min.) Show **Gramavisión** (*subjects and verbs in sentences*), *Video Program* (Videocassette 1) or *DVD Tutor* (Disc 1).
- (10 min.) Review subjects and verbs in sentences, p. 12.
- (20 min.) Have students do Activities 14–16, p. 13.

Wrap-Up

- (10 min.) Have students do the drawing part of the activity described in **Comunicación** (TE), p. 13. Take up the drawings at the end of class.

OPTIONAL RESOURCES

- (5 min.) See Slower Pace Learners, p. 13. ◆
- (5 min.) See Special Learning Needs, p. 13. ●
- You can find alternative quizzes in the Assessment Options on the next page.

▲ = Advanced Learners   ◆ = Slower Pace Learners   ● = Special Learning Needs   ■ = Heritage Speakers

Holt Spanish 1A

Lesson Planner

BLOCK 4 90-MINUTE LESSON PLAN

Practice Options
- *Lab Book*, pp. 9–10 ▲ ● ■
- ***Cuaderno de vocabulario y gramática***, pp. 4–6 ▲ ◆ ●
- ***Cuaderno de actividades***, pp. 1–4. ▲ ● ■
- *Teaching Transparencies:* Bell Work 1.3; ***Cuaderno de vocabulario y gramática*** Answers, pp. 4–6 ▲ ● ■
- *Video Guide*, pp. 4–5 ▲ ● ■
- *Grammar Tutor for Students of Spanish*, pp. 1–2 ◆ ●
- *Interactive Tutor* (Disc 1) or *DVD Tutor* (Disc 1) ▲ ● ■
- Online practice, Chapter 1 (go.hrw.com, Keyword: EXP1A CH1) ▲ ● ■

Assessment Options
- *Assessment Program*: **Prueba: Vocabulario 1**, pp. 1–2 ▲ ● ■
- Test Generator ▲ ● ■

▲ = Advanced Learners   ◆ = Slower Pace Learners   ● = Special Learning Needs   ■ = Heritage Speakers

¡Empecemos!

BLOCK 5 90-MINUTE LESSON PLAN

NATIONAL STANDARDS

Gramática en acción 1

Communication 1.1: Student engages in oral and written exchanges of learned material to socialize and to provide and obtain information.

Communication 1.2: Student demonstrates understanding of simple, clearly spoken, and written language such as simple stories, high-frequency commands, and brief instructions when dealing with familiar topics.

Cultures 2.1: Student demonstrates an understanding of the practices (what people do) and how they are related to the perspectives (how people perceive things) of the cultures studied.

Comparisons 4.1: Student demonstrates an understanding of the nature of language through comparisons of the student's own language and the language studied.

CORE INSTRUCTION

Warm-Up

- (10 min.) Have students do the activity described in **Comunicación** (TE), p. 13, using their drawings from yesterday.

Gramática en acción 1

- (5 min.) Have students do Bell Work 1.3, p. 14.
- (15 min.) Present **Gramática:** *Subject pronouns,* p. 14, using Teaching **Gramática,** #s 1–3, p. 14.
- (10 min.) Show **GramaVisión** *(subject pronouns), Video Program* (Videocassette 1) or *DVD Tutor* (Disc 1).
- (5 min.) Have students do Activity 17, p. 14.
- (10 min.) Play Audio CD 1, Tr. 4, for Activity 18, p. 15. ●
- (20 min.) Have students do Activities 19–20, p. 15.
- (10 min.) Review **Gramática 1,** pp. 12–15.

Wrap-Up

- (5 min.) Review topics for **Prueba: Gramática 1.**

OPTIONAL RESOURCES

- (5 min.) See Heritage Speakers, p. 14. ■
- (5 min.) See Slower Pace Learners, p. 15. ◆
- (5 min.) For students with learning disabilities/dyslexia, see Special Learning Needs, p. 15. ●
- (5 min.) See **Comunicación** (TE), p. 15.

▲ = Advanced Learners ◆ = Slower Pace Learners ● = Special Learning Needs ■ = Heritage Speakers

BLOCK 5 90-MINUTE LESSON PLAN

Practice Options

- *Lab Book*, pp. 9–10 ▲ ● ■
- ***Cuaderno de vocabulario y gramática***, pp. 4–6 ▲ ◆ ●
- ***Cuaderno de actividades***, pp. 1–4 ▲ ● ■
- *Activities for Communication*, pp. 1–2 ▲ ■
- *Teaching Transparencies:* Bell Work, 1.4; ***Cuaderno de vocabulario y gramática*** Answers pp. 4–6 ▲ ● ■
- *Video Guide*, pp. 4–5 ▲ ● ■
- *Grammar Tutor for Students of Spanish*, pp. 1–2 ◆ ●
- *Interactive Tutor* (Disc 1) Ch. 1 or *DVD Tutor* (Disc 1) ▲ ● ■
- Online practice, Chapter 1 (go.hrw.com, Keyword: EXP1A CH1) ▲ ● ■

▲ = Advanced Learners   ◆ = Slower Pace Learners   ● = Special Learning Needs   ■ = Heritage Speakers

Holt Spanish 1A

Lesson Planner

¡Empecemos!

BLOCK 6 90-MINUTE LESSON PLAN

NATIONAL STANDARDS

Gramática en acción 1

Communication 1.1: Student engages in oral and written exchanges of learned material to socialize and to provide and obtain information.

Communication 1.2: Student demonstrates understanding of simple, clearly spoken, and written language such as simple stories, high-frequency commands, and brief instructions when dealing with familiar topics.

Communication 1.3: Student presents information using familiar words, phrases, and sentences to listeners and readers.

Cultures 2.1: Student demonstrates an understanding of the practices (what people do) and how they are related to the perspectives (how people perceive things) of the cultures studied.

Comparisons 4.1: Student demonstrates an understanding of the nature of language through comparisons of the student's own language and the language studied.

Cultura

Communication 1.2: Student demonstrates understanding of simple, clearly spoken, and written language such as simple stories, high-frequency commands, and brief instructions when dealing with familiar topics.

Cultures 2.1: Student demonstrates an understanding of the practices (what people do) and how they are related to the perspectives (how people perceive things) of the cultures studied.

Connections 3.2: Student uses resources (that may include technology) in the language and cultures being studied to gain access to information.

Comparisons 4.2: Student demonstrates an understanding of the concept of culture through comparisons of the student's own culture and the cultures studied.

Communities 5.2: Student shows evidence of becoming a lifelong learner by using the language for personal enrichment and career development.

CORE INSTRUCTION

Warm-Up
- (5 min.) Have students do Bell Work 1.5, p. 18.

Gramática en acción 1
- (5 min.) Review **Gramática 1,** pp. 12–15.

Assessment
- (20 min.) Give **Prueba: Gramática 1.**

Cultura
- (20 min.) Present **Cultura,** p. 16–17, using Teaching **Cultura,** p. 16.
- (15 min.) Play the Audio CD 1, Tr. 5, 6, 7, or show **VideoCultura,** Ch. 1. ●
- (10 min.) Present **Comunidad,** p. 17.

Vocabulario en acción 2
- (10 min.) Present **Vocabulario 2,** p.18, using Teaching **Vocabulario,** #s 1–2, p.18.

Wrap-Up
- (5 min.) Have students make flash cards with the names of the numbers 0–10 written out in Spanish. ●

OPTIONAL RESOURCES
- (15 min.) See Map Activities, p. 16.
- (5 min.) See Language Note, p. 16.
- (5 min.) See Comparing and Contrasting, p. 17.
- (15 min.) See Advanced Learners, p. 17. ▲
- (15 min.) See Multiple Intelligences, p. 17. ●
- (15 min.) See Heritage Speakers, p. 17. ■
- You can find alternative quizzes in the Assessment Options on the next page.

▲ = Advanced Learners   ◆ = Slower Pace Learners   ● = Special Learning Needs   ■ = Heritage Speakers

BLOCK 6 90-MINUTE LESSON PLAN

Practice Options
- *Lab Book*, pp. 11–12, 34 ▲ ● ■
- *Cuaderno de vocabulario y gramática*, pp. 7–9 ▲ ◆ ●
- *Cuaderno de actividades*, pp. 7–9 ▲ ● ■
- *Cuaderno para hispanohablantes*, pp. 9–10 ■
- *Video Guide*, pp. 4–5, 7, 101–103 ▲ ● ■
- *Teaching Transparencies:* Bell Work, 1.5; **Vocabulario** 1.2; *Vocabulario y gramática* Answers, pp. 7–9
- *Interactive Tutor* (Disc 1) or *DVD Tutor* (Disc 1) ▲ ● ■
- Online practice, Chapter 1 (go.hrw.com, Keyword: EXP1A CH1) ▲ ● ■

Assessment Options
- *Assessment Program*: **Prueba: Gramática 1,** pp. 3–4 ▲ ● ■
- *Assessment Program*: **Prueba: Aplicación 1,** pp. 5–6 ▲ ● ■
- Test Generator ▲ ● ■

▲ = Advanced Learners   ◆ = Slower Pace Learners   ● = Special Learning Needs   ■ = Heritage Speakers

¡Empecemos!

BLOCK 7 90-MINUTE LESSON PLAN

NATIONAL STANDARDS

Vocabulario en acción 2

Communication 1.1: Student engages in oral and written exchanges of learned material to socialize and to provide and obtain information.

Communication 1.2: Student demonstrates understanding of simple, clearly spoken, and written language such as simple stories, high-frequency commands, and brief instructions when dealing with familiar topics.

Communication 1.3: Student presents information using familiar words, phrases, and sentences to listeners and readers.

Cultures 2.1: Student demonstrates an understanding of the practices (what people do) and how they are related to the perspectives (how people perceive things) of the cultures studied.

CORE INSTRUCTION

Warm-Up

- (5 min.) Present information from Practices and Perspectives, p. 19.

Vocabulario en acción 2

- (10 min.) Show **ExpresaVisión,** Ch. 1.
- (10 min.) Review **Vocabulario,** p. 18, using Teaching **Vocabulario,** #s 3–4, p. 18.
- (15 min.) Have students do Activities 21–22, p. 18.
- (10 min.) Play Audio CD 1, Tr. 8, for Activity 23, p. 19. ●
- (15 min.) Have students do Activities 24–25, p. 19.
- (20 min.) Present **Vocabulario: ¿Qué hora es?,** p. 20, using Teaching **Vocabulario,** #1–2, p. 20.

Wrap-Up

- (5 min.) Have students do Bell Work 1.6, p. 20.

OPTIONAL RESOURCES

- (10 min.) See TPR, p. 19. ●
- (10 min.) See **Comunicación** (TE), p. 19.
- (15 min.) See Multiple Intelligences, p. 19. ●
- (10 min.) See Advanced Learners, p. 19. ▲

▲ = Advanced Learners   ◆ = Slower Pace Learners   ● = Special Learning Needs   ■ = Heritage Speakers

BLOCK 7 90-MINUTE LESSON PLAN

Practice Options
- *Lab Book*, pp. 11–12, 34 ▲ ● ■
- ***Cuaderno de vocabulario y gramática***, pp. 7–9 ▲ ◆ ●
- *Teaching Transparencies:* Bell Work 1.6; Vocabulary 1.3, 1.4; ***Cuaderno de vocabulario y gramática*** Answers, pp. 7–9 ▲ ● ■
- *Video Guide*, pp. 4–5, 8 ▲ ● ■
- *Interactive Tutor* (Disc 1) or *DVD Tutor* (Disc 1) ▲ ● ■
- Online practice, Chapter 1 (go.hrw.com, Keyword: EXP1A CH1) ▲ ● ■

▲ = Advanced Learners   ◆ = Slower Pace Learners   ● = Special Learning Needs   ■ = Heritage Speakers

Holt Spanish 1A   **Lesson Planner**

CAPÍTULO
1

¡Empecemos!

BLOCK 8 90-MINUTE LESSON PLAN

NATIONAL STANDARDS

Vocabulario en acción 2
Communication 1.1: Student engages in oral and written exchanges of learned material to socialize and to provide and obtain information.
Communication 1.2: Student demonstrates understanding of simple, clearly spoken, and written language such as simple stories, high-frequency commands, and brief instructions when dealing with familiar topics.
Communication 1.3: Student presents information using familiar words, phrases, and sentences to listeners and readers.

CORE INSTRUCTION

Warm-Up
• (5 min.) Present Language Notes, p. 21.

Vocabulario en acción 2
• (5 min.) Have students do Bell Work 1.7, p. 24.
• (10 min.) Show **ExpresaVisión,** Ch. 1.
• (15 min.) Have students do Activities 26–27, p. 20.
• (20 min.) Present **Vocabulario** and **¡Exprésate!,** p. 21, using Teaching **Vocabulario,** #s 3–4, p. 20. Then present the seasons, p. 21.
• (10 min.) Have students do Activities 28–29, p. 21.
• (20 min.) Present **El alfabeto** and **¡Exprésate!,** pp. 22–23, using Teaching **¡Exprésate!,** p. 22.

Wrap-Up
• (5 min.) Present Language Note, p. 22.

OPTIONAL RESOURCES
• (5 min.) See Slower Pace Learners, p. 21. ◆
• (10 min.) See **Comunicación** (TE), p. 21.
• (15 min.) See Teacher to Teacher, p. 21.
• For students with visual impairments, see Special Learning Needs, p. 23. ●

▲ = Advanced Learners   ◆ = Slower Pace Learners   ● = Special Learning Needs   ■ = Heritage Speakers

(166)

BLOCK 8 90-MINUTE LESSON PLAN

Practice Options

- *Lab Book*, pp. 11–12, 34 ▲ ● ■
- ***Cuaderno de vocabulario y gramática***, pp. 7–9 ▲ ◆ ●
- *Teaching Transparencies:* Bell Work 1.7; Vocabulary 1.3, 1.4; ***Cuaderno de vocabulario y gramática*** Answers, pp. 7–9 ▲ ● ■
- *Video Guide*, pp. 4–5, 8 ▲ ● ■
- *Interactive Tutor* (Disc 1) or *DVD Tutor* (Disc 1) ▲ ● ■
- Online practice, Chapter 1 (go.hrw.com, Keyword: EXP1A CH1) ▲ ● ■

▲ = Advanced Learners   ◆ = Slower Pace Learners   ● = Special Learning Needs   ■ = Heritage Speakers

CAPÍTULO
1

¡Empecemos!

BLOCK 9 90-MINUTE LESSON PLAN

NATIONAL STANDARDS

Vocabulario en acción 2

Communication 1.1: Student engages in oral and written exchanges of learned material to socialize and to provide and obtain information.

Communication 1.2: Student demonstrates understanding of simple, clearly spoken, and written language such as simple stories, high-frequency commands, and brief instructions when dealing with familiar topics.

Communication 1.3: Student presents information using familiar words, phrases, and sentences to listeners and readers.

Gramática en acción 2

Communication 1.2: Student demonstrates understanding of simple, clearly spoken, and written language such as simple stories, high-frequency commands, and brief instructions when dealing with familiar topics.

CORE INSTRUCTION

Warm-Up
- (5 min.) Present Common Error Alert, p. 23. Write these words on the board for students to practice spelling aloud: **acción, amarillo, perro, filosofía.**

Vocabulario en acción 2
- (10 min.) Review **El alfabeto** and **¡Exprésate!,** pp. 22–23.
- (10 min.) Play Audio CD 1, Tr. 9, for Activity 30, p. 23. ●
- (15 min.) Have students do Activities 31–32, p. 23.

Gramática en acción 2
- (20 min.) Present **Gramática:** *The verb* **ser,** p. 24, using Teaching **Gramática,** p. 24.
- (10 min.) Show **GramaVisión** *(the verb* **ser***), Video Program* (Videocassette 1) or *DVD Tutor* (Disc 1).
- (15 min.) Have students do Activities 33–34, pp. 24–25.

Wrap-Up
- (5 min.) Teach students the song from Teacher to Teacher, p. 25. ●

OPTIONAL RESOURCES
- (5 min.) See Slower Pace Learners, p. 23. ◆
- (5 min.) See **Comunicación** (TE), p. 23.

▲ = Advanced Learners   ◆ = Slower Pace Learners   ● = Special Learning Needs   ■ = Heritage Speakers

Holt Spanish 1A

Lesson Planner

BLOCK 9 90-MINUTE LESSON PLAN

Practice Options

- *Lab Book*, pp. 11–12, 34 ▲ ● ■
- ***Cuaderno de vocabulario y gramática***, pp. 7–9, 11–12 ▲ ◆ ●
- ***Cuaderno de actividades***, pp. 5–7 ▲ ● ■
- *Activities for Communication*, pp. 3–4 ▲ ■
- *Teaching Transparencies:* Vocabulary 1.3, 1.4; ***Cuaderno de vocabulario y gramática*** Answers, pp. 7–9, 11–12 ▲ ● ■
- *Video Guide*, pp. 4–5, 8 ▲ ● ■
- *TPR Storytelling Book*, pp. 2–3 ▲ ●
- *Grammar Tutor for Students of Spanish*, pp. 3–6, 168–169 ◆ ●
- *Interactive Tutor* (Disc 1) or *DVD Tutor* (Disc 1) ▲ ● ■
- Online practice, Chapter 1 (go.hrw.com, Keyword: EXP1A CH1) ▲ ● ■

▲ = Advanced Learners   ◆ = Slower Pace Learners   ● = Special Learning Needs   ■ = Heritage Speakers

¡Empecemos!

BLOCK 10 90-MINUTE LESSON PLAN

NATIONAL STANDARDS

Vocabulario en acción 2

Communication 1.1: Student engages in oral and written exchanges of learned material to socialize and to provide and obtain information.

Communication 1.2: Student demonstrates understanding of simple, clearly spoken, and written language such as simple stories, high-frequency commands, and brief instructions when dealing with familiar topics.

Communication 1.3: Student presents information using familiar words, phrases, and sentences to listeners and readers.

Gramática en acción 2

Communication 1.1: Student engages in oral and written exchanges of learned material to socialize and to provide and obtain information.

Communication 1.2: Student demonstrates understanding of simple, clearly spoken, and written language such as simple stories, high-frequency commands, and brief instructions when dealing with familiar topics.

Communication 1.3: Student presents information using familiar words, phrases, and sentences to listeners and readers.

Comparisons 4.1: Student demonstrates an understanding of the nature of language through comparisons of the student's own language and the language studied.

CORE INSTRUCTION

Warm-Up
- (5 min.) Practice the song from Teacher to Teacher, p. 25. ●

Vocabulario en acción 2
- (10 min.) Review **Vocabulario 2,** pp. 18–23.

Assessment
- (20 min.) Give **Prueba: Vocabulario 2.**

Gramática en acción 2
- (15 min.) Have students do Activities 35–36, pp. 24–25.
- (15 min.) Present **Gramática:** *Punctuation marks and written accents,* p. 26, using Teaching **Gramática,** #s 1–3, p. 26.
- (15 min.) Have students do Activities 37–38, pp. 26–27.

Wrap-Up
- (5 min.) Have students work with a partner to check Activity 37, p. 26.

OPTIONAL RESOURCES
- (10 min.) See **GramaVisión** (*punctuation marks and written accents*), *Video Program* (Videocassette 1) or *DVD Tutor* (Disc 1).
- (5 min.) See Slower Pace Learners, p. 25. ◆
- See Special Learning Needs, p. 25. ●
- See Special Learning Needs, p. 27. ●
- You can find alternative quizzes in the Assessment Options on the next page.

▲ = Advanced Learners   ◆ = Slower Pace Learners   ● = Special Learning Needs   ■ = Heritage Speakers

BLOCK 10 90-MINUTE LESSON PLAN

Practice Options

- *Lab Book*, pp. 11–12, 34 ▲ ● ■
- ***Cuaderno de vocabulario y gramática***, pp. 10–12 ▲ ◆ ●
- ***Cuaderno de actividades***, pp. 5–7 ▲ ● ■
- *Activities for Communication*, pp. 3–4 ▲ ■
- ***Cuaderno para hispanohablantes***, Chapter 1 ■
- *Teaching Transparencies:* ***Cuaderno de vocabulario y gramática***
  Answers, pp. 10–12 ▲ ● ■
- *Video Guide*, pp. 4–5 ▲ ● ■
- *Grammar Tutor for Students of Spanish*, pp. 3–6, 168–169 ◆ ●
- *Interactive Tutor* (Disc 1) or *DVD Tutor* (Disc 1) ▲ ● ■
- Online practice, Chapter 1 (go.hrw.com, Keyword: EXP1A CH1) ▲ ● ■

Assessment Options

- *Assessment Program:* **Prueba: Vocabulario 2**, pp. 7–8 ▲ ● ■
- Test Generator ▲ ● ■

▲ = Advanced Learners   ◆ = Slower Pace Learners   ● = Special Learning Needs   ■ = Heritage Speakers

Holt Spanish 1A   **Lesson Planner**

¡Empecemos!

CAPÍTULO

BLOCK 11 90-MINUTE LESSON PLAN

NATIONAL STANDARDS

Gramática en acción 2

Communication 1.1: Student engages in oral and written exchanges of learned material to socialize and to provide and obtain information.

Communication 1.2: Student demonstrates understanding of simple, clearly spoken, and written language such as simple stories, high-frequency commands, and brief instructions when dealing with familiar topics.

Communication 1.3: Student presents information using familiar words, phrases, and sentences to listeners and readers.

Conexiones culturales

Communication 1.2: Student demonstrates understanding of simple, clearly spoken, and written language such as simple stories, high-frequency commands, and brief instructions when dealing with familiar topics.

Cultures 2.1: Student demonstrates an understanding of the practices (what people do) and how they are related to the perspectives (how people perceive things) of the cultures studied.

Cultures 2.2: Student demonstrates an understanding of the products (what people create) and how they are related to the perspectives (how people perceive things) of the cultures studied.

Connections 3.1: Student uses the language to obtain, reinforce, or expand knowledge of other subject areas.

Comparisons 4.2: Student demonstrates an understanding of the concept of culture through comparisons of the student's own culture and the cultures studied.

CORE INSTRUCTION

Warm-Up
- (5 min.) Have students do Bell Work 1.8, p. 26.

Gramática en acción 2
- (15 min.) Review **Gramática 2,** pp. 24–27.
- (15 min.) Have students do Activity 39, p. 27.

Assessment
- (20 min.) Give **Prueba: Gramática 2.**

Conexiones culturales
- (30 min.) Present **Conexiones culturales,** pp. 28–28, using Teaching **Conexiones culturales,** #s 1–5, p. 28.

Wrap-Up
- (5 min.) Present Practices and Perspectives, p. 28. Have students write out today's date, their birth date, and the date for Independence Day the way they would be written in Spanish-speaking countries.

OPTIONAL RESOURCES
- (15 min.) See Advanced Learners, p. 27. ▲
- (25 min.) See Advanced Learners, p. 29. ▲
- (25 min.) For students with learning disabilities/dyslexia, see Special Learning Needs, p. 29. ●
- You can find alternative quizzes in the Assessment Options on the next page.

▲ = Advanced Learners   ◆ = Slower Pace Learners   ● = Special Learning Needs   ■ = Heritage Speakers

BLOCK 11 90-MINUTE LESSON PLAN

Practice Options
- *Lab Book*, pp. 11–12 ▲ ● ■
- ***Cuaderno de vocabulario y gramática***, pp. 10–12 ▲ ◆ ●
- ***Cuaderno de actividades***, pp. 5–7 ▲ ● ■
- *Activities for Communication*, pp. 3–4 ▲ ■
- *Teaching Transparencies:* Bell Work 1.8; ***Cuaderno de vocabulario y gramática*** Answers, pp. 10–12 ▲ ● ■
- *Video Guide*, pp. 4–5 ▲ ● ■
- *Grammar Tutor for Students of Spanish*, pp. 3–6, 168–169 ◆ ●
- *Interactive Tutor* (Disc 1) or *DVD Tutor* (Disc 1) ▲ ● ■
- Online practice, Chapter 1 (go.hrw.com, Keyword: EXP1A CH1) ▲ ● ■

Assessment Options
- *Assessment Program*: **Prueba: Gramática 2,** pp. 9–10 ▲ ● ■
- *Assessment Program*: **Prueba: Aplicaión 2,** pp. 11–22 ▲ ● ■
- *Assessment Program*: Alternative Assessment, pp. 212, 219, 227 ▲ ● ■
- Test Generator ▲ ● ■

▲ = Advanced Learners   ◆ = Slower Pace Learners   ● = Special Learning Needs   ■ = Heritage Speakers

173

CAPÍTULO

1

¡Empecemos!

BLOCK 12 90-MINUTE LESSON PLAN

NATIONAL STANDARDS

Novela en video

Communication 1.2: Student demonstrates under-standing of simple, clearly spoken, and written language such as simple stories, high-frequency commands, and brief instructions when dealing with familiar topics.

Connections 3.2: Student uses resources (that may include technology) in the language and cultures being studied to gain access to information.

Leamos y escribamos

Communication 1.2: Student demonstrates under-standing of simple, clearly spoken, and written language such as simple stories, high-frequency commands, and brief instructions when dealing with familiar topics.

CORE INSTRUCTION

Warm-Up
• (5 min.) Have students read **Estrategia,** p. 30.

Novela en video
• (20 min.) Present **Novela en video,** p. 30–32, using Teaching **Novela en video,** p. 30.
• (10 min.) Show **VideoNovela,** Ch. 1.
• (15 min.) Have students do Activities 1–3, p. 33.

Leamos y escribamos
• (35 min.) Present the first part of **Leamos y escribamos,** p. 34, using Teaching **Leamos,** #s 1–3, p. 34. Have students read the selection on p. 34.

Wrap-Up
• (5 min.) See **Gestures,** p. 30.

OPTIONAL RESOURCES
• (10 min.) See Visual Learners, p. 30. ●
• (5 min.) See Comparing and Contrasting, p. 31.
• (10 min.) See **Comunicación** (TE), p. 32.
• (15 min.) See Advanced Learners, p. 33. ▲

▲ = Advanced Learners   ◆ = Slower Pace Learners   ● = Special Learning Needs   ■ = Heritage Speakers

BLOCK 12 90-MINUTE LESSON PLAN

Practice Options

- *Lab Book*, p. 35 ▲ ● ■
- ***Cuaderno de actividades***, p. 8 ▲ ● ■
- *Video Guide*, pp. 4–5, 9 ▲ ● ■
- Audio CD 1 Tr. 10 ●
- *Student Edition*, **Literatura y variedades**, pp. 228–229
- *Reading Strategies and Skills Handbook,* pp. xi–xii, 65, 14–17
- ***¡Lee conmigo!*** Level 1 Reader
- *Interactive Tutor* (Disc 1) or *DVD Tutor* (Disc 1) ▲ ● ■
- Online practice, Chapter 1 (go.hrw.com, Keyword: EXP1A CH1) ▲ ● ■

▲ = Advanced Learners ◆ = Slower Pace Learners ● = Special Learning Needs ■ = Heritage Speakers

¡Empecemos!

CAPÍTULO
1

BLOCK 13 90-MINUTE LESSON PLAN

NATIONAL STANDARDS

Leamos y escribamos

Communication 1.2: Student demonstrates understanding of simple, clearly spoken, and written language such as simple stories, high-frequency commands, and brief instructions when dealing with familiar topics.

Comparisons 4.1: Student demonstrates an understanding of the nature of language through comparisons of the student's own language and the language studied.

Repaso

Communication 1.2: Student demonstrates understanding of simple, clearly spoken, and written language such as simple stories, high-frequency commands, and brief instructions when dealing with familiar topics.

Communication 1.3: Student presents information using familiar words, phrases, and sentences to listeners and readers.

Cultures 2.1: Student demonstrates an understanding of the practices (what people do) and how they are related to the perspectives (how people perceive things) of the cultures studied.

CORE INSTRUCTION

Warm-Up

- (10 min.) Have students do the activity described in Advanced Learners, p. 35. ▲

Leamos y escribamos

- (20 min.) Present **Escribamos: Taller de escritor**, p. 35, using Teaching **Escribamos,** p. 34.

Review

- (25 min.) Have students do Activities 1–6, pp. 36–37.
- (10 min.) Play Audio CD 1, Tr. 12, for Activity 7, p. 37. ●
- (10 min.) Have students do Activity 8, p. 37.
- (10 min.) Play Audio CD 1, Tr. 13, 14, 15, for **Letra y sonido,** p. 38. ●

Wrap-Up

- (5 min.) Present Fold-N-Learn, p. 36. Suggest to students that they use the Fold-N-Learn activity as part of their preparation for the Chapter Test. ●

OPTIONAL RESOURCES

- (10 min.) See Special Learning Needs, p. 35. ●
- (20 min.) See Teacher to Teacher, p. 36.

▲ = Advanced Learners   ◆ = Slower Pace Learners   ● = Special Learning Needs   ■ = Heritage Speakers

(176)

BLOCK 13 90-MINUTE LESSON PLAN

Practice Options

- *Lab Book*, pp. 11–12, 36 ▲ ● ■
- *Activities for Communication*, pp. 43, 55–56 ▲ ■
- *Video Guide*, pp. 4–5, 10 ▲ ● ■
- *TPR Storytelling Book*, pp. 4–5 ▲ ●
- Reading Strategies and Skills Handbook, pp. 65, 14–17
- *Interactive Tutor* (Disc 1) or *DVD Tutor* (Disc 1) ▲ ● ■
- Online practice, Chapter 1 (go.hrw.com, Keyword: EXP1A CH1) ▲ ● ■

▲ = Advanced Learners ◆ = Slower Pace Learners ● = Special Learning Needs ■ = Heritage Speakers

CAPÍTULO
1

¡Empecemos!

NATIONAL STANDARDS

Integración

Communication 1.1: Student engages in oral and written exchanges of learned material to socialize and to provide and obtain information.

Communication 1.2: Student demonstrates understanding of simple, clearly spoken, and written language such as simple stories, high-frequency commands, and brief instructions when dealing with familiar topics.

Communication 1.3: Student presents information using familiar words, phrases, and sentences to listeners and readers.

CORE INSTRUCTION

Assessment

• (50 min.) Give the Chapter 1 Test.

Integración

• (10 min.) Play Audio CD 1, Tr. 16, for Activity 1, p. 40. ●
• (30 min.) Have students do Activities 2–4, pp. 40–41.

OPTIONAL RESOURCES

• You may also choose from the other modes of assessment listed in the Assessment Options box on the next page.

▲ = Advanced Learners   ◆ = Slower Pace Learners   ● = Special Learning Needs   ■ = Heritage Speakers

BLOCK 14 90-MINUTE LESSON PLAN

Practice Options
- *Cuaderno de actividades*, pp. 9–10, 52–53 ▲ ● ■
- *Teaching Transparencies:* Fine Art, Ch. 1 ▲ ● ■
- *Lab Book*, pp. 11–12, 36 ▲ ● ■

Assessment Options
- *Assessment Program,* **Prueba: Lectura,** pp. 13, 19 ▲ ● ■
- *Assessment Program,* **Prueba: Escritura,** pp. 14, 19 ▲ ● ■
- Test Generator ▲ ● ■
- *Assessment Program,* **Examen: Capítulo 1,** pp. 105–115 ▲ ● ■
- *Assessment Program,* **Examen Oral: Capítulo 1,** p. 116 ▲ ● ■

▲ = Advanced Learners   ◆ = Slower Pace Learners   ● = Special Learning Needs   ■ = Heritage Speakers

Holt Spanish 1A   Lesson Planner

¡A conocernos!

BLOCK 1 90-MINUTE LESSON PLAN

NATIONAL STANDARDS

Chapter Opener
Communication 1.2: Student demonstrates understanding of simple, clearly spoken, and written language such as simple stories, high-frequency commands, and brief instructions when dealing with familiar topics.

Vocabulario 1
Communication 1.1: Student engages in oral and written exchanges of learned material to socialize and to provide and obtain information.

Communication 1.2: Student demonstrates understanding of simple, clearly spoken, and written language such as simple stories, high-frequency commands, and brief instructions when dealing with familiar topics.

Communication 1.3: Student presents information using familiar words, phrases, and sentences to listeners and readers.

Comparisons 4.1: Student demonstrates an understanding of the nature of language through comparisons of the student's own language and the language studied.

Comparisons 4.2: Student demonstrates an understanding of the concept of culture through comparisons of the student's own culture and the cultures studied.

Before starting **Capítulo 2,** you may wish to teach **Geocultura: Puerto Rico,** pp. 42–45. For teaching suggestions, see pp. xv–xvi of this *Lesson Planner.*

CORE INSTRUCTION

Warm-Up
- (5 min.) See Learning and Pacing Tips, p. 47.

Chapter Opener
- (5 min.) Present information from Using the Photo and **Más vocabulario,** p. 46.
- (5 min.) Present **Objetivos,** p. 46.

Vocabulario en acción 1
- (15 min.) Present **Vocabulario,** pp. 48–49, using Teaching **Vocabulario,** p. 48.
- (15 min.) Present **¡Exprésate!,** p. 49.
- (10 min.) Show **ExpresaVisión,** Ch 2.
- (5 min.) Present **Nota cultural,** p. 50.
- (10 min.) Play Audio CD 2, Tr. 1, for Activity 1, p. 50. ●
- (15 min.) Have students to Activities 2–3, p. 50.

Wrap-Up
- (5 min.) Have students do Bell Work 2.1, p. 48.

OPTIONAL RESOURCES
- (15 min.) See Teacher to Teacher, p. 49.
- (5 min.) See Slower Pace Learners, p. 49. ◆
- (5 min.) See Special Learning Needs, p. 49. ●
- (15 min.) See TPR, p. 49. ▲ ●
- (10 min.) See Fold-N-Learn, p. 50. ●
- (5 min.) See Common Error Alert, p. 50.

▲ = Advanced Learners ◆ = Slower Pace Learners ● = Special Learning Needs ■ = Heritage Speakers

BLOCK 1 90-MINUTE LESSON PLAN

Practice Options
- *Lab Book*, pp. 2, 13–14, 37, 38 ▲ ● ■
- *Cuaderno de vocabulario y gramática*, pp. 13–15 ▲ ◆ ●
- *Teaching Transparencies*: Map 4; Bell Work, 2.1; **Vocabulario** 2.1, 2.2; *Vocabulario y gramática* Answers, pp. 13–15 ▲ ● ■
- *Video Guide*, pp. 11, 12, 14–15, 16 ▲ ● ■
- *Interactive Tutor* (Disc 1) or *DVD Tutor* (Disc 1) ▲ ● ■
- Online practice, Chapter 2 (go.hrw.com, Keyword: EXP1A CH2) ▲ ● ■

▲ = Advanced Learners   ◆ = Slower Pace Learners   ● = Special Learning Needs   ■ = Heritage Speakers

CAPÍTULO
2

¡A conocernos!

BLOCK 2 90-MINUTE LESSON PLAN

NATIONAL STANDARDS

Vocabulario en acción 1

Communication 1.1: Student engages in oral and written exchanges of learned material to socialize and to provide and obtain information.

Communication 1.2: Student demonstrates understanding of simple, clearly spoken, and written language such as simple stories, high-frequency commands, and brief instructions when dealing with familiar topics.

Communication 1.3: Student presents information using familiar words, phrases, and sentences to listeners and readers.

Connections 3.2: Student uses resources (that may include technology) in the language and cultures being studied to gain access to information.

Connections 3.1: Student uses the language to obtain, reinforce, or expand knowledge of other subject areas.

CORE INSTRUCTION

Warm-Up

- (5 min.) Have students do Bell Work 2.2, p. 54.

Vocabulario en acción 1

- (10 min.) Have students do Activities 4–5, p. 51.
- (15 min.) Present **¡Exprésate!,** p. 52. See Teaching **¡Exprésate!,** p. 52.
- (10 min.) Present **Nota cultural,** p. 52.
- (30 min.) Have students do Activities 6–9, pp. 52–53.
- (10 min.) Review **Vocabulario 1** and **¡Exprésate!,** pp. 48–53.

Wrap-Up

- (10 min.) Have students do Activity 9, p. 53. Then remind the class to study for **Prueba: Vocabulario 1.**

OPTIONAL RESOURCES

- (5 min.) See Common Error Alert, p. 51.
- (5 min.) See **Más práctica,** p. 51.
- (20 min.) See Slower Pace Learners, p. 51. ◆
- (25 min.) See Multiple Intelligences, p. 51. ●
- (5 min.) See Common Error Alert, p. 52.
- (5 min.) See Practices and Perspectives, p. 53.
- (10 min.) See Advanced Learners, p. 53. ▲
- (5 min.) See Multiple Intelligences, p. 53. ●

▲ = Advanced Learners ◆ = Slower Pace Learners ● = Special Learning Needs ■ = Heritage Speakers

BLOCK 2 90-MINUTE LESSON PLAN

Practice Options
- *Lab Book*, pp. 13–14, 38 ▲ ● ■
- ***Cuaderno de vocabulario y gramática***, pp. 13–15 ▲ ◆ ●
- *Teaching Transparencies*: Bell Work, 2.2; **Vocabulario** 2.1, 2.2; ***Vocabulario y gramática*** Answers, pp. 13–15 ▲ ● ■
- *Video Guide*, pp. 14–15, 16 ▲ ● ■
- *Interactive Tutor* (Disc 1) or *DVD Tutor* (Disc 1) ▲ ● ■
- Online practice, Chapter 2 (go.hrw.com, Keyword: EXP1A CH2) ▲ ● ■

▲ = Advanced Learners   ◆ = Slower Pace Learners   ● = Special Learning Needs   ■ = Heritage Speakers

¡A conocernos!

BLOCK 3 90-MINUTE LESSON PLAN

NATIONAL STANDARDS

Vocabulario en acción 1

Communication 1.1: Student engages in oral and written exchanges of learned material to socialize and to provide and obtain information.

Communication 1.2: Student demonstrates understanding of simple, clearly spoken, and written language such as simple stories, high-frequency commands, and brief instructions when dealing with familiar topics.

Communication 1.3: Student presents information using familiar words, phrases, and sentences to listeners and readers.

Gramática en acción 1

Communication 1.1: Student engages in oral and written exchanges of learned material to socialize and to provide and obtain information.

Communication 1.2: Student demonstrates understanding of simple, clearly spoken, and written language such as simple stories, high-frequency commands, and brief instructions when dealing with familiar topics.

Communication 1.3: Student presents information using familiar words, phrases, and sentences to listeners and readers.

CORE INSTRUCTION

Warm-Up

- (10 min.) Have students do the activity described in **Comunicación** (TE), p. 53.

Vocabulario en acción 1

- (15 min.) Review **Vocabulario 1,** pp. 48–53.

Assessment

- (20 min.) Give **Prueba: Vocabulario 1.**

Gramática en acción 1

- (15 min.) Present **Gramática: Ser** *with adjectives,* p. 54, using Teaching **Gramática,** p. 54.
- (10 min.) Show **GramaVisión** (**ser** *with adjectives*), *Video Program* (Videocassette 1) or *DVD Tutor* (Disc 1).
- (15 min.) Have students do Activities 10–11, pp. 54–55.

Wrap-Up

- (5 min.) Have students share their responses to Activity 10, p. 54.

OPTIONAL RESOURCES

- (5 min.) See **Más práctica,** p. 54.
- (15 min.) See Special Learning Needs, p. 55. ●
- You can find alternative quizzes in the Assessment Options on the next page.

▲ = Advanced Learners   ◆ = Slower Pace Learners   ● = Special Learning Needs   ■ = Heritage Speakers

Holt Spanish 1A

Lesson Planner

BLOCK 3 90-MINUTE LESSON PLAN

Practice Options
- *Lab Book*, pp. 13–14, 38 ▲ ● ■
- ***Cuaderno de vocabulario y gramática***, pp. 16–18 ▲ ◆ ●
- ***Cuaderno de actividades***, pp. 11–13 ▲ ● ■
- *Activities for Communication*, pp. 5–6, 57–58 ▲ ■
- *Teaching Transparencies*: **Vocabulario y gramática** Answers, pp. 16–18 ▲ ● ■
- *Video Guide*, pp. 14–15 ▲ ● ■
- *Grammar Tutor for Students of Spanish*, pp. 7–10, 169 ◆ ●
- *Interactive Tutor* (Disc 1) or *DVD Tutor* (Disc 1) ▲ ● ■
- Online practice, Chapter 2 (go.hrw.com, Keyword: EXP1A CH2) ▲ ● ■

Assessment Options
- *Assessment Program*: **Prueba: Vocabulario 1**, pp. 21–22 ▲ ● ■
- Test Generator ▲ ● ■

▲ = Advanced Learners ◆ = Slower Pace Learners ● = Special Learning Needs ■ = Heritage Speakers

Holt Spanish 1A　　　　　　　　　　　　　　　　　　　　　　　　　　　**Lesson Planner**

　　　　(**185**)

¡A conocernos!

BLOCK 4 90-MINUTE LESSON PLAN

NATIONAL STANDARDS

Gramática en acción 1

Communication 1.1: Student engages in oral and written exchanges of learned material to socialize and to provide and obtain information.

Communication 1.2: Student demonstrates understanding of simple, clearly spoken, and written language such as simple stories, high-frequency commands, and brief instructions when dealing with familiar topics.

Communication 1.3: Student presents information using familiar words, phrases, and sentences to listeners and readers.

CORE INSTRUCTION

Warm-Up
- (5 min.) Have students do Bell Work 2.3, p. 56.

Gramática en acción 1
- (15 min.) Have students do Activities 12–13, pp. 55.
- (15 min.) Present **Gramática:** *Gender and adjective agreement,* p. 56, using Teaching **Gramática,** p. 56.
- (10 min.) Show **GramaVisión** *(gender and adjective agreement), Video Program* (Videocassette 1) or *DVD Tutor* (Disc 1).
- (30 min.) Have students to Activities 14–17, pp. 56–57.

Wrap-Up
- (15 min.) Have students do Activity 17, p. 57.
- Ask them to prepare pairs of index cards as indicated in **Comunicación** (TE), p. 57.

OPTIONAL RESOURCES
- (10 min.) See Advanced Learners, p. 55. ▲
- (10 min.) See Slower Pace Learners, p. 57. ◆
- (10 min.) See Special Learning Needs, p. 57. ●

▲ = Advanced Learners   ◆ = Slower Pace Learners   ● = Special Learning Needs   ■ = Heritage Speakers

BLOCK 4 90-MINUTE LESSON PLAN

Practice Options
- *Lab Book*, pp. 13–14 ▲ ● ■
- **Cuaderno de vocabulario y gramática**, pp. 16–18 ▲ ◆ ●
- **Cuaderno de actividades**, pp. 11–13 ▲ ● ■
- *Activities for Communication*, pp. 5–6, 57–58 ▲ ■
- *Teaching Transparencies*: Bell Work 2.3; **Vocabulario y gramática**
  Answers, pp. 16–18 ▲ ● ■
- *Video Guide*, pp. 14–15 ▲ ● ■
- *Grammar Tutor for Students of Spanish*, pp. 7–10, 169 ◆ ●
- *Interactive Tutor* (Disc 1) or *DVD Tutor* (Disc 1) ▲ ● ■
- Online practice, Chapter 2 (go.hrw.com, Keyword: EXP1A CH2) ▲ ● ■

▲ = Advanced Learners   ◆ = Slower Pace Learners   ● = Special Learning Needs   ■ = Heritage Speakers

¡A conocernos!

BLOCK 5 90-MINUTE LESSON PLAN

NATIONAL STANDARDS

Gramática en acción 1

Communication 1.1: Student engages in oral and written exchanges of learned material to socialize and to provide and obtain information.

Communication 1.2: Student demonstrates understanding of simple, clearly spoken, and written language such as simple stories, high-frequency commands, and brief instructions when dealing with familiar topics.

Communication 1.3: Student presents information using familiar words, phrases, and sentences to listeners and readers.

Cultures 2.1: Student demonstrates an understanding of the practices (what people do) and how they are related to the perspectives (how people perceive things) of the cultures studied.

Comparisons 4.2: Student demonstrates an understanding of the concept of culture through comparisons of the student's own culture and the cultures studied.

CORE INSTRUCTION

Warm-Up

- (5 min.) Name some famous people (or show pictures) and ask volunteers to describe them.

Gramática en acción 1

- (15 min.) Present **Gramática:** *Question formation,* p. 58, using Teaching **Gramática,** p. 58.
- (10 min.) Show **GramaVisión** *(question formation), Video Program* (Videocassette 1) or *DVD Tutor* (Disc 1).
- (10 min.) Play Audio CD 2, Tr. 2, for Activity 18, p. 58. ●
- (20 min.) Have students do Activities 19–22, pp. 58–59.
- (10 min.) Present **Nota cultural,** p. 59.
- (10 min.) Review **Gramática 1,** pp. 54–59.

Wrap-Up

- (10 min.) Have students write an answer to the e-mail in Activity 21, p. 59. Then remind them to study for **Prueba: Gramática 1.**

OPTIONAL RESOURCES

- (10 min.) See Advanced Learners, p. 59. ▲
- (10 min.) See Special Learning Needs, p. 59. ●
- (10 min.) See Common Error Alert, p. 59.
- (10 min.) See **Comunicación** (TE), p. 59.

▲ = Advanced Learners   ◆ = Slower Pace Learners   ● = Special Learning Needs   ■ = Heritage Speakers

BLOCK 5 90-MINUTE LESSON PLAN

Practice Options
- *Lab Book*, pp. 13–14 ▲ ● ■
- ***Cuaderno de vocabulario y gramática***, pp. 16–18 ▲ ◆ ●
- ***Cuaderno de actividades***, pp. 11–13 ▲ ● ■
- *Activities for Communication*, pp. 5–6, 57–58 ▲ ■
- ***Cuaderno para hispanohablantes***, Chapter 2 ■
- *Teaching Transparencies*: ***Vocabulario y gramática*** Answers, pp. 16–18 ▲ ● ■
- *Video Guide*, pp. 14–15 ▲ ● ■
- *Grammar Tutor for Students of Spanish*, pp. 7–10, 169 ◆ ●
- *Interactive Tutor* (Disc 1) or *DVD Tutor* (Disc 1) ▲ ● ■
- Online practice, Chapter 2 (go.hrw.com, Keyword: EXP1A CH2) ▲ ● ■

▲ = Advanced Learners   ◆ = Slower Pace Learners   ● = Special Learning Needs   ■ = Heritage Speakers

(189)

¡A conocernos!

NATIONAL STANDARDS

Gramática en acción 1

Communication 1.1: Student engages in oral and written exchanges of learned material to socialize and to provide and obtain information.

Communication 1.2: Student demonstrates understanding of simple, clearly spoken, and written language such as simple stories, high-frequency commands, and brief instructions when dealing with familiar topics.

Communication 1.3: Student presents information using familiar words, phrases, and sentences to listeners and readers.

Cultures 2.1: Student demonstrates an understanding of the practices (what people do) and how they are related to the perspectives (how people perceive things) of the cultures studied.

Comparisons 4.2: Student demonstrates an understanding of the concept of culture through comparisons of the student's own culture and the cultures studied.

Cultura

Communication 1.2: Student demonstrates understanding of simple, clearly spoken, and written language such as simple stories, high-frequency commands, and brief instructions when dealing with familiar topics.

Communication 1.3: Student presents information using familiar words, phrases, and sentences to listeners and readers.

Cultures 2.1: Student demonstrates an understanding of the practices (what people do) and how they are related to the perspectives (how people perceive things) of the cultures studied.

Comparisons 4.2: Student demonstrates an understanding of the concept of culture through comparisons of the student's own culture and the cultures studied.

Vocabulario en acción 2

Communication 1.2: Student demonstrates understanding of simple, clearly spoken, and written language such as simple stories, high-frequency commands, and brief instructions when dealing with familiar topics.

CORE INSTRUCTION

Warm-Up

- (10 min.) Play Twenty Questions with your students. Give statements about famous people using forms of **ser** with adjectives and have students guess at the identities of the people.

Gramática en acción 1

- (10 min.) Review **Gramática 1,** pp. 54–59.

Assessment

- (20 min.) Give **Prueba: Gramática 1.**

Cultura

- (15 min.) Present **Cultura,** pp. 60–61, using Teaching **Cultura,** #s 1–4, p. 60.
- (5 min.) Show **Video Cultura,** Ch. 2.
- (5 min.) Discuss **Para pensar y hablar,** p. 61.

Vocabulario en acción 2

- (20 min.) Present **Vocabulario** and **¡Exprésate!,** pp. 62–63, using Teaching **Vocabulario,** p. 62.

Wrap-Up

- (5 min.) Have students do Bell Work 2.5, p. 62.

OPTIONAL RESOURCES

- (10 min.) See Map Activities, p. 60.
- (5 min.) See Language to Language, p. 61.
- (15 min.) See Advanced Learners, p. 61. ▲
- (15 min.) See Multiple Intelligences, p. 61. ●
- (5 min.) See Language to Language, p. 63.
- (10 min.) See Special Learning Needs, p. 63. ●
- You can find alternative quizzes in the Assessment Options on p. 191.

▲ = Advanced Learners ◆ = Slower Pace Learners ● = Special Learning Needs ■ = Heritage Speakers

BLOCK 6 90-MINUTE LESSON PLAN

Practice Options
- *Lab Book*, pp. 13–14, 39 ▲ ● ■
- *Cuaderno de vocabulario y gramática*, pp. 16–18 ▲ ◆ ●
- *Cuaderno de actividades*, pp. 11–13, 14 ▲ ● ■
- *Activities for Communication*, pp. 5–6, 57–58 ▲ ■
- *Cuaderno para hispanohablantes*, pp. 19–20 ■
- *Teaching Transparencies*: Bell Work 2.5; *Vocabulario y gramática* Answers, pp. 16–18 ▲ ● ■
- *Video Guide*, pp. 14–15, 17 ▲ ● ■
- *Grammar Tutor for Students of Spanish*, pp. 7–10, 169 ◆ ●
- *Interactive Tutor* (Disc 1) or *DVD Tutor* (Disc 1) ▲ ● ■
- Online practice, Chapter 2 (go.hrw.com, Keyword: EXP1A CH2) ▲ ● ■

Assessment Options
- *Assessment Program*: **Prueba: Gramática 1,** pp. 23–24 ▲ ● ■
- *Assessment Program*: **Prueba: Aplicación 1,** pp. 25–26 ▲ ● ■
- Test Generator ▲ ● ■

▲ = Advanced Learners   ◆ = Slower Pace Learners   ● = Special Learning Needs   ■ = Heritage Speakers

¡A conocernos!

BLOCK 7 90-MINUTE LESSON PLAN

NATIONAL STANDARDS

Vocabulario en acción 2

Communication 1.1: Student engages in oral and written exchanges of learned material to socialize and to provide and obtain information.

Communication 1.2: Student demonstrates understanding of simple, clearly spoken, and written language such as simple stories, high-frequency commands, and brief instructions when dealing with familiar topics.

Communication 1.3: Student presents information using familiar words, phrases, and sentences to listeners and readers.

Cultures 2.1: Student demonstrates an understanding of the practices (what people do) and how they are related to the perspectives (how people perceive things) of the cultures studied.

Comparisons 4.2: Student demonstrates an understanding of the concept of culture through comparisons of the student's own culture and the cultures studied.

CORE INSTRUCTION

Warm-Up
- (5 min.) Have students do Bell Work 2.6, p. 68.

Vocabulario en acción 2
- (10 min.) Show **ExpresaVisión,** Ch. 2.
- (10 min.) Review **Vocabulario 2,** pp. 62–63.
- (5 min.) Present **Nota cultural,** p. 64.
- (5 min.) Have students do Activity 23, p. 64.
- (10 min.) Play Audio CD 2, Tr. 6, for Activity 24, p. 64. ●
- (20 min.) Have students do Activities 25–27, pp. 64–65.
- (20 min.) Present **¡Exprésate!,** p. 66, using Teaching **¡Exprésate!,** p. 66.

Wrap-Up
- (5 min.) Ask the questions in Activity 27, p. 65, to several students. Then remind the class to study for **Prueba: Vocabulario 2.**

OPTIONAL RESOURCES
- (10 min.) See TPR, p. 63.
- (5 min.) See **También se puede decir... ,** p. 63.
- (15 min.) See Slower Pace Learners, p. 63. ◆
- (20 min.) See Game, p. 64. ●
- (10 min.) See Special Learning Needs, p. 65. ●
- (5 min.) See Products and Perspectives, p. 65.
- (15 min.) See Group Activity suggestion, p. 65.
- (20 min.) See Advanced Learners, p. 65. ▲
- (15 min.) See Multicultural Link, p. 66.

▲ = Advanced Learners   ◆ = Slower Pace Learners   ● = Special Learning Needs   ■ = Heritage Speakers

BLOCK 7 90-MINUTE LESSON PLAN

Practice Options

- *Lab Book*, pp. 15–16, 40 ▲ ● ■
- ***Cuaderno de vocabulario y gramática***, pp. 19–21 ▲ ◆ ●
- *Teaching Transparencies*: Bell Work 2.6; ***Vocabulario*** 2.3, 2.4; ***Vocabulario y gramática*** Answers, pp. 19–21 ▲ ● ■
- *Video Guide*, pp. 14–15, 18 ▲ ● ■
- *Interactive Tutor* (Disc 1) or *DVD Tutor* (Disc 1) ▲ ● ■
- Online practice, Chapter 2 (go.hrw.com, Keyword: EXP1A CH2) ▲ ● ■

▲ = Advanced Learners   ◆ = Slower Pace Learners   ● = Special Learning Needs   ■ = Heritage Speakers

(193)

CAPÍTULO
2

¡A conocernos!

BLOCK 8 90-MINUTE LESSON PLAN

NATIONAL STANDARDS

Vocabulario en acción 2

Communication 1.1: Student engages in oral and written exchanges of learned material to socialize and to provide and obtain information.

Communication 1.2: Student demonstrates understanding of simple, clearly spoken, and written language such as simple stories, high-frequency commands, and brief instructions when dealing with familiar topics.

Communication 1.3: Student presents information using familiar words, phrases, and sentences to listeners and readers.

Cultures 2.1: Student demonstrates an understanding of the practices (what people do) and how they are related to the perspectives (how people perceive things) of the cultures studied.

Comparisons 4.2: Student demonstrates an understanding of the concept of culture through comparisons of the student's own culture and the cultures studied.

Gramática en acción 2

Communication 1.2: Student demonstrates understanding of simple, clearly spoken, and written language such as simple stories, high-frequency commands, and brief instructions when dealing with familiar topics.

Comparisons 4.1: Student demonstrates an understanding of the nature of language through comparisons of the student's own language and the language studied.

CORE INSTRUCTION

Warm-Up

- (5 min.) Review **¡Exprésate!,** p. 66, by asking students questions such as **¿Cómo es la comida china?**

Vocabulario en acción 2

- (25 min.) Have students do Activities 28–31, pp. 66–67.
- (15 min.) Review **Vocabulario 2,** pp. 62–67.

Assessment

- (20 min.) Give **Prueba: Vocabulario 2.**

Gramática en acción 2

- (20 min.) Present **Gramática:** *Nouns and definite articles,* p. 68. See Teaching **Gramática,** p. 68.

Wrap-Up

- (5 min.) See Thinking Critically, p. 69.

OPTIONAL RESOURCES

- (15 min.) See Advanced Learners, p. 67. ▲
- (15 min.) See Multiple Intelligences, p. 67. ●
- (15 min.) See Advanced Learners, p. 69. ▲
- You can find alternative quizzes in the Assessment Options on the next page.

▲ = Advanced Learners ◆ = Slower Pace Learners ● = Special Learning Needs ■ = Heritage Speakers

BLOCK 8 90-MINUTE LESSON PLAN

Practice Options
- *Lab Book*, pp. 14–16, 40 ▲ ● ■
- ***Cuaderno de vocabulario y gramática***, pp. 22–24 ▲ ◆ ●
- *Activities for Communication*, pp. 5–6, 57–58 ▲ ■
- *Teaching Transparencies*: **Vocabulario y gramática** Answers, pp. 22–24 ▲ ● ■
- *Video Guide*, pp. 14–15, 18 ▲ ● ■
- *Grammar Tutor for Students of Spanish*, pp. 11–14, 169 ◆ ●
- *Interactive Tutor* (Disc 1) or *DVD Tutor* (Disc 1) ▲ ● ■
- Online practice, Chapter 2 (go.hrw.com, Keyword: EXP1A CH2) ▲ ● ■

Assessment Options
- *Assessment Program*: **Prueba: Vocabulario 2**, pp. 27–28 ▲ ● ■
- Test Generator ▲ ● ■

▲ = Advanced Learners   ◆ = Slower Pace Learners   ● = Special Learning Needs   ■ = Heritage Speakers

Holt Spanish 1A   Lesson Planner

CAPÍTULO
2

¡A conocernos!

BLOCK 9 90-MINUTE LESSON PLAN

NATIONAL STANDARDS

Gramática en acción 2

Communication 1.1: Student engages in oral and written exchanges of learned material to socialize and to provide and obtain information.

Communication 1.2: Student demonstrates understanding of simple, clearly spoken, and written language such as simple stories, high-frequency commands, and brief instructions when dealing with familiar topics.

Communication 1.3: Student presents information using familiar words, phrases, and sentences to listeners and readers.

Cultures 2.1: Student demonstrates an understanding of the practices (what people do) and how they are related to the perspectives (how people perceive things) of the cultures studied.

CORE INSTRUCTION

Warm-Up
- (5 min.) Have students do Bell Work 2.7, p. 70.

Gramática en acción 2
- (10 min.) Show **GramaVisión** *(nouns and definite articles), Video Program* (Videocassette 1) or *DVD Tutor* (Disc 1).
- (10 min.) Review nouns and definite articles.
- (25 min.) Have students do Activities 32–35, pp. 68–69.
- (15 min.) Present **Gramática:** *The verb* **gustar, ¿por qué?,** *and* **porque**, p. 70, using Teaching **Gramática**, p. 70.
- (10 min.) Play Audio CD 2, Tr. 7, for Activity 36, p. 70. ●
- (10 min.) Have students do Activity 37, p. 71.

Wrap-Up
- (5 min.) Present the information in Practices and Perspectives, p. 71.

OPTIONAL RESOURCES
- (10 min.) Have students do Activity 35, p. 69.
- (5 min.) See Common Error Alert, p. 71.

▲ = Advanced Learners   ◆ = Slower Pace Learners   ● = Special Learning Needs   ■ = Heritage Speakers

BLOCK 9 90-MINUTE LESSON PLAN

Practice Options

- *Lab Book*, pp. 15–16 ▲ ● ■
- ***Cuaderno de vocabulario y gramática***, pp. 22–24 ▲ ◆ ●
- ***Cuaderno de actividades***, pp. 15–17 ▲ ● ■
- *Activities for Communication*, pp. 7–8, 57–58 ▲ ■
- *Teaching Transparencies*: Bell Work, 2.7; ***Vocabulario y gramática***
  Answers, pp. 22–24 ▲ ● ■
- *Video Guide*, pp. 14–15 ▲ ● ■
- *Grammar Tutor for Students of Spanish*, pp. 11–14 ◆ ●
- *Interactive Tutor* (Disc 1) or *DVD Tutor* (Disc 1) ▲ ● ■
- Online practice, Chapter 2 (go.hrw.com, Keyword: EXP1A CH2) ▲ ● ■

▲ = Advanced Learners   ◆ = Slower Pace Learners   ● = Special Learning Needs   ■ = Heritage Speakers

¡A conocernos!

BLOCK 10 90-MINUTE LESSON PLAN

NATIONAL STANDARDS

Gramática en acción 2

Communication 1.1: Student engages in oral and written exchanges of learned material to socialize and to provide and obtain information.

Communication 1.2: Student demonstrates understanding of simple, clearly spoken, and written language such as simple stories, high-frequency commands, and brief instructions when dealing with familiar topics.

Communication 1.3: Student presents information using familiar words, phrases, and sentences to listeners and readers.

CORE INSTRUCTION

Warm-Up
- (5 min.) Have students share answers from Activity 34, p. 69.

Gramática en acción 2
- (5 min.) Have students do Bell Work 2.8, p. 72.
- (10 min.) Show **GramaVisión** (**gustar, ¿por qué?,** *and* **porque**), *Video Program* (Videocassette 1) or *DVD Tutor* (Disc 1).
- (10 min.) Review **gustar, ¿por qué?,** and **porque.**
- (20 min.) Have students do Activities 38–39, p. 71.
- (15 min.) Present **Gramática:** *The preposition* **de,** p. 72, using Teaching **Gramática,** p. 72.
- (10 min.) Have students do Activities 40–41, pp. 72–73.
- (10 min.) Play Audio CD 2, Tr. 8, for Activity 42, p. 73. ●

Wrap-Up
- (5 min.) Share and check answers to Activity 41.
- Remind students to study for **Prueba: Gramática 2.**

OPTIONAL RESOURCES
- (10 min.) See **GramaVisión** (*the preposition* **de**), *Video Program* (Videocassette 1) or *DVD Tutor* (Disc 1).
- (10 min.) See Advanced Learners, p. 71. ▲
- (10 min.) See Special Learning Needs, p. 71. ●
- (5 min.) See Slower Pace Learners, p. 73. ◆
- (15 min.) See Special Learning Needs, p. 73. ●

▲ = Advanced Learners ◆ = Slower Pace Learners ● = Special Learning Needs ■ = Heritage Speakers

BLOCK 10 90-MINUTE LESSON PLAN

Practice Options

- *Lab Book*, pp. 15–16 ▲ ● ■
- ***Cuaderno de vocabulario y gramática***, pp. 22–24 ▲ ◆ ●
- ***Cuaderno de actividades***, pp. 15–17 ▲ ● ■
- *Activities for Communication*, pp. 7–8, 57–58 ▲ ■
- *Teaching Transparencies*: Bell Work 2.8; ***Vocabulario y gramática*** Answers, pp. 22–24 ▲ ● ■
- *Video Guide*, pp. 14–15 ▲ ● ■
- *Grammar Tutor for Students of Spanish*, pp. 11–14, 169 ◆ ●
- *Interactive Tutor* (Disc 1) or *DVD Tutor* (Disc 1) ▲ ● ■
- Online practice, Chapter 2 (go.hrw.com, Keyword: EXP1A CH2) ▲ ● ■

▲ = Advanced Learners   ◆ = Slower Pace Learners   ● = Special Learning Needs   ■ = Heritage Speakers

¡A conocernos!

NATIONAL STANDARDS

Gramática en acción 2

Communication 1.1: Student engages in oral and written exchanges of learned material to socialize and to provide and obtain information.

Communication 1.2: Student demonstrates understanding of simple, clearly spoken, and written language such as simple stories, high-frequency commands, and brief instructions when dealing with familiar topics.

Communication 1.3: Student presents information using familiar words, phrases, and sentences to listeners and readers.

Conexiones culturales

Communication 1.1: Student engages in oral and written exchanges of learned material to socialize and to provide and obtain information.

Connections 3.2: Student uses resources (that may include technology) in the language and cultures being studied to gain access to information.

Connections 3.1: Student uses the language to obtain, reinforce, or expand knowledge of other subject areas.

CORE INSTRUCTION

Warm-Up

- (5 min.) Have each student tell a partner in Spanish where he or she is from.

Gramática en acción 2

- (15 min.) Have students do Activity 43, p. 73.
- (20 min.) Review **Gramática 2,** pp. 68–73.

Assessment

- (20 min.) Give **Prueba: Gramática 2.**

Conexiones culturales

- (25 min.) Present **Conexiones culturales,** p. 74, using Teaching **Conexiones culturales**, #s 1–3, p. 74.

Wrap-Up

- (5 min.) Remind students of the Spanish-speaking countries by pointing them out on a map and having students repeat the name of each one.

OPTIONAL RESOURCES

- (10 min.) See AP Language Examination note, p. 73.
- (30 min.) See **Más práctica,** p. 75.
- You can find alternative quizzes in the Assessment Options on the next page.

▲ = Advanced Learners ◆ = Slower Pace Learners ● = Special Learning Needs ■ = Heritage Speakers

Holt Spanish 1A

Lesson Planner

BLOCK 11 90-MINUTE LESSON PLAN

Practice Options
- *Lab Book*, pp. 15–16, 40 ▲ ● ■
- ***Cuaderno de vocabulario y gramática***, pp. 22–24 ▲ ◆ ●
- ***Cuaderno de actividades***, pp. 15–17 ▲ ● ■
- *Activities for Communication*, pp. 7–8, 57–58 ▲ ■
- *Teaching Transparencies*: ***Vocabulario y gramática*** Answers, pp. 22–24 ▲ ● ■
- *Video Guide*, pp. 14–15 ▲ ● ■
- *Grammar Tutor for Students of Spanish*, pp. 11–14 ◆ ●
- *Interactive Tutor* (Disc 1) or *DVD Tutor* (Disc 1) ▲ ● ■
- Online practice, Chapter 2 (go.hrw.com, Keyword: EXP1A CH2)

Assessment Options
- *Assessment Program:* **Prueba: Gramática 2**, pp. 29–30 ▲ ● ■
- *Assessment Program:* **Prueba: Aplicación 2**, pp. 31–32 ▲ ● ■
- Test Generator ▲ ● ■

▲ = Advanced Learners   ◆ = Slower Pace Learners   ● = Special Learning Needs   ■ = Heritage Speakers

Holt Spanish 1A

Lesson Planner

CAPÍTULO

¡A conocernos!

(2)

BLOCK 12 90-MINUTE LESSON PLAN

NATIONAL STANDARDS

Conexiones culturales

Connections 3.2: Student uses resources (that may include technology) in the language and cultures being studied to gain access to information.

Connections 3.1: Student uses the language to obtain, reinforce, or expand knowledge of other subject areas.

Novela en video

Communication 1.2: Student demonstrates understanding of simple, clearly spoken, and written language such as simple stories, high-frequency commands, and brief instructions when dealing with familiar topics.

Cultures 2.1: Student demonstrates an understanding of the practices (what people do) and how they are related to the perspectives (how people perceive things) of the cultures studied.

Connections 3.2: Student uses resources (that may include technology) in the language and cultures being studied to gain access to information.

Comparisons 4.2: Student demonstrates an understanding of the concept of culture through comparisons of the student's own culture and the cultures studied.

Leamos y escribamos

Communication 1.2: Student demonstrates understanding of simple, clearly spoken, and written language such as simple stories, high-frequency commands, and brief instructions when dealing with familiar topics.

Communication 1.3: Student presents information using familiar words, phrases, and sentences to listeners and readers.

Connections 3.2: Student uses resources (that may include technology) in the language and cultures being studied to gain access to information.

CORE INSTRUCTION

Warm-Up

- (5 min.) Have students find Bolivia, Guatemala, the Dominican Republic, and Spain on the maps on pages R2–R6.

Conexiones culturales

- (15 min.) Present **Conexiones culturales**, p. 74–75, using Teaching **Conexiones culturales**, #s 4–5, p. 74.

Novela en video

- (25 min.) Present **Novela en video,** using Teaching **Novela en video,** #s 1–4, p. 76.
- (5 min.) Discuss Gestures, p. 78, and Language Note, p. 77.

Leamos y escribamos

- (25 min.) Present **Leamos,** p. 80, using Teaching **Leamos,** #s 1–4, p. 80.
- (5 min.) Play Audio CD 2, Tr. 9, for **¿De qué color eres?** p. 80. ●

Wrap-Up

- (10 min.) See Applying the Strategies, p. 80. ■

OPTIONAL RESOURCES

- (15 min.) See Slower Pace Learners, p. 75. ◆
- (20 min.) See Multiple Intelligences, p. 75. ●
- (10 min.) See Visual Learners, p. 76. ●
- (20 min.) See Multiple Intelligences, p. 81. ●

▲ = Advanced Learners ◆ = Slower Pace Learners ● = Special Learning Needs ■ = Heritage Speakers

BLOCK 12 90-MINUTE LESSON PLAN

Practice Options
- *Lab Book*, p. 41 ▲ ● ■
- *Video Guide*, pp. 14–15, 19 ▲ ● ■
- ***Cuaderno de actividades***, p. 18 ▲ ● ■
- *Student Edition*, **Literatura y variedades,** pp. 230–231 ▲ ● ■
- *Reading Strategies and Skills Handbook*, pp. 66, 22–25 ▲ ● ■
- ***¡Lee conmigo!*** Level 1 Reader ▲ ■
- *Interactive Tutor* (Disc 1) or *DVD Tutor* (Disc 1) ▲ ● ■
- Online practice, Chapter 2 (go.hrw.com, Keyword: EXP1A CH2) ▲ ● ■

Assessment Options
- *Assessment Program:* **Prueba: Lectura,** pp. 33, 39 ▲ ● ■
- *Assessment Program:* **Prueba: Escritura,** pp. 34, 39 ▲ ● ■

▲ = Advanced Learners   ◆ = Slower Pace Learners   ● = Special Learning Needs   ■ = Heritage Speakers

Holt Spanish 1A   Lesson Planner

CAPÍTULO
2

¡A conocernos!

BLOCK 13 90-MINUTE LESSON PLAN

NATIONAL STANDARDS

Leamos y escribamos
Communication 1.3: Student presents information using familiar words, phrases, and sentences to listeners and readers.

Repaso
Communication 1.1: Student engages in oral and written exchanges of learned material to socialize and to provide and obtain information.

Communication 1.2: Student demonstrates understanding of simple, clearly spoken, and written language such as simple stories, high-frequency commands, and brief instructions when dealing with familiar topics.

Communication 1.3: Student presents information using familiar words, phrases, and sentences to listeners and readers. **Cultures 2.1:** Student demonstrates an understanding of the practices (what people do) and how they are related to the perspectives (how people perceive things) of the cultures studied.

CORE INSTRUCTION

Warm-Up
- (5 min.) Review with students the writing rubric you intend to use to evaluate the **Taller del escritor** assignment, p. 81.

Repaso
- (20 min.) Present **Taller del escritor,** p. 81, using Teaching **Escribamos,** p. 80.
- (25 min.) Have students do Activities 1–5, pp. 82–83.
- (10 min.) Play Audio CD 2, Tr. 11, for Activity 6, p. 83. ●
- (10 min.) Have students do Activity 7, p. 83.
- (10 min.) Play Audio CD 2, Tr. 12, 13, 14, for **Letra y sonido,** p. 84. ●

Wrap-Up
- (10 min.) Read aloud from AP Language Examination, p. 83, as students look at the pictures in Activity 7, p. 83. Then remind the class to study for the Chapter Test.

OPTIONAL RESOURCES
- (20 min.) See Advanced Learners, p. 81. ▲
- (30 min.) See Teacher to Teacher, p. 82.
- (15 min.) See Fold-N-Learn, p. 82. ●
- (15 min.) See Language Arts Link, p. 85.

▲ = Advanced Learners ◆ = Slower Pace Learners ● = Special Learning Needs ■ = Heritage Speakers

Holt Spanish 1A

Lesson Planner

BLOCK 13 90-MINUTE LESSON PLAN

Practice Options

- *Lab Book*, pp. 15–16, 42 ▲ ● ■
- *Activities for Communication*, pp. 44, 57–58 ▲ ■
- *Teaching Transparencies:* Situation; Picture Sequences ▲ ● ■
- *Video Guide*, pp. 15–19, 20 ▲ ● ■
- *TPR Storytelling Book*, pp. 10–11 ▲ ●
- *Grammar Tutor for Students of Spanish*, pp. 66–69, 169 ◆ ●
- *Interactive Tutor* (Disc 1) or *DVD Tutor* (Disc 1) ▲ ● ■
- Online practice, Chapter 2 (go.hrw.com, Keyword: EXP1A CH2) ▲ ● ■

▲ = Advanced Learners   ◆ = Slower Pace Learners   ● = Special Learning Needs   ■ = Heritage Speakers

Holt Spanish 1A   Lesson Planner

¡A conocernos!

BLOCK 14 90-MINUTE LESSON PLAN

NATIONAL STANDARDS

Integración

Communication 1.1: Student engages in oral and written exchanges of learned material to socialize and to provide and obtain information.

Communication 1.2: Student demonstrates understanding of simple, clearly spoken, and written language such as simple stories, high-frequency commands, and brief instructions when dealing with familiar topics.

Communication 1.3: Student presents information using familiar words, phrases, and sentences to listeners and readers.

CORE INSTRUCTION

Assessment
- (50 min.) Give the Chapter 2 Test.

Integración
- (10 min.) Play Audio CD 2, Tr. 17, for Activity 1, p. 86. ●
- (25 min.) Have students do Activities 2–4, pp. 86–87.

OPTIONAL RESOURCES
- (25 min.) See Game, p. 83. ●
- (20 min.) See Culture Project, p. 86.
- (15 min.) See Fine Art Connection, p. 87.
- You may also choose from the other modes of assessment listed in the Assessment Options box on the next page.

▲ = Advanced Learners ◆ = Slower Pace Learners ● = Special Learning Needs ■ = Heritage Speakers

Holt Spanish 1A

Lesson Planner

BLOCK 14 90-MINUTE LESSON PLAN

Practice Options
- *Lab Book*, pp. 15–16 ▲ ● ■
- *Activities for Communication*, pp. 44, 57–58 ▲ ■
- **Cuaderno de actividades**, pp. 19–20, 54–55 ▲ ● ■
- *Teaching Transparencies*: Fine Art, Chapter 2 ▲ ● ■
- *Grammar Tutor for Students of Spanish*, pp. 63–66, 169–170 ◆ ●
- *Interactive Tutor* (Disc 1) or *DVD Tutor* (Disc 1) ▲ ● ■
- Online practice, Chapter 2 (go.hrw.com, Keyword: EXP1A CH2) ▲ ● ■

Assessment Options
- *Assessment Program:* **Exam, Capítulo 2,** pp. 117–127 ▲ ● ■
- *Assessment Program:* **Examen oral,** pp. 128 ▲ ● ■
- *Assessment Program:* Alternative Assessment, pp. 213, 219, 226 ▲ ● ■
- Audio CD 2, Tr. 18–19 ●
- Test Generator ▲ ● ■

▲ = Advanced Learners   ◆ = Slower Pace Learners   ● = Special Learning Needs   ■ = Heritage Speakers

(207)

¿Qué te gusta hacer?

BLOCK 1 90-MINUTE LESSON PLAN

NATIONAL STANDARDS

Chapter Opener

Communication 1.2: Student demonstrates understanding of simple, clearly spoken, and written language such as simple stories, high-frequency commands, and brief instructions when dealing with familiar topics.

Vocabulario en acción 1

Communication 1.1: Student engages in oral and written exchanges of learned material to socialize and to provide and obtain information.

Communication 1.2: Student demonstrates understanding of simple, clearly spoken, and written language such as simple stories, high-frequency commands, and brief instructions when dealing with familiar topics.

Communication 1.3: Student presents information using familiar words, phrases, and sentences to listeners and readers.

Comparisons 4.2: Student demonstrates an understanding of the concept of culture through comparisons of the student's own culture and the cultures studied.

Before starting **Capítulo 3,** you may wish to teach **Geocultura: Texas,** pp. 88–91. For teaching suggestions, see pp. xv–xvi of this *Lesson Planner.*

CORE INSTRUCTION

Warm-Up

- (5 min.) See Learning and Pacing Tips, p. 93.

Chapter Opener

- (5 min.) Have students do Bell Work 3.1, p. 94.
- (5 min.) Present information from Using the Photo and **Más vocabulario,** p. 92.
- (5 min.) Present **Objetivos,** p. 92.

Vocabulario en acción 1

- (30 min.) Present **Vocabulario**, pp. 94–95, using Teaching **Vocabulario,** p. 94.
- (10 min.) Show **ExpresaVisión,** Ch. 3.
- (5 min.) Present **Nota cultural,** p. 96.
- (5 min.) Play Audio CD 3, Tr. 1 for activity 1, p. 96. ●
- (10 min.) Have students do Activity 2, p. 96.

Wrap-Up

- (10 min.) Get students started on the Fold-N-Learn project described on p. 96. ●

OPTIONAL RESOURCES

- (5 min.) See Language Note, p. 95.
- (15 min.) See Advanced Learners, p. 95. ▲
- (5 min.) See Special Learning Needs, p. 95. ●

▲ = Advanced Learners   ◆ = Slower Pace Learners   ● = Special Learning Needs   ■ = Heritage Speakers

BLOCK 1 90-MINUTE LESSON PLAN

Practice Options
- *Lab Book*, pp. 3, 17–18, 43, 44 ▲ ● ■
- ***Cuaderno de vocabulario y gramática***, pp. 25–27 ▲ ◆ ●
- *Teaching Transparencies*: Bell Work 3.1; **Vocabulario** 3.1, 3.2; Situation; ***Vocabulario y gramática*** Answers, pp. 25–27 ▲ ● ■
- *Video Guide*, pp. 21–22, 24–25, 26 ▲ ● ■
- *Interactive Tutor* (Disc 1) or *DVD Tutor* (Disc 1) ▲ ● ■
- Online practice, Chapter 3 (go.hrw.com, Keyword: EXP1A CH3) ▲ ● ■

▲ = Advanced Learners   ◆ = Slower Pace Learners   ● = Special Learning Needs   ■ = Heritage Speakers

Holt Spanish 1A

Lesson Planner

CAPÍTULO
3

¿Qué te gusta hacer?

BLOCK 2 90-MINUTE LESSON PLAN

NATIONAL STANDARDS

Vocabulario en acción 1

Communication 1.1: Student engages in oral and written exchanges of learned material to socialize and to provide and obtain information.

Communication 1.2: Student demonstrates understanding of simple, clearly spoken, and written language such as simple stories, high-frequency commands, and brief instructions when dealing with familiar topics.

Communication 1.3: Student presents information using familiar words, phrases, and sentences to listeners and readers.

Comparisons 4.3: Student demonstrates an understanding of the influence of one language and culture on another.

CORE INSTRUCTION

Warm-Up
- (5 min.) Have students do Bell Work 3.1, p. 94.

Vocabulario en acción 1
- (10 min.) Review **Vocabulario 1** and **¡Exprésate!**, pp. 94–95.
- (25 min.) Have students do Activities 3–5, pp. 96–97.
- (15 min.) Present **¡Exprésate!**, p. 98, using Teaching **¡Exprésate!**, p. 98.
- (25 min.) Have students do Activities 6–9, pp. 98–99.

Wrap-Up
- (10 min.) Have students do the activity described in **Comunicación** (TE), p. 97.
- Remind the class to study for **Prueba: Vocabulario en acción 1.**

OPTIONAL RESOURCES
- (15 min.) See **Más práctica,** p. 97.
- (10 min.) See Slower Learners, p. 97. ◆
- (15 min.) See Multiple Intelligences, p. 97. ●
- (5 min.) See Common Error Alert, p. 99.
- (15 min.) See **Más práctica,** p. 99.

▲ = Advanced Learners   ◆ = Slower Pace Learners   ● = Special Learning Needs   ■ = Heritage Speakers

BLOCK 2 90-MINUTE LESSON PLAN

Practice Options
- *Lab Book*, pp. 17–18, 44 ▲ ● ■
- ***Cuaderno de vocabulario y gramática***, pp. 25–27 ▲ ◆ ●
- *Teaching Transparencies*: Bell Work 3.1; **Vocabulario** 3.1, 3.2; ***Vocabulario y gramática*** Answers, pp. 25–27 ▲ ● ■
- *Video Guide*, pp. 24–25, 26 ▲ ● ■
- *Interactive Tutor* (Disc 1) or *DVD Tutor* (Disc 1) ▲ ● ■
- Online practice, Chapter 3 (go.hrw.com, Keyword: EXP1A CH3) ▲ ● ■

▲ = Advanced Learners   ◆ = Slower Pace Learners   ● = Special Learning Needs   ■ = Heritage Speakers

¿Qué te gusta hacer?

BLOCK 3 90-MINUTE LESSON PLAN

NATIONAL STANDARDS

Vocabulario en acción 1

Communication 1.1: Student engages in oral and written exchanges of learned material to socialize and to provide and obtain information.

Communication 1.2: Student demonstrates understanding of simple, clearly spoken, and written language such as simple stories, high-frequency commands, and brief instructions when dealing with familiar topics.

Communication 1.3: Student presents information using familiar words, phrases, and sentences to listeners and readers.

Comparisons 4.2: Student demonstrates an understanding of the concept of culture through comparisons of the student's own culture and the cultures studied.

Gramática en acción 1

Communication 1.1: Student engages in oral and written exchanges of learned material to socialize and to provide and obtain information.

Communication 1.2: Student demonstrates understanding of simple, clearly spoken, and written language such as simple stories, high-frequency commands, and brief instructions when dealing with familiar topics.

Communication 1.3: Student presents information using familiar words, phrases, and sentences to listeners and readers.

CORE INSTRUCTION

Warm-Up
- (5 min.) Have students do Bell Work 3.2, p. 100.

Vocabulario en acción 1
- (15 min.) Review **Vocabulario en acción 1,** pp. 94–99.

Assessment
- (20 min.) Give **Prueba: Vocabulario 1.**

Gramática en acción 1
- (20 min.) Present **Gramática: Gustar** *with infinitives,* p. 100, using Teaching **Gramática,** p. 100.
- (10 min.) Show **GramaVisión (gustar** *with infinitives), Video Program* (Videocassette 3) or *DVD Tutor* (Disc 1).
- (15 min.) Have students do Activities 10–11, pp. 100–101.

Wrap-Up
- (5 min.) Have students review their answers to Activity 11 with a partner.

OPTIONAL RESOURCES
- (15 min.) See Advanced Learners, p. 99. ▲
- (15 min.) See Special Learning Needs, p. 99. ●
- (15 min.) See Teacher to Teacher, p. 101.
- You can find alternative quizzes in the Assessment Options on the next page.

▲ = Advanced Learners   ◆ = Slower Pace Learners   ● = Special Learning Needs   ■ = Heritage Speakers

BLOCK 3 90-MINUTE LESSON PLAN

Practice Options
- *Lab Book*, pp. 17–18, 44 ▲ ● ■
- ***Cuaderno de vocabulario y gramática***, pp. 28–30 ▲ ◆ ●
- ***Cuaderno de actividades***, pp. 21–23 ▲ ● ■
- *Activities for Communication*, pp. 9–10, 59–60 ▲ ■
- *Teaching Transparencies*: Bell Work 3.2; ***Vocabulario y gramática*** Answers, pp. 28–30 ▲ ● ■
- *Video Guide*, pp. 24–25 ▲ ● ■
- *Grammar Tutor for Students of Spanish*, pp. 15–18, 170–171 ◆ ●
- *Interactive Tutor* (Disc 1) or *DVD Tutor* (Disc 1) ▲ ● ■
- Online practice, Chapter 3 (go.hrw.com, Keyword: EXP1A CH3) ▲ ● ■

Assessment Options
- *Assessment Program:* **Prueba, Vocabulario 1,** pp. 41–42 ▲ ● ■
- Test Generator ▲ ● ■

▲ = Advanced Learners   ◆ = Slower Pace Learners   ● = Special Learning Needs   ■ = Heritage Speakers

¿Qué te gusta hacer?

BLOCK 4 90-MINUTE LESSON PLAN

NATIONAL STANDARDS

Gramática en acción 1

Communication 1.1: Student engages in oral and written exchanges of learned material to socialize and to provide and obtain information.

Communication 1.2: Student demonstrates understanding of simple, clearly spoken, and written language such as simple stories, high-frequency commands, and brief instructions when dealing with familiar topics.

Communication 1.3: Student presents information using familiar words, phrases, and sentences to listeners and readers.

CORE INSTRUCTION

Warm-Up

- (5 min.) Have students do Bell Work 3.3, p. 102.

Gramática en acción 1

- (15 min.) Have students do Activities 12–13, p. 101.
- (20 min.) Present **Gramática:** *Pronouns after prepositions,* p. 102, using Teaching **Gramática,** p. 102.
- (10 min.) Show **GramaVisión** *(pronouns after prepositions), Video Program* (Videocassette 3) or *DVD Tutor* (Disc 1).
- (35 min.) Have students do Activities 14–17, pp. 102–103.

Wrap-Up

- (5 min.) Have students get in small groups and read the letter from Activity 14 aloud.

OPTIONAL RESOURCES

- (10 min.) See Advanced Learners, p. 101. ▲
- (15 min.) See Special Learning Needs, p. 101. ●
- (10 min.) See Multiple Intelligences, p. 103. ●
- (5 min.) See Slower Pace Learners, p. 103. ◆
- (5 min.) See Heritage Speakers, p. 103. ■
- (15 min.) See **Comunicación** (TE), p. 103.

▲ = Advanced Learners　◆ = Slower Pace Learners　● = Special Learning Needs　■ = Heritage Speakers

BLOCK 4 90-MINUTE LESSON PLAN

Practice Options

- *Lab Book*, pp. 17–18 ▲ ● ■
- ***Cuaderno de vocabulario y gramática***, pp. 28–30 ▲ ◆ ●
- ***Cuaderno de actividades***, pp. 21–23 ▲ ● ■
- *Activities for Communication*, pp. 9–10, 59–60 ▲ ■
- *Teaching Transparencies*: Bell Work 3.3; ***Vocabulario y gramática*** Answers, pp. 28–30 ▲ ● ■
- *Video Guide*, pp. 24–25 ▲ ● ■
- *Grammar Tutor for Students of Spanish*, pp. 15–18, 170–171 ◆ ●
- *TPR Storytelling Book*, pp. 12–13 ▲ ●
- *Interactive Tutor* (Disc 1) or *DVD Tutor* (Disc 1) ▲ ● ■
- Online practice, Chapter 3 (go.hrw.com, Keyword: EXP1A CH3) ▲ ● ■

▲ = Advanced Learners   ◆ = Slower Pace Learners   ● = Special Learning Needs   ■ = Heritage Speakers

215

¿Qué te gusta hacer?

BLOCK 5 90-MINUTE LESSON PLAN

NATIONAL STANDARDS

Gramática en acción 1

Communication 1.1: Student engages in oral and written exchanges of learned material to socialize and to provide and obtain information.

Communication 1.2: Student demonstrates understanding of simple, clearly spoken, and written language such as simple stories, high-frequency commands, and brief instructions when dealing with familiar topics.

Communication 1.3: Student presents information using familiar words, phrases, and sentences to listeners and readers.

Cultures 2.1: Student demonstrates an understanding of the practices (what people do) and how they are related to the perspectives (how people perceive things) of the cultures studied.

Comparisons 4.2: Student demonstrates an understanding of the concept of culture through comparisons of the student's own culture and the cultures studied.

CORE INSTRUCTION

Warm-Up

- (5 min.) Have students do Bell Work 3.4, p. 104.

Gramática en acción 1

- (15 min.) Present **Gramática:** *Present tense of* **querer** *with infinitives,* p. 104, using Teaching **Gramática,** p. 104.
- (10 min.) Show **GramaVisión (querer** *with infinitives), Video Program* (Videocassette 2) or *DVD Tutor* (Disc 1).
- (10 min.) Have students do Activities 18–19, p. 104.
- (5 min.) Present **Nota cultural,** p. 104.
- (10 min.) Have students do Activity 20, p. 105.
- (10 min.) Play Audio CD 3, Tr. 2, for Activity 21, p. 105. ●
- (10 min.) Have students do Activity 22, p. 105.
- (10 min.) Review **Gramática 1,** pp. 100–105.

Wrap-Up

- (5 min.) Have students do the activity described in **Comunicación** (TE), p. 105.
- Remind the class to study for **Prueba: Gramática 1.**

OPTIONAL RESOURCES

- (10 min.) See Slower Pace Learners, p. 105. ◆
- (10 min.) See Special Learning Needs, p. 105. ●

▲ = Advanced Learners   ◆ = Slower Pace Learners   ● = Special Learning Needs   ■ = Heritage Speakers

BLOCK 5 90-MINUTE LESSON PLAN

Practice Options

- *Lab Book*, pp. 17–18 ▲ ● ■
- ***Cuaderno de vocabulario y gramática***, pp. 28–30 ▲ ◆ ●
- ***Cuaderno de actividades***, pp. 21–23 ▲ ● ■
- *Activities for Communication*, pp. 9–10, 59–60 ▲ ■
- *Teaching Transparencies*: Bell Work 3.4; ***Vocabulario y gramática*** Answers, pp. 28–30 ▲ ● ■
- *Video Guide*, pp. 24–25 ▲ ● ■
- *Grammar Tutor for Students of Spanish*, pp. 15–18, 170–171 ◆ ●
- *TPR Storytelling Book*, pp. 12–13 ▲ ●
- *Interactive Tutor* (Disc 1) or *DVD Tutor* (Disc 1) ▲ ● ■
- Online practice, Chapter 3 (go.hrw.com, Keyword: EXP1A CH3) ▲ ● ■

▲ = Advanced Learners   ◆ = Slower Pace Learners   ● = Special Learning Needs   ■ = Heritage Speakers

(217)

¿Qué te gusta hacer?

BLOCK 6 90-MINUTE LESSON PLAN

NATIONAL STANDARDS

Gramática en acción 1

Communication 1.1: Student engages in oral and written exchanges of learned material to socialize and to provide and obtain information.

Communication 1.2: Student demonstrates understanding of simple, clearly spoken, and written language such as simple stories, high-frequency commands, and brief instructions when dealing with familiar topics.

Communication 1.3: Student presents information using familiar words, phrases, and sentences to listeners and readers.

Cultures 2.1: Student demonstrates an understanding of the practices (what people do) and how they are related to the perspectives (how people perceive things) of the cultures studied.

Comparisons 4.2: Student demonstrates an understanding of the concept of culture through comparisons of the student's own culture and the cultures studied.

Cultura

Communication 1.2: Student demonstrates understanding of simple, clearly spoken, and written language such as simple stories, high-frequency commands, and brief instructions when dealing with familiar topics.

Cultures 2.1: Student demonstrates an understanding of the practices (what people do) and how they are related to the perspectives (how people perceive things) of the cultures studied.

Comparisons 4.2: Student demonstrates an understanding of the concept of culture through comparisons of the student's own culture and the cultures studied.

Communities 5.2: Student shows evidence of becoming a lifelong learner by using the language for personal enrichment and career development.

Vocabulario en acción 2

Communication 1.1: Student engages in oral and written exchanges of learned material to socialize and to provide and obtain information.

Communication 1.2: Student demonstrates understanding of simple, clearly spoken, and written language such as simple stories, high-frequency commands, and brief instructions when dealing with familiar topics.

CORE INSTRUCTION

Warm-Up
- (5 min.) Have students do Bell Work 3.5, p. 100.

Gramática en acción 1
- (10 min.) Review **Gramática 1,** pp. 100–105.

Assessment
- (20 min.) Give **Prueba: Gramática 1.**

Cultura
- (20 min.) Present **Cultura,** pp. 106–107, using Teaching **Cultura,** p. 106, #s 1–3.
- (5 min.) Play Audio CD 3, Tr. 3, 4, 5 or show the **Video Cultura** video for chapter 3, *Video Program* (Videocassette 2) or *DVD Tutor* (Disc 1). ●
- (5 min.) Present **Comunidad,** p. 107.

Vocabulario en acción 2
- (20 min.) Present **Vocabulario 2,** pp. 108–109, using Teaching **Vocabulario,** #s 1–2, p. 108.

Wrap-Up
- (5 min.) Present Common Error Alert, p. 108.

OPTIONAL RESOURCES
- (10 min.) See Map Activities, p. 106.
- (10 min.) See Language Note, p. 107.
- (10 min.) See Heritage Speakers, p. 107. ■
- (10 min.) See Advanced Learners, p. 107. ▲
- (10 min.) See Multiple Intelligences, p. 107. ●
- (10 min.) See Slower Pace Learners, p. 109. ◆
- You can find alternative quizzes in the Assessment Options on the next page.

▲ = Advanced Learners   ◆ = Slower Pace Learners   ● = Special Learning Needs   ■ = Heritage Speakers

BLOCK 6 90-MINUTE LESSON PLAN

Practice Options

- *Lab Book*, pp. pp. 19–20, 45–46 ▲ ● ■
- *Cuaderno de vocabulario y gramática*, pp. 31–33 ▲ ◆ ●
- *Cuaderno de actividades*, p. 24 ▲ ● ■
- *Teaching Transparencies*: **Vocabulario** 3.3, 3.4; *Vocabulario y gramática*
  Answers, pp. 31–33 ▲ ● ■
- *Video Guide*, pp. 24–25, 27, 28 ▲ ● ■
- *Interactive Tutor* (Disc 1) or *DVD Tutor* (Disc 1) ▲ ● ■
- Online practice, Chapter 3 (go.hrw.com, Keyword: EXP1A CH3) ▲ ● ■

Assessment Options

- *Assessment Program:* **Prueba: Gramática 1**, pp. 43–44 ▲ ● ■
- *Assessment Program:* **Prueba: Aplicación 1**, pp. 45–46 ▲ ● ■
- Audio CD 3, Tr. 16 ▲ ●
- Test Generator ▲ ● ■

▲ = Advanced Learners   ◆ = Slower Pace Learners   ● = Special Learning Needs   ■ = Heritage Speakers

CAPÍTULO
3

¿Qué te gusta hacer?

BLOCK 7 90-MINUTE LESSON PLAN

NATIONAL STANDARDS

Vocabulario en acción 2

Communication 1.1: Student engages in oral and written exchanges of learned material to socialize and to provide and obtain information.

Communication 1.2: Student demonstrates understanding of simple, clearly spoken, and written language such as simple stories, high-frequency commands, and brief instructions when dealing with familiar topics.

Communication 1.3: Student presents information using familiar words, phrases, and sentences to listeners and readers.

Comparisons 4.2: Student demonstrates an understanding of the concept of culture through comparisons of the student's own culture and the cultures studied.

CORE INSTRUCTION

Warm-Up

- (5 min.) Have students do the activity described in Slower Pace Learners, p. 109. ◆

Vocabulario en acción 2

- (10 min.) Show **ExpresaVisión,** Ch. 3.
- (5 min.) Review **Vocabulario 2,** pp. 108–113.
- (15 min.) Present **Vocabulario,** pp. 108–109, using Teaching **Vocabulario,** #s 3–4, p. 108.
- (5 min.) Present **Nota cultural,** p. 110.
- (25 min.) Have students do Activities 23–26, pp. 110–111.
- (20 min.) Present **¡Exprésate!,** p. 112, using Teaching **¡Exprésate!,** p. 112.

Wrap-Up

- (5 min.) Have students do the activity described in **Más práctica,** p. 111.

OPTIONAL RESOURCES

- (15 min.) See TPR, p. 109. ●
- (15 min.) See Multiple Intelligences, p. 109. ●
- (5 min.) See **También se puede decir…,** p. 109.
- (20 min.) See Game, p. 110.
- (25 min.) See **Comunicación** (TE), p. 111.
- (10 min.) See Advanced Learners, p. 111. ▲
- (15 min.) See Multiple Intelligences, p. 111. ●

▲ = Advanced Learners   ◆ = Slower Pace Learners   ● = Special Learning Needs   ■ = Heritage Speakers

Holt Spanish 1A

Lesson Planner

BLOCK 7 90-MINUTE LESSON PLAN

Practice Options

- *Lab Book*, pp. 19–20, 46 ▲ ● ■
- ***Cuaderno de vocabulario y gramática***, pp. 31–33 ▲ ◆ ●
- *Teaching Transparencies*: **Vocabulario** 3.3, 3.4; ***Vocabulario y gramática*** Answers, pp. 31–33 ▲ ● ■
- *Video Guide*, pp. 24–25, 28 ▲ ● ■
- *Interactive Tutor* (Disc 1) or *DVD Tutor* (Disc 1) ▲ ● ■
- Online practice, Chapter 3 (go.hrw.com, Keyword: EXP1A CH3) ▲ ● ■

▲ = Advanced Learners   ◆ = Slower Pace Learners   ● = Special Learning Needs   ■ = Heritage Speakers

¿Qué te gusta hacer?

BLOCK 8 90-MINUTE LESSON PLAN

NATIONAL STANDARDS

Vocabulario en acción 2

Communication 1.1: Student engages in oral and written exchanges of learned material to socialize and to provide and obtain information.

Communication 1.2: Student demonstrates understanding of simple, clearly spoken, and written language such as simple stories, high-frequency commands, and brief instructions when dealing with familiar topics.

Communication 1.3: Student presents information using familiar words, phrases, and sentences to listeners and readers.

Gramática en acción 2

Communication 1.2: Student demonstrates understanding of simple, clearly spoken, and written language such as simple stories, high-frequency commands, and brief instructions when dealing with familiar topics.

Communication 1.3: Student presents information using familiar words, phrases, and sentences to listeners and readers.

CORE INSTRUCTION

Warm-Up

- (5 min.) Have students review the answers for Activity 24, p. 110.

Vocabulario en acción 2

- (10 min.) Review **Más vocabulario** and **¡Exprésate!**, p. 112.
- (10 min.) Play Audio CD 3, Tr. 6, for Activity 27, p. 112. ●
- (25 min.) Have students do Activities 28–30, pp. 112–113.

Gramática en acción 2

- (20 min.) Present **Gramática:** *The present tense of regular* **-ar** *verbs*, p. 114, using Teaching **Gramática,** p. 114.
- (15 min.) Have students do Activities 31–32, pp. 114–115.

Wrap-Up

- (5 min.) Have students do Bell Work 3.6, p. 114.
- Remind the class to study for **Prueba: Vocabulario 2.**

OPTIONAL RESOURCES

- (5 min.) See Practices and Perspectives, p. 110.
- (20 min.) See Extension, p. 113.
- (10 min.) See **Más práctica,** p. 113.
- (10 min.) See **Comunicación** (TE), p. 113.
- (10 min.) See Slower Pace Learners, p. 113. ◆
- (10 min.) See Special Learning Needs, p. 113. ●
- (5 min.) See Language to Language, p. 115.
- (10 min.) See Slower Pace Learners, p. 115. ◆

▲ = Advanced Learners   ◆ = Slower Pace Learners   ● = Special Learning Needs   ■ = Heritage Speakers

BLOCK 8 90-MINUTE LESSON PLAN

Practice Options

- *Lab Book*, pp. 19–20, 46 ▲ ● ■
- ***Cuaderno de vocabulario y gramática***, pp. 31–33, 34–36 ▲ ◆ ●
- ***Cuaderno de actividades***, pp. 25–27 ▲ ● ■
- *Activities for Communication*, pp. 11–12, 59–60 ▲ ■
- *Teaching Transparencies*: Bell Work 3.6; **Vocabulario** 3.3, 3.4; *Vocabulario y gramática* Answers, pp. 31–33, 34–36 ▲ ● ■
- *TPR Storytelling Book*, pp. 14–15 ▲ ●
- *Video Guide*, pp. 24–25, 28 ▲ ● ■
- *Grammar Tutor for Students of Spanish*, pp. 19–20, 170–171 ◆ ●
- *Interactive Tutor* (Disc 1) or *DVD Tutor* (Disc 1) ▲ ● ■
- Online practice, Chapter 3 (go.hrw.com, Keyword: EXP1A CH3) ▲ ● ■

▲ = Advanced Learners   ◆ = Slower Pace Learners   ● = Special Learning Needs   ■ = Heritage Speakers

Holt Spanish 1A

Lesson Planner

¿Qué te gusta hacer?

BLOCK 9 90-MINUTE LESSON PLAN

NATIONAL STANDARDS

Vocabulario en acción 2

Communication 1.1: Student engages in oral and written exchanges of learned material to socialize and to provide and obtain information.

Communication 1.2: Student demonstrates understanding of simple, clearly spoken, and written language such as simple stories, high-frequency commands, and brief instructions when dealing with familiar topics.

Communication 1.3: Student presents information using familiar words, phrases, and sentences to listeners and readers.

Gramática en acción 2

Communication 1.1: Student engages in oral and written exchanges of learned material to socialize and to provide and obtain information.

Communication 1.2: Student demonstrates understanding of simple, clearly spoken, and written language such as simple stories, high-frequency commands, and brief instructions when dealing with familiar topics.

Communication 1.3: Student presents information using familiar words, phrases, and sentences to listeners and readers.

CORE INSTRUCTION

Warm-Up
- (5 min.) Ask students **¿Qué haces los fines de semana?**

Vocabulario en acción 2
- (10 min.) Review **Vocabulario 2,** pp. 108–113.

Assessment
- (20 min.) Give **Prueba: Vocabulario 2.**

Gramática en acción 2
- (5 min.) Have students do Bell Work 3.7, p. 116.
- (10 min.) Show **GramaVisión** *(the present-tense of* **-ar** *verbs), Video Program* (Videocassette 2) or *DVD Tutor* (Disc 1).
- (5 min.) Review the present-tense conjugations of **-ar** verbs, p. 114.
- (10 min.) Have students do Activities 33–34, p. 115.
- (20 min.) Present **Gramática:** *The present tense of* **ir** *and* **jugar,** p. 116, using Teaching **Gramática,** p. 116.

Wrap-Up
- (5 min.) Present Language to Language, p. 115.

OPTIONAL RESOURCES
- (10 min.) See Special Learning Needs, p. 115. ●
- (15 min.) See **Comunicación** (TE), p. 115.
- You can find alternative quizzes in the Assessment Options on the next page.

▲ = Advanced Learners   ◆ = Slower Pace Learners   ● = Special Learning Needs   ■ = Heritage Speakers

BLOCK 9 90-MINUTE LESSON PLAN

Practice Options

- *Lab Book*, pp. 19–20 ▲ ● ■
- *Cuaderno de vocabulario y gramática*, pp. 34–36 ▲ ◆ ●
- *Cuaderno de actividades*, pp. 25–27 ▲ ● ■
- *Activities for Communication*, pp. 11–12, 59–60 ▲ ■
- *Teaching Transparencies*: Bell Work 3.7; **Vocabulario** 3.3, 3.4; *Vocabulario y gramática* Answers, pp. 34–36 ▲ ● ■
- *Video Guide*, pp. 24–25 ▲ ● ■
- *TPR Storytelling Book*, pp. 14–15 ▲ ●
- *Grammar Tutor for Students of Spanish*, pp. 19–20, 170–171 ◆ ●
- *Interactive Tutor* (Disc 1) or *DVD Tutor* (Disc 1) ▲ ● ■
- Online practice, Chapter 3 (go.hrw.com, Keyword: EXP1A CH3) ▲ ● ■

Assessment Options

- *Assessment Program:* **Prueba: Vocabulario 2**, pp. 47–48 ▲ ● ■
- Test Generator ▲ ● ■

▲ = Advanced Learners   ◆ = Slower Pace Learners   ● = Special Learning Needs   ■ = Heritage Speakers

Holt Spanish 1A

¿Qué te gusta hacer?

BLOCK 10 90-MINUTE LESSON PLAN

NATIONAL STANDARDS

Gramática en acción 2

Communication 1.1: Student engages in oral and written exchanges of learned material to socialize and to provide and obtain information.

Communication 1.2: Student demonstrates understanding of simple, clearly spoken, and written language such as simple stories, high-frequency commands, and brief instructions when dealing with familiar topics.

Communication 1.3: Student presents information using familiar words, phrases, and sentences to listeners and readers.

CORE INSTRUCTION

Warm-Up
- (5 min.) Have students do Bell Work 3.8, p. 118.

Gramática en acción 2
- (10 min.) Show **GramaVisión** (**ir, jugar**), *Video Program* (Videocassette 2) or *DVD Tutor* (Disc 1).
- (20 min.) Have students do Activities 35–38, pp. 116–117.
- (10 min.) Show **GramaVisión** (*weather expressions*), *Video Program* (Videocassette 2) or *DVD Tutor* (Disc 1).
- (15 min.) Present **Gramática:** *Weather expressions,* p. 118, using Teaching **Gramática,** p. 118.
- (5 min.) Have students do Activity 39, p. 118.
- (10 min.) Play Audio CD 3, Tr. 7, for Activity 40, p. 119. ●
- (10 min.) Have students do Activity 41, p. 119.

Wrap-Up
- (5 min.) Have students write a sentence about each picture in Activity 40.
- Remind them to study for **Prueba: Gramática 2.**

OPTIONAL RESOURCES
- (10 min.) See Special Learning Needs, p. 117. ●
- (15 min.) See Advanced Learners, p. 117. ▲
- (15 min.) See **Comunicación** (TE), p. 117.
- (10 min.) See Advanced Learners, p. 119. ▲

▲ = Advanced Learners   ◆ = Slower Pace Learners   ● = Special Learning Needs   ■ = Heritage Speakers

Lesson Planner

BLOCK 10 90-MINUTE LESSON PLAN

Practice Options
- *Lab Book*, pp. 19–20 ▲ ● ■
- ***Cuaderno de vocabulario y gramática***, pp. 34–36 ▲ ◆ ●
- ***Cuaderno de actividades***, pp. 25–27 ▲ ● ■
- *Activities for Communication*, pp. 11–12, 59–60 ▲ ■
- *Teaching Transparencies*: Bell Work, 3.8. ***Vocabulario y gramática*** Answers, pp. 34–36 ▲ ● ■
- *Video Guide*, pp. 24–25 ▲ ● ■
- *Grammar Tutor for Students of Spanish*, pp. 19–20, 170–171 ◆ ●
- *Interactive Tutor* (Disc 1) or *DVD Tutor* (Disc 1) ▲ ● ■
- Online practice, Chapter 3 (go.hrw.com, Keyword: EXP1A CH3) ▲ ● ■

▲ = Advanced Learners   ◆ = Slower Pace Learners   ● = Special Learning Needs   ■ = Heritage Speakers

(227)

¿Qué te gusta hacer?

NATIONAL STANDARDS

Gramática en acción 2

Communication 1.1: Student engages in oral and written exchanges of learned material to socialize and to provide and obtain information.

Communication 1.2: Student demonstrates understanding of simple, clearly spoken, and written language such as simple stories, high-frequency commands, and brief instructions when dealing with familiar topics.

Communication 1.3: Student presents information using familiar words, phrases, and sentences to listeners and readers.

Comparisons 4.1: Student demonstrates an understanding of the nature of language through comparisons of the student's own language and the language studied.

Conexiones culturales

Communication 1.2: Student demonstrates understanding of simple, clearly spoken, and written language such as simple stories, high-frequency commands, and brief instructions when dealing with familiar topics.

Cultures 2.2: Student demonstrates an understanding of the products (what people create) and how they are related to the perspectives (how people perceive things) of the cultures studied.

Connections 3.1: Student uses the language to obtain, reinforce, or expand knowledge of other subject areas.

Comparisons 4.2: Student demonstrates an understanding of the concept of culture through comparisons of the student's own culture and the cultures studied.

CORE INSTRUCTION

Warm-Up

- (5 min.) Ask students to complete the following sentences: **Cuando hace calor, yo… / Cuando hace frío, yo… / Cuando llueve, yo…**

Gramática en acción 2

- (10 min.) Have students do Activity 42, p. 119.
- (30 min.) Review **Gramática 2,** pp. 114–119.

Assessment

- (20 min.) Give **Prueba: Gramática 2.**

Conexiones culturales

- (20 min.) Present **Conexiones culturales,** pp. 120–121, using Teaching **Conexiones culturales,** #s 1–4, p. 120.

Wrap-Up

- (5 min.) Present Practices and Products, p. 120.

OPTIONAL RESOURCES

- (5 min.) See Multiple Intelligences, p. 119. ●
- (5 min.) See **Comunicación** (TE), p. 119.
- (5 min.) See Language Note, p. 121.
- You can find alternative quizzes in the Assessment Options on the next page.

▲ = Advanced Learners ◆ = Slower Pace Learners ● = Special Learning Needs ■ = Heritage Speakers

BLOCK 11 90-MINUTE LESSON PLAN

Practice Options
- *Lab Book*, pp. 19–20 ▲ ● ■
- **Cuaderno de vocabulario y gramática**, pp. 34–36 ▲ ◆ ●
- **Cuaderno de actividades**, pp. 25–27 ▲ ● ■
- *Activities for Communication*, pp. 11–12, 59–60 ▲ ■
- *Teaching Transparencies*: **Vocabulario y gramática** Answers, pp. 34–36 ▲ ● ■
- *Video Guide*, pp. 24–25 ▲ ● ■
- *Grammar Tutor for Students of Spanish*, pp. 19–20, 170–171 ◆ ●
- *Interactive Tutor* (Disc 1) or *DVD Tutor* (Disc 1) ▲ ● ■
- Online practice, Chapter 3 (go.hrw.com, Keyword: EXP1A CH3) ▲ ● ■

Assessment Options
- *Assessment Program:* **Prueba: Gramática 2**, pp. 49–50 ▲ ● ■
- *Assessment Program:* **Prueba: Aplicación 2**, pp. 51–52 ▲ ● ■
- Test Generator ▲ ● ■

▲ = Advanced Learners   ◆ = Slower Pace Learners   ● = Special Learning Needs   ■ = Heritage Speakers

CAPÍTULO
3

¿Qué te gusta hacer?

BLOCK 12 90-MINUTE LESSON PLAN

NATIONAL STANDARDS

Conexiones culturales

Communication 1.1: Student engages in oral and written exchanges of learned material to socialize and to provide and obtain information.

Communication 1.3: Student presents information using familiar words, phrases, and sentences to listeners and readers.

Cultures 2.1: Student demonstrates an understanding of the practices (what people do) and how they are related to the perspectives (how people perceive things) of the cultures studied.

Connections 3.1: Student uses the language to obtain, reinforce, or expand knowledge of other subject areas.

Novela en video

Communication 1.2: Student demonstrates understanding of simple, clearly spoken, and written language such as simple stories, high-frequency commands, and brief instructions when dealing with familiar topics.

Connections 3.2: Student uses resources (that may include technology) in the language and cultures being studied to gain access to information.

Leamos y escribamos

Communication 1.2: Student demonstrates understanding of simple, clearly spoken, and written language such as simple stories, high-frequency commands, and brief instructions when dealing with familiar topics.

Communication 1.3: Student presents information using familiar words, phrases, and sentences to listeners and readers.

Cultures 2.1: Student demonstrates an understanding of the practices (what people do) and how they are related to the perspectives (how people perceive things) of the cultures studied.

Connections 3.2: Student uses resources (that may include technology) in the language and cultures being studied to gain access to information.

Comparisons 4.2: Student demonstrates an understanding of the concept of culture through comparisons of the student's own culture and the cultures studied.

CORE INSTRUCTION

Warm-Up
- (5 min.) Present Language Note, p. 121.

Conexiones culturales
- (10 min.) Present **Conexiones culturales,** pp. 120–212, using Teaching **Conexiones culturales,** #s 5–6, p. 120.

Novela en video
- (40 min.) Present **Novela en video,** pp. 122–125, using Teaching **Novela en video,** p. 122.

Leamos y escribamos
- (25 min.) Present **Leamos,** p. 126, using Teaching **Leamos,** #s 1–3, p. 126.
- (5 min.) Play Audio CD 3, Tr. 8. for **Los cuatro elementos** p. 126. ●

Wrap-Up
- (5 min.) Have volunteers read parts of the story aloud, p. 126.

OPTIONAL RESOURCES
- (35 min.) See Advanced Learners, p. 121. ▲
- (35 min.) See Multiple Intelligences, p. 121. ●
- (15 min.) See Visual Learners, p. 122. ●
- (5 min.) See Gestures, p. 122.
- (5 min.) See Slower Pace Learners, p. 125. ◆
- For students with learning disabilities/ADD, see Special Learning Needs, p. 127. ●

▲ = Advanced Learners ◆ = Slower Pace Learners ● = Special Learning Needs ■ = Heritage Speakers

Holt Spanish 1A

Lesson Planner

BLOCK 12 90-MINUTE LESSON PLAN

Practice Options
- *Lab Book,* p. 47 ▲ ● ■
- *Video Guide,* pp. 24–25, 29 ▲ ● ■
- **Cuaderno de actividades,** p. 28 ▲ ●
- *Student Edition,* **Literatura y variedades,** pp. 232–233 ▲ ● ■
- *Reading Strategies and Skills Handbook,* pp. 67–68, 50–53 ▲ ● ■
- **¡Lee conmigo!** Level 1 Reader ▲ ■
- *Interactive Tutor* (Disc 1) or *DVD Tutor* (Disc 1) ▲ ● ■
- Online practice, Chapter 3 (go.hrw.com, Keyword: EXP1A CH3) ▲ ● ■

Assessment Options
- *Assessment Program:* **Prueba: Lectura,** pp. 53, 59 ▲ ● ■
- *Assessment Program:* **Prueba: Escritura,** pp. 54, 59 ▲ ● ■

▲ = Advanced Learners   ◆ = Slower Pace Learners   ● = Special Learning Needs   ■ = Heritage Speakers

Lesson Planner

(231)

Teacher's Name _____ Class _____ Date _____

¿Qué te gusta hacer?

BLOCK 13 90-MINUTE LESSON PLAN

NATIONAL STANDARDS

Leamos y escribamos
Communication 1.2: Student demonstrates understanding of simple, clearly spoken, and written language such as simple stories, high-frequency commands, and brief instructions when dealing with familiar topics.
Communication 1.3: Student presents information using familiar words, phrases, and sentences to listeners and readers.

Repaso
Communication 1.1: Student engages in oral and written exchanges of learned material to socialize and to provide and obtain information.
Communication 1.2: Student demonstrates understanding of simple, clearly spoken, and written language such as simple stories, high-frequency commands, and brief instructions when dealing with familiar topics.

Communication 1.3: Student presents information using familiar words, phrases, and sentences to listeners and readers.
Cultures 2.1: Student demonstrates an understanding of the practices (what people do) and how they are related to the perspectives (how people perceive things) of the cultures studied.
Comparisons 4.2: Student demonstrates an understanding of the concept of culture through comparisons of the student's own culture and the cultures studied.

CORE INSTRUCTION

Warm-Up
- (5 min.) Have students reread **Leamos,** p. 126.

Leamos y escribamos
- (30 min.) Present **Taller del escritor,** p. 127, using Teaching **Escribamos,** p. 126.

Review
- (20 min.) Have students do Activities 1–5, pp. 128–129.
- (10 min.) Play Audio CD 3, Tr. 10, for Activity 6, p. 129. ●
- (10 min.) Have students do Activity 7, p. 129.
- (10 min.) Play Audio CD 3, Tr. 11–13, for **Letra y sonido,** p. 130. ●

Wrap-Up
- (5 min.) Have students make up sentences that include the following words: **quiero, queremos, voy, vamos, hablo, hablamos.** They should say the sentences aloud to the class.
- Remind students to study for the Chapter Test.

OPTIONAL RESOURCES
- (10 min.)See Computer Science Link, p. 127.
- (10 min.)See Science Link, p. 128.
- (25 min.) See Fold-N-Learn, p. 128. ●
- (5 min.) See Common Error Alert, p. 130.
- (35 min.) See Teacher to Teacher, p. 131.

▲ = Advanced Learners   ◆ = Slower Pace Learners   ● = Special Learning Needs   ■ = Heritage Speakers

Holt Spanish 1A

Lesson Planner

(232)

BLOCK 13 90-MINUTE LESSON PLAN

Practice Options
- *Lab Book*, p. 19–20, 48 ▲ ● ■
- *Activities for Communication*, pp. 45, 59–60 ▲ ■
- *Teaching Transparencies*: Situation; Picture Sequences ▲ ● ■
- *TPR Storytelling Book*, pp. 16–17 ▲ ●
- *Interactive Tutor* (Disc 1) or *DVD Tutor* (Disc 1) ▲ ● ■
- Online practice, Chapter 3 (go.hrw.com, Keyword: EXP1A CH3) ▲ ● ■

▲ = Advanced Learners   ◆ = Slower Pace Learners   ● = Special Learning Needs   ■ = Heritage Speakers

(233)

¿Qué te gusta hacer?

BLOCK 14 90-MINUTE LESSON PLAN

NATIONAL STANDARDS

Integración

Communication 1.1: Student engages in oral and written exchanges of learned material to socialize and to provide and obtain information.

Communication 1.2: Student demonstrates understanding of simple, clearly spoken, and written language such as simple stories, high-frequency commands, and brief instructions when dealing with familiar topics.

Communication 1.3: Student presents information using familiar words, phrases, and sentences to listeners and readers.

CORE INSTRUCTION

Assessment

- (50 min.) Give the Chapter 3 Test.

Integración

- (10 min.) Play Audio CD 3, Tr. 14, for Activity 1, p. 132.●
- (30 min.) Have students do Activities 2–5, pp. 132–133.

OPTIONAL RESOURCES

- You may also choose from the other modes of assessment listed in the Assessment Options box on the next page.

▲ = Advanced Learners ◆ = Slower Pace Learners ● = Special Learning Needs ■ = Heritage Speakers

Teacher's Name _____ Class _____ Date _____

BLOCK 14 90-MINUTE LESSON PLAN

Practice Options
- *Lab Book*, pp. 19–20, 48 ▲ ● ■
- ***Cuaderno de Actividades***, pp. 29–30 ▲ ● ■
- *Activities for Communication*, pp. 45, 59–60 ▲ ■
- *Teaching Transparencies*: Fine Art, Chapter 3 ▲ ● ■
- *Video Guide*, pp. 24–25, 30 ▲ ● ■
- *TPR Storytelling Book*, pp. 16–17 ▲ ●
- *Interactive Tutor* (Disc 1) or *DVD Tutor* (Disc 1) ▲ ● ■
- Online practice, Chapter 3 (go.hrw.com, Keyword: EXP1A CH3) ▲ ● ■

Assessment Options
- *Assessment Program:* **Examen: Capítulo 3,** pp. 129–139 ▲ ● ■
- *Assessment Program:* **Examen oral: Capítulo 3,** p. 140 ▲ ● ■
- *Assessment Program:* Alternative Assessment, pp. 214, 220, 227 ▲ ● ■
- Audio CD 3, Tr. 18–19 ●
- *Assessment Program:* **Examen parcial: Capítulos 1–3,** pp. 141–155 ▲ ● ■
- Audio CD 3, Tr. 20–21 ●
- Test Generator ▲ ● ■

▲ = Advanced Learners ◆ = Slower Pace Learners ● = Special Learning Needs ■ = Heritage Speakers

Holt Spanish 1A

Lesson Planner

La vida escolar

BLOCK 1 90-MINUTE LESSON PLAN

NATIONAL STANDARDS

Chapter Opener

Communication 1.2: Student demonstrates understanding of simple, clearly spoken, and written language such as simple stories, high-frequency commands, and brief instructions when dealing with familiar topics.

Vocabulario en acción 1

Communication 1.2: Student demonstrates understanding of simple, clearly spoken, and written language such as simple stories, high-frequency commands, and brief instructions when dealing with familiar topics.

Cultures 2.1: Student demonstrates an understanding of the practices (what people do) and how they are related to the perspectives (how people perceive things) of the cultures studied.

Before starting **Capítulo 4,** you may wish to teach **Geocultura: Costa Rica,** pp. 134–137. For teaching suggestions, see pp. xv–xvi of this *Lesson Planner*.

CORE INSTRUCTION

Warm-Up
* (5 min.) See Learning and Pacing Tips, p. 139.

Chapter Opener
* (5 min.) Present information from Using the Photo and **Más vocabulario,** p. 138.
* (5 min.) Present **Objetivos,** p. 138.

Vocabulario en acción 1
* (10 min.) Show **ExpresaVisión,** Ch. 4.
* (30 min.) Present **Vocabulario,** pp. 140–141, using Teaching **Vocabulario,** p. 140.
* (10 min.) Present **¡Exprésate!,** p. 141.
* (10 min.) Present **Nota cultural,** p. 142.
* (10 min.) Play Audio CD 4, Tr. 1, for Activity 1, p. 142. ●

Wrap-Up
* (5 min.) Have students do Bell Work 4.1 p. 140.

OPTIONAL RESOURCES
* (5 min.) See **También se puede decir… ,** p. 141.
* (5 min.) See Common Error Alert, p. 141.
* (15 min.) See TPR, p. 141. ●
* (15 min.) See Advanced Learners, p. 141. ▲
* (15 min.) See Multiple Intelligences, p. 141. ●

▲ = Advanced Learners   ◆ = Slower Pace Learners   ● = Special Learning Needs   ■ = Heritage Speakers

236

BLOCK 1 90-MINUTE LESSON PLAN

Practice Options

- *Lab Book*, pp. 4, 21–22, 49, 50 ▲ ● ■
- ***Cuaderno de vocabulario y gramática***, pp. 37–39 ▲ ◆ ●
- *Teaching Transparencies:* Map 4; Bell Work 4.1; **Vocabulario** 4.1, 4.2; Situation;
  Vocabulario y gramática Answers, pp. 37–39 ▲ ● ■
- *Video Guide*, pp. 31–32, 34–35, 36 ▲ ● ■
- *Interactive Tutor* (Disc 1) or *DVD Tutor* (Disc 1) ▲ ● ■
- Online practice, Chapter 4 (go.hrw.com, Keyword: EXP1A CH4) ▲ ● ■

▲ = Advanced Learners   ◆ = Slower Pace Learners   ● = Special Learning Needs   ■ = Heritage Speakers

CAPÍTULO
4

La vida escolar

BLOCK 2 90-MINUTE LESSON PLAN

NATIONAL STANDARDS

Vocabulario en acción 1

Communication 1.1: Student engages in oral and written exchanges of learned material to socialize and to provide and obtain information.

Communication 1.2: Student demonstrates understanding of simple, clearly spoken, and written language such as simple stories, high-frequency commands, and brief instructions when dealing with familiar topics.

Communication 1.3: Student presents information using familiar words, phrases, and sentences to listeners and readers.

Comparisons 4.2: Student demonstrates an understanding of the concept of culture through comparisons of the student's own culture and the cultures studied.

CORE INSTRUCTION

Warm-Up
- (5 min.) Have students do Bell Work 4.2, p. 146.

Vocabulario en acción 1
- (35 min.) Have students do Activities 2–6, pp. 142–143.
- (15 min.) Present **¡Exprésate!,** p. 144, using Teaching **¡Exprésate!,** p. 144.
- (10 min.) Present **Nota cultural**, p. 145.
- (20 min.) Have students do Activities 7–9, pp. 144–145.

Wrap-Up
- (5 min.) Pull object out of a student backpack. As each item is pulled out, students should say the name of the item in Spanish. Then remind the class to study for **Prueba: Vocabulario 1.**

OPTIONAL RESOURCES
- (20 min.) See Fold-N-Learn, p. 142. ●
- (5 min.) See **Más práctica,** p. 142.
- (5 min.) See Language Note, p. 143.
- (5 min.) See Practices and Perspectives, p. 143.
- (15 min.) See **Comunicación** (TE), p. 143.
- (15 min.) See Slower Pace Learners, p.143. ◆
- (20 min.) See Multiple Intelligences, p. 143. ●
- (10 min.) See **Comunicación** (TE), p. 145.
- (25 min.) See Special Learning Needs, p. 145. ●

▲ = Advanced Learners   ◆ = Slower Pace Learners   ● = Special Learning Needs   ■ = Heritage Speakers

(238)

BLOCK 2 90-MINUTE LESSON PLAN

Practice Options

- *Lab Book*, pp. 21–22, 50 ▲ ● ■
- ***Cuaderno de vocabulario y gramática***, pp. 37–39 ▲ ◆ ●
- *Teaching Transparencies:* **Vocabulario** 4.1, 4.2; ***Vocabulario y gramática***
  Answers, pp. 37–39 ▲ ● ■
- *Video Guide*, pp. 34–35, 36 ▲ ● ■
- *Interactive Tutor* (Disc 1) or *DVD Tutor* (Disc 1) ▲ ● ■
- Online practice, Chapter 4 (go.hrw.com, Keyword: EXP1A CH4) ▲ ● ■

▲ = Advanced Learners   ◆ = Slower Pace Learners   ● = Special Learning Needs   ■ = Heritage Speakers

239

CAPÍTULO

4

La vida escolar

BLOCK 3 90-MINUTE LESSON PLAN

NATIONAL STANDARDS

Vocabulario en acción 1

Communication 1.1: Student engages in oral and written exchanges of learned material to socialize and to provide and obtain information.

Communication 1.2: Student demonstrates understanding of simple, clearly spoken, and written language such as simple stories, high-frequency commands, and brief instructions when dealing with familiar topics.

Communication 1.3: Student presents information using familiar words, phrases, and sentences to listeners and readers.

Comparisons 4.2: Student demonstrates an understanding of the concept of culture through comparisons of the student's own culture and the cultures studied.

Gramática en acción 1

Communication 1.2: Student demonstrates understanding of simple, clearly spoken, and written language such as simple stories, high-frequency commands, and brief instructions when dealing with familiar topics.

Comparisons 4.1: Student demonstrates an understanding of the nature of language through comparisons of the student's own language and the language studied.

CORE INSTRUCTION

Warm-Up

- (5 min.) Have students read the paragraph from Activity 8, p. 144, aloud with a partner.

Vocabulario en acción 1

- (10 min.) Have students do Activity 10, p. 145.
- (15 min.) Review **Vocabulario 1,** pp. 140–145.

Assessment

- (20 min.) Give **Prueba: Vocabulario 1.**

Gramática en acción 1

- (20 min.) Present **Gramática:** *Indefinite articles;* **¿cuánto?, mucho,** *and* **poco,** p. 146, using Teaching **Gramática,** #s 2–4, p. 146.
- (15 min.) Have students do Activities 11–12, pp. 146–147.

Wrap-Up

- (5 min.) Present Common Error Alert, p. 147.

OPTIONAL RESOURCES

- (10 min.) See Slower Pace Learners, p. 145. ◆
- (5 min.) See Common Error Alert, p. 147.
- (15 min.) See **Comunicación** (TE), p. 147.
- You can find alternative quizzes in the Assessment Options on the next page.

▲ = Advanced Learners   ◆ = Slower Pace Learners   ● = Special Learning Needs   ■ = Heritage Speakers

(240)

BLOCK 3 90-MINUTE LESSON PLAN

Practice Options

- *Lab Book*, pp. 21–22, 50 ▲ ● ■
- ***Cuaderno de vocabulario y gramática***, pp. 40–42 ▲ ◆ ●
- ***Cuaderno de actividades***, pp. 31–33 ▲ ■
- *Activities for Communication*, pp. 13–14, 61–62 ▲ ■
- *Teaching Transparencies:* **Vocabulario** 4.1, 4.2; *Vocabulario y gramática*
  Answers, pp. 40–42 ▲ ● ■
- *Video Guide*, pp. 34–35 ▲ ● ■
- *TPR Storytelling Book*, pp. 18–19 ▲ ●
- *Grammar Tutor for Students of Spanish*, pp. 21–22, 171–172 ◆ ●
- *Interactive Tutor* (Disc 1) or *DVD Tutor* (Disc 1) ▲ ● ■
- Online practice, Chapter 4 (go.hrw.com, Keyword: EXP1A CH4) ▲ ● ■

Assessment Options

- *Assessment Program:* **Prueba: Vocabulario 1**, pp. 61–62 ▲ ● ■
- Test Generator ▲ ● ■

▲ = Advanced Learners ◆ = Slower Pace Learners ● = Special Learning Needs ■ = Heritage Speakers

(241)

La vida escolar

BLOCK 4 90-MINUTE LESSON PLAN

NATIONAL STANDARDS

Gramática en acción 1

Communication 1.1: Student engages in oral and written exchanges of learned material to socialize and to provide and obtain information.

Communication 1.2: Student demonstrates understanding of simple, clearly spoken, and written language such as simple stories, high-frequency commands, and brief instructions when dealing with familiar topics.

Communication 1.3: Student presents information using familiar words, phrases, and sentences to listeners and readers.

CORE INSTRUCTION

Warm-Up

- (5 min.) Have students do Bell Work 4.3, p. 148.

Gramática en acción 1

- (10 min.) Show **GramaVisión** (*indefinite articles; ¿cuánto?, mucho, poco*), *Video Program* (Videocassette 2) or *DVD Tutor* (Disc 1).
- (10 min.) Have students do Activity 13, p. 147.
- (10 min.) Play Audio CD 4, Tr. 2, for Activity 14, p. 147. ●
- (10 min.) Have students do Activity 15, p. 147.
- (15 min.) Present **Gramática:** *The present tense of* **tener** *and some* **tener** *idioms,* p. 148, using Teaching **Gramática,** p. 148.
- (10 min.) Play Audio CD 4, Tr. 3, for Activity 16, p. 148. ●
- (25 min.) Have students do Activities 17–19, p. 149.

Wrap-Up

- (5 min.) Have students do Bell Work 4.4, p. 150.

OPTIONAL RESOURCES

- (10 min.) See **GramaVisión** (*the present tense of* **tener** *and some tener idioms*), *Video Program* (Videocassette 2) or *DVD Tutor* (Disc 1).
- (10 min.) See Advanced Learners, p. 147.▲
- (15 min.) See Multiple Intelligences, p. 147. ●
- (5 min.) See Language to Language, p. 149.
- (5 min.) See Heritage Speakers, p. 149. ■
- (25 min.) See Advanced Learners, p. 149. ▲
- (10 min.) See Special Learning Needs, p. 149. ●
- (15 min.) See **Comunicación** (TE), p. 149.

▲ = Advanced Learners   ◆ = Slower Pace Learners   ● = Special Learning Needs   ■ = Heritage Speakers

Holt Spanish 1A

Lesson Planner

BLOCK 4 90-MINUTE LESSON PLAN

Practice Options

- *Lab Book*, pp. 21–22 ▲ ● ■
- ***Cuaderno de vocabulario y gramática***, pp. 40–42 ▲ ◆ ●
- ***Cuaderno de actividades***, pp. 31–33 ▲ ● ■
- *Activities for Communication*, pp. 13–14, 61–62 ▲ ■
- *Teaching Transparencies:* Bell Work 4.3, 4.4; ***Vocabulario y gramática*** Answers, pp. 40–42 ▲ ● ■
- *Video Guide*, pp. 34–35 ▲ ● ■
- *TPR Storytelling Book*, pp. 18–19 ▲ ●
- *Grammar Tutor for Students of Spanish*, pp. 21–22, 171–172 ◆ ●
- *Interactive Tutor* (Disc 1) or *DVD Tutor* (Disc 1) ▲ ● ■
- Online practice, Chapter 4 (go.hrw.com, Keyword: EXP1A CH4) ▲ ● ■

▲ = Advanced Learners   ◆ = Slower Pace Learners   ● = Special Learning Needs   ■ = Heritage Speakers

（243）

La vida escolar

NATIONAL STANDARDS

Gramática en acción 1

Communication 1.1: Student engages in oral and written exchanges of learned material to socialize and to provide and obtain information.

Communication 1.2: Student demonstrates under-standing of simple, clearly spoken, and written language such as simple stories, high-frequency commands, and brief instructions when dealing with familiar topics.

Communication 1.3: Student presents information using familiar words, phrases, and sentences to listeners and readers.

Connections 3.2: Student uses resources (that may include technology) in the language and cultures being studied to gain access to information.

CORE INSTRUCTION

Warm-Up

- (5 min.) Ask students to answer the following questions with words and gestures: **¿Tienes hambre? / ¿Tienes sed? / ¿Tienes ganas de descansar? / ¿Tienes un bolígrafo?**

Gramática en acción 1

- (10 min.) Show **GramaVisión** (**venir** *and* **a** + *time*), *Video Program* (Videocassette 2) or *DVD Tutor* (Disc 1).
- (15 min.) Present **Gramática:** *The verb* **venir** *and* **a** + *time*, p. 150, using Teaching **Gramática,** p. 150.
- (10 min.) Play Audio CD 4, Tr. 4, for Activity 20, p. 150. ●
- (30 min.) Have students do Activities 21–23, pp. 150–151.
- (15 min.) Review **Gramática 1,** pp. 146–151.

Wrap-Up

- (5 min.) Have students do Bell Work 4.5, p. 154.
- Then remind the class to study for **Prueba: Gramática 1.**

OPTIONAL RESOURCES

- (10 min.) See Slower Pace Learners, p. 151. ◆
- (5 min.) See Special Learning Needs, p. 151. ●
- (5 min.) See Practices and Perspectives, p. 151.

▲ = Advanced Learners   ◆ = Slower Pace Learners   ● = Special Learning Needs   ■ = Heritage Speakers

BLOCK 5 90-MINUTE LESSON PLAN

Practice Options
- *Lab Book*, pp. 21–22 ▲ ● ■
- ***Cuaderno de vocabulario y gramática***, pp. 40–42 ▲ ◆ ●
- ***Cuaderno de actividades***, pp. 31–33 ▲ ● ■
- *Activities for Communication*, pp. 13–14, 61–62 ▲ ■
- *Teaching Transparencies:* Bell Work 4.5; ***Vocabulario y gramática***
  Answers, pp. 40–42 ▲ ● ■
- *Video Guide*, pp. 34–35 ▲ ● ■
- *TPR Storytelling Book*, pp. 18–19 ▲ ● ■
- *Grammar Tutor for Students of Spanish*, pp. 21–22, 171–172 ◆ ●
- *Interactive Tutor* (Disc 1) or *DVD Tutor* (Disc 1) ▲ ● ■
- Online practice, Chapter 4 (go.hrw.com, Keyword: EXP1A CH4) ▲ ● ■

▲ = Advanced Learners   ◆ = Slower Pace Learners   ● = Special Learning Needs   ■ = Heritage Speakers

〔245〕

La vida escolar

BLOCK 6 90-MINUTE LESSON PLAN

NATIONAL STANDARDS

Gramática en acción 1
Communication 1.1: Student engages in oral and written exchanges of learned material to socialize and to provide and obtain information.
Communication 1.2: Student demonstrates understanding of simple, clearly spoken, and written language such as simple stories, high-frequency commands, and brief instructions when dealing with familiar topics.
Communication 1.3: Student presents information using familiar words, phrases, and sentences to listeners and readers.
Connections 3.2: Student uses resources (that may include technology) in the language and cultures being studied to gain access to information.

Cultura
Communication 1.2: Student demonstrates understanding of simple, clearly spoken, and written language such as simple stories, high-frequency commands, and brief instructions when dealing with familiar topics.
Communities 5.1: Student uses the language both within and beyond the school setting through activities such as participating in cultural events and using technology to communicate.

Vocabulario en acción 2
Communication 1.2: Student demonstrates understanding of simple, clearly spoken, and written language such as simple stories, high-frequency commands, and brief instructions when dealing with familiar topics.

CORE INSTRUCTION

Warm-Up
• (5 min.) Have students do the first part of the activity described in **Comunicación** (TE), p. 151.

Gramática en acción 1
• (10 min.) Review **Gramática 1,** pp. 146–151.

Assessment
• (20 min.) Give **Prueba: Gramática 1.**

Cultura
• (15 min.) Present **Cultura,** pp. 152–153, using Teaching **Cultura,** #s 1–3, p. 152.
• (10 min.) Show **Video Cultura,** Ch. 4
• (5 min.) Present and assign **Comunidad,** p. 153.

Vocabulario en acción 2
• (15 min.) Present **Vocabulario,** pp. 154–155, using Teaching **Vocabulario,** #s 1–2, p. 154.

Wrap-Up
• (10 min.) See Map Activities, p. 152.

OPTIONAL RESOURCES
• (5 min.) See Language Note, p. 153.
• (15 min.) See Special Learning Needs, p. 153. ●
• (15 min.) See Advanced Learners, p. 153. ▲
• (10 min.) See Thinking Critically, p. 153 ▲
• (5 min.) See Common Error Alert, p. 155.
• (5 min.) See Language Note, p. 155.
• You can find alternative quizzes in the Assessment Options on the next page.

▲ = Advanced Learners ◆ = Slower Pace Learners ● = Special Learning Needs ■ = Heritage Speakers

BLOCK 6 90-MINUTE LESSON PLAN

Practice Options
- *Lab Book*, pp. 23–24, 51, 52 ▲ ● ■
- *Cuaderno de actividades*, pp. 34
- *Cuaderno de vocabulario y gramática*, pp. 43–45 ▲ ◆ ●
- *Teaching Transparencies:* **Vocabulario** 4.3, 4.4; *Vocabulario y gramática* Answers, pp. 43–45 ▲ ● ■
- *Video Guide*, pp. 34–35, 37, 38 ▲ ● ■
- *Interactive Tutor* (Disc 1) or *DVD Tutor* (Disc 1) ▲ ● ■
- Online practice, Chapter 4 (go.hrw.com, Keyword: EXP1A CH4) ▲ ● ■

Assessment Options
- *Assessment Program:* **Prueba: Gramática 1,** pp. 63–64 ▲ ● ■
- *Assessment Program:* **Prueba: Aplicación 1,** pp. 65–66 ▲ ● ■
- Audio CD 4, Tr. 19 ●
- Test Generator ▲ ● ■

▲ = Advanced Learners   ◆ = Slower Pace Learners   ● = Special Learning Needs   ■ = Heritage Speakers

CAPÍTULO
4

La vida escolar

BLOCK 7 90-MINUTE LESSON PLAN

NATIONAL STANDARDS

Vocabulario en acción 2
Communication 1.1: Student engages in oral and written exchanges of learned material to socialize and to provide and obtain information.

Communication 1.2: Student demonstrates understanding of simple, clearly spoken, and written language such as simple stories, high-frequency commands, and brief instructions when dealing with familiar topics.

Communication 1.3: Student presents information using familiar words, phrases, and sentences to listeners and readers.

Cultures 2.1: Student demonstrates an understanding of the practices (what people do) and how they are related to the perspectives (how people perceive things) of the cultures studied.

Comparisons 4.2: Student demonstrates an understanding of the concept of culture through comparisons of the student's own culture and the cultures studied.

CORE 1INSTRUCTION

Warm-Up
• (10 min.) Do the first part of Advanced Learners, p. 155 with the class. ▲

Vocabulario en acción 2
• (10 min.) Show **ExpresaVisión,** Ch. 4.
• (10 min.) See Teaching **Vocabulario,** #s 3–4, p. 154.
• (10 min.) Present other expressions from **¡Exprésate!,** p. 155.
• (10 min.) Play Audio CD 4, Tr. 8, for Activity 24, p. 156. ●
• (10 min.) Have students do Activities 25–26, p. 156.
• (10 min.) Present **Nota cultural,** p. 156.
• (15 min.) Have students do Activities 27–28, p. 157.

Wrap-Up
• (5 min.) Have students write out five of the sentences required for Activity 26, p. 156.

OPTIONAL RESOURCES
• (10 min.) See TPR, p. 155. ●
• (10 min.) See Special Learning Needs, p. 155. ●
• (20 min.) See **Comunicación** (TE), p. 156.
• (20 min.) See Game, p. 156.
• (5 min.) See Common Error Alert, p. 157.
• (10 min.) See Comparing and Contrasting, p. 157.
• (10 min.) See **Comunicación** (TE), p. 157.
• (10 min.) See Advanced Learners, p. 157. ▲
• (25 min.) See Multiple Intelligences, p. 157. ●

▲ = Advanced Learners   ◆ = Slower Pace Learners   ● = Special Learning Needs   ■ = Heritage Speakers

BLOCK 7 90-MINUTE LESSON PLAN

Practice Options

- *Lab Book*, pp. 23–24, 52 ▲ ● ■
- ***Cuaderno de vocabulario y gramática***, pp. 43–45 ▲ ◆ ●
- *Teaching Transparencies:* **Vocabulario** 4.3, 4.4; ***Vocabulario y gramática***
  Answers, pp. 43–45 ▲ ● ■
- *Video Guide*, pp. 34–35, 38 ▲ ● ■
- *Interactive Tutor* (Disc 1) or *DVD Tutor* (Disc 1) ▲ ● ■
- Online practice, Chapter 4 (go.hrw.com, Keyword: EXP1A CH4) ▲ ● ■

▲ = Advanced Learners   ◆ = Slower Pace Learners   ● = Special Learning Needs   ■ = Heritage Speakers

La vida escolar

BLOCK 8 90-MINUTE LESSON PLAN

NATIONAL STANDARDS

Vocabulario en acción 2

Communication 1.1: Student engages in oral and written exchanges of learned material to socialize and to provide and obtain information.

Communication 1.2: Student demonstrates understanding of simple, clearly spoken, and written language such as simple stories, high-frequency commands, and brief instructions when dealing with familiar topics.

Communication 1.3: Student presents information using familiar words, phrases, and sentences to listeners and readers.

Comparisons 4.1: Student demonstrates an understanding of the nature of language through comparisons of the student's own language and the language studied.

Gramática en acción 2

Communication 1.2: Student demonstrates understanding of simple, clearly spoken, and written language such as simple stories, high-frequency commands, and brief instructions when dealing with familiar topics.

Communication 1.3: Student presents information using familiar words, phrases, and sentences to listeners and readers.

CORE INSTRUCTION

Warm-Up

• (5 min.) See Language Note, p. 159.

Vocabulario en acción 2

• (10 min.) Present ¡Exprésate!, p. 158, using Teaching ¡Exprésate!, p. 158.

• (10 min.) Play Audio CD 4, Tr. 9, for Activity 29, p. 158. ●

• (25 min.) Have students do Activities 30–33, pp. 158–159.

• (15 min.) Review **Vocabulario 2,** pp. 154–159.

Gramática en acción 2

• (20 min.) Present **Gramática: ir a** with infinitive, p. 160, using Teaching **Gramática,** p. 160.

Wrap-Up

• (5 min.) Have students do Bell Work 4.6, p. 160. Then remind the class to study for **Prueba: Vocabulario 2.**

OPTIONAL RESOURCES

• (10 min.) See **GramaVisión** (**ir a** *with infinitive*), *Video Program* (Videocassette 2) or *DVD Tutor* (Disc 1).

• (5 min.) See Heritage Speakers, p. 159. ■

• (25 min.) See **Comunicación** (TE), p. 159.

• (20 min.) See Advanced Learners, p. 159. ▲

• (60 min.) See Multiple Intelligences, p. 159. ●

▲ = Advanced Learners   ◆ = Slower Pace Learners   ● = Special Learning Needs   ■ = Heritage Speakers

Holt Spanish 1A

Lesson Planner

BLOCK 8 90-MINUTE LESSON PLAN

Practice Options
- *Lab Book*, pp. 23–24, 52 ▲ ● ■
- ***Cuaderno de vocabulario y gramática***, pp. 43–45, 46–48 ▲ ◆ ●
- ***Cuaderno de actividades***, pp. 35–37 ▲ ● ■
- *Activities for Communication*, pp. 15–16, 61–62 ▲ ■
- *Teaching Transparencies:* Bell Work 4.5, 4.6; **Vocabulario** 4.3, 4.4; ***Vocabulario y gramática*** Answers, pp. 43–45, 46–48 ▲ ● ■
- *TPR Storytelling Book*, pp. 20–21 ▲ ●
- *Video Guide*, pp. 34–35, 38 ▲ ● ■
- *Grammar Tutor for Students of Spanish*, pp. 23–24, 171–172 ◆ ●
- *Interactive Tutor* (Disc 1) or *DVD Tutor* (Disc 1) ▲ ● ■
- Online practice, Chapter 4 (go.hrw.com, Keyword: EXP1A CH4) ▲ ● ■

▲ = Advanced Learners   ◆ = Slower Pace Learners   ● = Special Learning Needs   ■ = Heritage Speakers

CAPÍTULO

4

La vida escolar

BLOCK 9 90-MINUTE LESSON PLAN

Vocabulario en acción 2

Communication 1.1: Student engages in oral and written exchanges of learned material to socialize and to provide and obtain information.

Communication 1.2: Student demonstrates understanding of simple, clearly spoken, and written language such as simple stories, high-frequency commands, and brief instructions when dealing with familiar topics.

Communication 1.3: Student presents information using familiar words, phrases, and sentences to listeners and readers.

Gramática en acción 2

Communication 1.1: Student engages in oral and written exchanges of learned material to socialize and to provide and obtain information.

Communication 1.2: Student demonstrates understanding of simple, clearly spoken, and written language such as simple stories, high-frequency commands, and brief instructions when dealing with familiar topics.

Communication 1.3: Student presents information using familiar words, phrases, and sentences to listeners and readers.

CORE INSTRUCTION

Warm-Up

- (5 min.) Ask students the following question: **¿A qué hora sales del colegio hoy?**

Vocabulario en acción 2

- (5 min.) Review **Vocabulario 2,** pp. 154–159.

Assessment

- (20 min.) Give **Prueba: Vocabulario 2.**

Gramática en acción 2

- (5 min.) Review **ir a** *with an infinitive,* p. 160.
- (10 min.) Play Audio CD 4, Tr. 10, for Activity 34, p. 160. ●
- (20 min.) Have students do Activities 35–38, pp. 160–161.
- (20 min.) Present **Gramática: -er** and **-ir** *verbs; tag questions,* p. 162, using Teaching **Gramática,** #s 1–4, p. 162.

Wrap-Up

- (5 min.) Have students do Bell Work 4.7, p. 162.

OPTIONAL RESOURCES

- (5 min.) See Slower Pace Learners, p. 161. ◆
- (10 min.) See Multiple Intelligences, p. 161. ●
- (15 min.) See **Comunicación** (TE), p. 161.
- You can find alternative quizzes in the Assessment Options on the next page.

▲ = Advanced Learners   ◆ = Slower Pace Learners   ● = Special Learning Needs   ■ = Heritage Speakers

Holt Spanish 1A

Lesson Planner

BLOCK 9 90-MINUTE LESSON PLAN

Practice Options

- *Lab Book*, pp. 23–24 ▲ ● ■
- ***Cuaderno de vocabulario y gramática***, pp. 43–45, 46–48 ▲ ◆ ●
- ***Cuaderno de actividades***, pp. 35–37 ▲ ● ■
- *Activities for Communication*, pp. 15–16, 61–62 ▲ ■
- *Teaching Transparencies:* Bell Work 4.7; **Vocabulario** 4.3, 4.4; ***Vocabulario y gramática*** Answers, pp. 43–45, 46–48 ▲ ● ■
- *TPR Storytelling Book*, pp. 20–21 ▲ ●
- *Video Guide*, pp. 34–35 ▲ ● ■
- *Grammar Tutor for Students of Spanish*, pp. 23–26, 171–172 ◆ ●
- *Interactive Tutor* (Disc 1) or *DVD Tutor* (Disc 1) ▲ ● ■
- Online practice, Chapter 4 (go.hrw.com, Keyword: EXP1A CH4) ▲ ● ■

Assessment Options

- *Assessment Program:* **Prueba: Vocabulario 2**, pp. 67–68 ▲ ● ■
- Test Generator ▲ ● ■

▲ = Advanced Learners   ◆ = Slower Pace Learners   ● = Special Learning Needs   ■ = Heritage Speakers

(253)

CAPÍTULO
4

La vida escolar

BLOCK 10 90-MINUTE LESSON PLAN

NATIONAL STANDARDS

Gramática en acción 2

Communication 1.1: Student engages in oral and written exchanges of learned material to socialize and to provide and obtain information.

Communication 1.2: Student demonstrates understanding of simple, clearly spoken, and written language such as simple stories, high-frequency commands, and brief instructions when dealing with familiar topics.

Communication 1.3: Student presents information using familiar words, phrases, and sentences to listeners and readers.

Cultures 2.1: Student demonstrates an understanding of the practices (what people do) and how they are related to the perspectives (how people perceive things) of the cultures studied.

Comparisons 4.2: Student demonstrates an understanding of the concept of culture through comparisons of the student's own culture and the cultures studied.

CORE INSTRUCTION

Warm-Up
- (5 min.) Have students do Bell Work 4.8, p. 164.

Gramática en acción 2
- (10 min.) Show **GramaVisión** (*-er and -ir verbs and tag question*), *Video Program* (Videocassette 2) or *DVD Tutor* (Disc 1).
- (5 min.) Review **-er** and **-ir** verbs and tag questions, p. 162.
- (10 min.) See Teaching **Gramática**, #5, p. 162.
- (20 min.) Have students do Activities 39–42, pp. 162–163.
- (5 min.) Present **Nota cultural,** p. 162.
- (20 min.) Present **Gramática:** *Some* **–er/-ir** *verbs with irregular* **yo** *forms,* p. 164, using Teaching **Gramática,** p. 164.
- (5 min.) Have students do Activity 43, p. 164.

Wrap-Up
- (10 min.) Have students do the activity described in Advanced Learners, p. 163.
- Remind the class to study for **Prueba: Gramática 2.** ▲

OPTIONAL RESOURCES
- (10 min.) See **GramaVisión** (*some* **–er/-ir** *verbs with irregular* **yo** *forms*), *Video Program* (Videocassette 2) or *DVD Tutor* (Disc 1).
- (10 min.) See Special Learning Needs, p. 163. ●
- (10 min.) See Teacher to Teacher, p. 163.
- (15 min.) See **Comunicación** (TE), p. 163.
- (10 min.) See Multiple Intelligences, p. 165. ●

▲ = Advanced Learners   ◆ = Slower Pace Learners   ● = Special Learning Needs   ■ = Heritage Speakers

Holt Spanish 1A

Lesson Planner

BLOCK 10 90-MINUTE LESSON PLAN

Practice Options

- *Lab Book*, pp. 23–24, 52 ▲ ● ■
- ***Cuaderno de vocabulario y gramática***, pp. 46–48 ▲ ◆ ●
- ***Cuaderno de actividades***, pp. 35–37 ▲ ● ■
- *Activities for Communication*, pp. 15–16, 61–62 ▲ ■
- *Teaching Transparencies:* Bell Work 4.8; ***Vocabulario y gramática***
  Answers, pp. 46–48 ▲ ● ■
- *TPR Storytelling Book*, pp. 20–21 ▲ ●
- *Video Guide*, pp. 34–35 ▲ ● ■
- *Grammar Tutor for Students of Spanish*, pp. 23–26, 171–172 ◆ ●
- *Interactive Tutor* (Disc 1) or *DVD Tutor* (Disc 1) ▲ ● ■
- Online practice, Chapter 4 (go.hrw.com, Keyword: EXP1A CH4) ▲ ● ■

▲ = Advanced Learners   ◆ = Slower Pace Learners   ● = Special Learning Needs   ■ = Heritage Speakers

255

CAPÍTULO
4

La vida escolar

BLOCK 11 90-MINUTE LESSON PLAN

NATIONAL STANDARDS

Gramática en acción 2

Communication 1.1: Student engages in oral and written exchanges of learned material to socialize and to provide and obtain information.

Communication 1.2: Student demonstrates understanding of simple, clearly spoken, and written language such as simple stories, high-frequency commands, and brief instructions when dealing with familiar topics.

Communication 1.3: Student presents information using familiar words, phrases, and sentences to listeners and readers.

Cultures 2.1: Student demonstrates an understanding of the practices (what people do) and how they are related to the perspectives (how people perceive things) of the cultures studied.

Comparisons 4.2: Student demonstrates an understanding of the concept of culture through comparisons of the student's own culture and the cultures studied.

Conexiones culturales

Communication 1.1: Student engages in oral and written exchanges of learned material to socialize and to provide and obtain information.

Communication 1.2: Student demonstrates understanding of simple, clearly spoken, and written language such as simple stories, high-frequency commands, and brief instructions when dealing with familiar topics.

Cultures 2.2: Student demonstrates an understanding of the products (what people create) and how they are related to the perspectives (how people perceive things) of the cultures studied.

CORE INSTRUCTION

Warm-Up
- (5 min.) Have students write out the present-tense conjugations of **saber, ver,** and **hacer.**

Gramática en acción 2
- (20 min.) Have students do Activities 44–46, p. 165.
- (10 min.) Review **Gramática 2,** pp. 160–165.

Assessment
- (20 min.) Give **Prueba: Gramática 2.**

Conexiones culturales
- (30 min.) Present **Conexiones culturales,** pp. 166–167, using Teaching **Conexiones culturales,** #s 1–3, p. 166.

Wrap-Up
- (5 min.) Do Step 4 of Teaching Conexiones Culturales with students

OPTIONAL RESOURCES
- (15 min.) See Slower Pace Learners, p. 165. ◆
- (15 min.) See **Comunicación** (TE), p. 165.
- (5 min.) See Advanced Learners, p. 167. ▲
- (20 min.) See Multiple Intelligences, p. 167. ●
- You can find alternative quizzes in the Assessment Options on the next page.

▲ = Advanced Learners ◆ = Slower Pace Learners ● = Special Learning Needs ■ = Heritage Speakers

BLOCK 11 90-MINUTE LESSON PLAN

Practice Options
- *Lab Book*, pp. 23–24 ▲ ● ■
- ***Cuaderno de vocabulario y gramática***, pp. 46–48 ▲ ◆ ●
- ***Cuaderno de actividades***, pp. 35–37 ▲ ● ■
- *Activities for Communication*, pp. 15–16, 61–62 ▲ ■
- *Teaching Transparencies:* ***Vocabulario y gramática*** Answers, pp. 46–48 ▲ ● ■
- *Video Guide*, pp. 34–35 ▲ ● ■
- *Grammar Tutor for Students of Spanish*, pp. 23–26, 171–172 ◆ ●
- *Interactive Tutor* (Disc 1) or *DVD Tutor* (Disc 1) ▲ ● ■
- Online practice, Chapter 4 (go.hrw.com, Keyword: EXP1A CH4) ▲ ● ■

Assessment Options
- *Assessment Program:* **Prueba: Gramática 2**, pp. 69–70 ▲ ● ■
- *Assessment Program:* **Prueba: Aplicación 2**, pp. 71–72 ▲ ● ■
- Audio CD 4, Tr. 19 ●
- Test Generator ▲ ● ■

▲ = Advanced Learners   ◆ = Slower Pace Learners   ● = Special Learning Needs   ■ = Heritage Speakers

CAPÍTULO

4

La vida escolar

BLOCK 12 90-MINUTE LESSON PLAN

NATIONAL STANDARDS

Conexiones culturales

Cultures 2.1: Student demonstrates an understanding of the practices (what people do) and how they are related to the perspectives (how people perceive things) of the cultures studied.

Cultures 2.2: Student demonstrates an understanding of the products (what people create) and how they are related to the perspectives (how people perceive things) of the cultures studied.

Novela en video

Communication 1.2: Student demonstrates understanding of simple, clearly spoken, and written language such as simple stories, high-frequency commands, and brief instructions when dealing with familiar topics.

Connections 3.2: Student uses resources (that may include technology) in the language and cultures being studied to gain access to information.

Leamos y escribamos

Communication 1.1: Student engages in oral and written exchanges of learned material to socialize and to provide and obtain information.

Communication 1.2: Student demonstrates understanding of simple, clearly spoken, and written language such as simple stories, high-frequency commands, and brief instructions when dealing with familiar topics.

CORE INSTRUCTION

Warm-Up
- (10 min.) Have students do the activity described in Math Link, p. 167.

Conexiones culturales
- (15 min.) See Teaching **Conexiones,** #s 5–6, p. 166.

Novela en video
- (45 min.) See Teaching **Novela en video,** #s 1–4, p. 168.

Leamos y escribamos
- (15 min.) See Teaching **Leamos,** #s 1–3, p. 172.

Wrap-Up
- (5 min.) Have students work with a partner to describe the two pictures on p. 172 in Spanish.

OPTIONAL RESOURCES
- (10 min.) See Visual Learners, p. 168. ●
- (5 min.) See Gestures, p. 169.
- (5 min.) See Comparing and Contrasting, p. 169. ▲
- (5 min.) See Thinking Critically, p. 170. ▲
- (15 min.) See **Comunicación** (TE), p. 171.
- (5 min.) See Slower Pace Learners, p. 171. ◆
- (15 min.) See Multiple Intelligences, p. 171. ●
- (15 min.) See Applying the Strategies, p. 172.
- (10 min.) See Special Learning Needs, p. 173. ●

▲ = Advanced Learners ◆ = Slower Pace Learners ● = Special Learning Needs ■ = Heritage Speakers

Holt Spanish 1A

Lesson Planner

BLOCK 12 90-MINUTE LESSON PLAN

Practice Options

- *Lab Book*, p. 53 ▲ ● ■
- **Cuaderno de actividades**, p. 38 ▲ ● ■
- *Student Edition*, **Literatura y variedades,** pp. 234–235 ▲ ● ■
- *Reading Strategies and Skills Handbook*, pp. 69, 34–37 ▲ ● ■
- *¡Lee conmigo!* Level 1 Reader
- *Video Guide*, pp. 34–35, 39 ▲ ● ■
- *Interactive Tutor* (Disc 1) or *DVD Tutor* (Disc 1) ▲ ● ■
- Online practice, Chapter 4 (go.hrw.com, Keyword: EXP1A CH4) ▲ ● ■

▲ = Advanced Learners   ◆ = Slower Pace Learners   ● = Special Learning Needs   ■ = Heritage Speakers

La vida escolar

BLOCK 13 90-MINUTE LESSON PLAN

NATIONAL STANDARDS

Leamos y escribamos

Communication 1.2: Student demonstrates understanding of simple, clearly spoken, and written language such as simple stories, high-frequency commands, and brief instructions when dealing with familiar topics.

Communication 1.3: Student presents information using familiar words, phrases, and sentences to listeners and readers.

Repaso

Communication 1.1: Student engages in oral and written exchanges of learned material to socialize and to provide and obtain information.

Communication 1.2: Student demonstrates understanding of simple, clearly spoken, and written language such as simple stories, high-frequency commands, and brief instructions when dealing with familiar topics.

Communication 1.3: Student presents information using familiar words, phrases, and sentences to listeners and readers.

Comparisons 4.2: Student demonstrates an understanding of the concept of culture through comparisons of the student's own culture and the cultures studied.

CORE INSTRUCTION

Warm Up
- (5 min.) Ask students to describe the three characters in **Pepito, el niño precoz.**

Leamos y escribamos
- (10 min.) See Teaching **Leamos,** #4, p. 172.
- (25 min.) Present **Taller del escritor,** p. 173, using Teaching **Escribamos,** #s 1–4, p. 172.

Review
- (20 min.) Have students do Activities 1–5, p. 174–175.
- (10 min.) Play Audio CD 4, Tr. 13, for Activity 6, p. 175. ●
- C Have students do Activity 7, p. 175.
- (10 min.) Play Audio CD 4, Tr. 14–16, for **Letra y sonido,** p. 176. ●

Wrap-Up
- (5 min.) Present the Fold-N-Learn activity suggestion on p. 174. Suggest that students use the Fold-N-Learn activity as part of their review for the Chapter Test. ●

OPTIONAL RESOURCES
- (20 min.) See Advanced Learners, p. 173. ▲
- (25 min.) See Reteaching, p. 174.
- (5 min.) See Test-Taking Strategy, p. 174.
- (5 min.) See **Más práctica,** p. 174.
- (20 min.) See Game, p. 177. ●

▲ = Advanced Learners   ◆ = Slower Pace Learners   ● = Special Learning Needs   ■ = Heritage Speakers

Teacher's Name _____ Class _____ Date _____

BLOCK 13 90-MINUTE LESSON PLAN

Practice Options
- *Lab Book*, pp. 23–24, 54 ▲ ● ■
- ***Cuaderno de actividades***, p. 38 ▲ ◆ ●
- *Activities for Communication*, pp. 46, 61–62 ▲ ■
- *Student Edition*, **Literatura y Variedades,** pp. 234–235 ▲ ● ■
- *Reading Strategies and Skills Handbook*, pp. xi–xii, 34–37, 69 ▲ ● ■
- ***¡Lee conmigo!*** Level 1 Reader ▲ ■
- *Teaching Transparencies:* Situation; Picture Sequences ▲ ● ■
- *Video Guide*, pp. 34–35, 40 ▲ ● ■
- *TPR Storytelling Book*, **Cuento final** pp. 22–23 ▲ ●
- *Interactive Tutor* (Disc 1) or *DVD Tutor* (Disc 1) ▲ ● ■
- Online practice, Chapter 4 (go.hrw.com, Keyword: EXP1A CH4) ▲ ● ■

Assessment Options
- *Assessment Program:* **Prueba: Lectura,** pp. 73, 79 ▲ ● ■
- *Assessment Program:* **Prueba: Escritura** , pp. 74, 79 ▲ ● ■

▲ = Advanced Learners   ◆ = Slower Pace Learners   ● = Special Learning Needs   ■ = Heritage Speakers

Holt Spanish 1A

Lesson Planner

La vida escolar

BLOCK 14 90-MINUTE LESSON PLAN

NATIONAL STANDARDS

Integración

Communication 1.1: Student engages in oral and written exchanges of learned material to socialize and to provide and obtain information.

Communication 1.2: Student demonstrates understanding of simple, clearly spoken, and written language such as simple stories, high-frequency commands, and brief instructions when dealing with familiar topics.

Communication 1.3: Student presents information using familiar words, phrases, and sentences to listeners and readers.

CORE INSTRUCTION

Assessment

- (50 min.) Give the Chapter 4 Test.

Integración

- (10 min.) Play Audio CD 4, Tr. 17, for Activity 1, p. 178. ●
- (30 min.) Have students do Activities 2–4, pp. 178–179.

OPTIONAL RESOURCES

- You may also choose from the other modes of assessment listed in the Assessment Options box on the next page.

▲ = Advanced Learners ◆ = Slower Pace Learners ● = Special Learning Needs ■ = Heritage Speakers

BLOCK 14 90-MINUTE LESSON PLAN

Practice Options

- *Lab Book*, pp. 23–24, 54 ▲ ● ■
- ***Cuaderno de actividades***, pp. 39–40 ▲ ● ■
- *Teaching Transparencies:* Fine Art ▲ ● ■
- *Video Guide*, pp. 34–35, 40 ▲ ● ■
- *Interactive Tutor* (Disc 1) or *DVD Tutor* (Disc 1) ▲ ● ■
- Online practice, Chapter 4 (go.hrw.com, Keyword: EXP1A CH4) ▲ ● ■

Assessment Options

- *Assessment Program:* **Examen: Capítulo 4,** pp. 157–167 ▲ ● ■
- *Assessment Program:* **Examen oral: Capítulo 4,** p. 168 ▲ ● ■
- Audio CD 4, Tr. 20, 21 ▲ ●
  Assessment Program: Alternative Assessment, pp. 215, 221, 228 ▲ ● ■
- Test Generator ▲ ● ■

▲ = Advanced Learners ◆ = Slower Pace Learners ● = Special Learning Needs ■ = Heritage Speakers

CAPÍTULO

En casa con la familia

BLOCK 1 90-MINUTE LESSON PLAN

NATIONAL STANDARDS

Chapter Opener

Communication 1.2: Student demonstrates understanding of simple, clearly spoken, and written language such as simple stories, high-frequency commands, and brief instructions when dealing with familiar topics.

Vocabulario en acción 1

Communication 1.1: Student engages in oral and written exchanges of learned material to socialize and to provide and obtain information.

Communication 1.2: Student demonstrates understanding of simple, clearly spoken, and written language such as simple stories, high-frequency commands, and brief instructions when dealing with familiar topics.

Comparisons 4.2: Student demonstrates an understanding of the concept of culture through comparisons of the student's own culture and the cultures studied.

Before starting **Capítulo 5,** you may wish to teach **Geocultura: Chile,** pp. 180–183. For teaching suggestions, see pp. xv–xvi of this *Lesson Planner.*

CORE INSTRUCTION

Warm-Up

- (5 min.) See Learning and Pacing Tips, p. 185.

Chapter Opener

- (5 min.) Present information from Using the Photo and **Más vocabulario,** p. 184.
- (5 min.) Present **Objetivos,** p. 184.

Vocabulario en acción 1

- (10 min.) Show **ExpresaVisión,** Ch. 5.
- (20 min.) Present **Vocabulario,** pp. 186–187, using Teaching **Vocabulario,** p. 186.
- (10 min.) Present **¡Exprésate!,** p. 187.
- (10 min.) Present **Nota cultural,** p. 188.
- (10 min.) Play Audio CD 5, Tr. 1, for Activity 1, p. 188. ●
- (10 min.) Have students do Activity 2, p. 188.

Wrap-Up

- (5 min.) Present the Fold-N-Learn activity suggestion, p. 188. ●

OPTIONAL RESOURCES

- (5 min.) See Language to Language, p. 187.
- (5 min.) See **También se puede decir…** , p. 187.
- (20 min.) See Special Learning Needs, p. 187. ●
- (20 min.) See Advanced Learners, p. 187. ▲
- (25 min.) See **Más práctica,** p. 188.
- (15 min.) See Practices and Perspectives, p. 188.
- (5 min.) See Slower Pace Learners, p. 189. ◆

▲ = Advanced Learners ◆ = Slower Pace Learners ● = Special Learning Needs ■ = Heritage Speakers

BLOCK 1 90-MINUTE LESSON PLAN

Practice Options
- *Lab Book*, pp. 25–26, 55, 56 ▲ ● ■
- ***Cuaderno de vocabulario y gramática***, pp. 49–51 ▲ ◆ ●
- *Teaching Transparencies:* Map 3; Bell Work, 5.1; **Vocabulario** 5.1, 5.2; Situation; ***Cuaderno de vocabulario y gramática*** Answers, pp. 49–51▲ ● ■
- *Video Guide*, pp. 41–42, 44–45, 46 ▲ ● ■
- *Interactive Tutor* (Disc 1) or *DVD Tutor* (Disc 1) ▲ ● ■
- Online practice, Chapter 5 (go.hrw.com, Keyword: EXP1A CH5) ▲ ● ■

▲ = Advanced Learners   ◆ = Slower Pace Learners   ● = Special Learning Needs   ■ = Heritage Speakers

Holt Spanish 1A   Lesson Planner

En casa con la familia

BLOCK 2 90-MINUTE LESSON PLAN

NATIONAL STANDARDS

Vocabulario en acción 1

Communication 1.1: Student engages in oral and written exchanges of learned material to socialize and to provide and obtain information.

Communication 1.2: Student demonstrates understanding of simple, clearly spoken, and written language such as simple stories, high-frequency commands, and brief instructions when dealing with familiar topics.

Communication 1.3: Student presents information using familiar words, phrases, and sentences to listeners and readers.

Comparisons 4.1: Student demonstrates an understanding of the nature of language through comparisons of the student's own language and the language studied.

CORE INSTRUCTION

Warm-Up
- (10 min.) Present Language Note, p. 190.

Vocabulario en acción 1
- (5 min.) Have students do Bell Work 5.2, p. 192.
- (15 min.) Review **Vocabulario 1** and **¡Exprésate!**, pp. 186–187.
- (55 min.) Have students do Activities 3–10, pp. 188–191.

Wrap-Up
- (5 min.) Have students tell a partner in Spanish about one of the family members they described for Activity 8, p. 191.
- Remind the class to study for **Prueba: Vocabulario 1.**

OPTIONAL RESOURCES
- (10 min.) See TPR, p. 187. ●
- (20 min.) See **Comunicación** (TE), p. 189.
- (15 min.) See Multiple Intelligences, p. 189. ●
- (10 min.) See Circumlocution, p. 190. ▲ ●
- (10 min.) See Heritage Speakers, p. 190. ■
- (10 min.) See Slower Pace Learners, p. 191. ◆
- (15 min.) See Special Learning Needs, p. 191. ●
- (30 min.) See **Comunicación** (TE), p. 191.

▲ = Advanced Learners ◆ = Slower Pace Learners ● = Special Learning Needs ■ = Heritage Speakers

Holt Spanish 1A

Lesson Planner

BLOCK 2 90-MINUTE LESSON PLAN

Practice Options

- *Lab Book*, pp. 25–26, 56 ▲ ● ■
- ***Cuaderno de vocabulario y gramática***, pp. 49–51 ▲ ◆ ●
- *Teaching Transparencies:* Bell Work, 5.2; **Vocabulario** 5.1, 5.2;
  Cuaderno de vocabulario y gramática Answers, pp. 49–51 ▲ ● ■
- *Video Guide*, pp. 44–45, 46 ▲ ● ■
- *Interactive Tutor* (Disc 1) or *DVD Tutor* (Disc 1) ▲ ● ■
- Online practice, Chapter 5 (go.hrw.com, Keyword: EXP1A CH5) ▲ ● ■

▲ = Advanced Learners   ◆ = Slower Pace Learners   ● = Special Learning Needs   ■ = Heritage Speakers

(267)

En casa con la familia

BLOCK 3 90-MINUTE LESSON PLAN

NATIONAL STANDARDS

Vocabulario en acción 1

Communication 1.1: Student engages in oral and written exchanges of learned material to socialize and to provide and obtain information.

Communication 1.2: Student demonstrates understanding of simple, clearly spoken, and written language such as simple stories, high-frequency commands, and brief instructions when dealing with familiar topics.

Communication 1.3: Student presents information using familiar words, phrases, and sentences to listeners and readers.

Comparisons 4.1: Student demonstrates an understanding of the nature of language through comparisons of the student's own language and the language studied.

Gramática en acción 1

Communication 1.1: Student engages in oral and written exchanges of learned material to socialize and to provide and obtain information.

Communication 1.2: Student demonstrates understanding of simple, clearly spoken, and written language such as simple stories, high-frequency commands, and brief instructions when dealing with familiar topics.

Cultures 2.1: Student demonstrates an understanding of the practices (what people do) and how they are related to the perspectives (how people perceive things) of the cultures studied.

Comparisons 4.2: Student demonstrates an understanding of the concept of culture through comparisons of the student's own culture and the cultures studied.

CORE INSTRUCTION

Warm-Up

- (5 min.) Have students do Activity 10, p. 191, again with a different partner.

Vocabulario en acción 1

- (15 min.) Review **Vocabulario 1,** pp. 186–191.

Assessment

- (20 min.) Give **Prueba: Vocabulario 1.**

Gramática en acción 1

- (15 min.) Present **Gramática:** *Possessive adjectives,* p. 192, using Teaching **Gramática,** p. 192.
- (5 min.) Have students do Activity 11, p. 192.
- (10 min.) Present **Nota cultural,** p. 193.
- (10 min.) Play Audio CD 5, Tr. 2, for Activity 12, p. 193. ●

Wrap-Up

- (5 min.) Have students check Activity 11, p. 192, with a partner.

OPTIONAL RESOURCES

- (10 min.) See **GramaVisión** (*possessive adjectives*), *Video Program* (Videocassette 3) or *DVD Tutor* (Disc 1).
- (5 min.) See Common Error Alert, p. 193.
- (5 min.) See Practices and Perspectives, p. 193.
- (5 min.) See Slower Pace Learners, p. 193. ◆

▲ = Advanced Learners   ◆ = Slower Pace Learners   ● = Special Learning Needs   ■ = Heritage Speakers

BLOCK 3 90-MINUTE LESSON PLAN

Practice Options

- *Lab Book*, pp. 25–26, 56 ▲ ● ■
- ***Cuaderno de vocabulario y gramática***, pp. 49–51, 52–54 ▲ ◆ ●
- ***Cuaderno de actividades***, pp. 41–43 ▲ ●
- *Activities for Communication*, pp. 17–18, 63–64 ▲ ■
- *Teaching Transparencies:* **Vocabulario** 5.1, 5.2; ***Cuaderno de vocabulario y gramática*** Answers, pp. 49–51, 52–54 ▲ ● ■
- *Video Guide*, pp. 44–45, 46 ▲ ● ■
- *TPR Storytelling Book*, pp. 24–25 ▲ ●
- *Interactive Tutor* (Disc 1) or *DVD Tutor* (Disc 1) ▲ ● ■
- Online practice, Chapter 5 (go.hrw.com, Keyword: EXP1A CH5) ▲ ● ■

Assessment Options

- *Assessment Program:* **Prueba: Vocabulario 1**, pp. 81–82 ▲ ● ■
- Test Generator ▲ ● ■

▲ = Advanced Learners   ◆ = Slower Pace Learners   ● = Special Learning Needs   ■ = Heritage Speakers

Holt Spanish 1A   Lesson Planner

CAPÍTULO

5

En casa con la familia

BLOCK 4 90-MINUTE LESSON PLAN

NATIONAL STANDARDS

Gramática en acción 1

Communication 1.1: Student engages in oral and written exchanges of learned material to socialize and to provide and obtain information.

Communication 1.2: Student demonstrates understanding of simple, clearly spoken, and written language such as simple stories, high-frequency commands, and brief instructions when dealing with familiar topics.

Communication 1.3: Student presents information using familiar words, phrases, and sentences to listeners and readers.

Comparisons 4.2: Student demonstrates an understanding of the concept of culture through comparisons of the student's own culture and the cultures studied.

CORE INSTRUCTION

Warm-Up
- (5 min.) See Bell Work 5.3, p. 194.

Gramática en acción 1
- (10 min.) Review possessive adjectives, p. 192.
- (15 min.) Have students do Activities 13–14, p. 193.
- (15 min.) Present **Gramática:** *Stem–changing verbs:* **o→ue,** p. 194, using Teaching **Gramática,** p. 194.
- (10 min.) Present **Nota cultural,** p. 194.
- (30 min.) Have students do Activities 15–17, pp. 194–195.

Wrap-Up
- (5 min.) Assign Family Link, p. 195, as homework.

OPTIONAL RESOURCES
- (10 min.) See **GramaVisión** (*stem–changing verbs:* **o→ue**), *Video Program* (Videocassette 3) or *DVD Tutor* (Disc 1).
- (15 min.) See **Comunicación** (TE), p. 193.
- (20 min.) See Advanced Learners, p. 195. ▲
- (5 min.) See Special Learning Needs, p. 195. ●
- (20 min.) See **Comunicación** (TE), p. 195.

▲ = Advanced Learners   ◆ = Slower Pace Learners   ● = Special Learning Needs   ■ = Heritage Speakers

(270)

CAPÍTULO
5

BLOCK 4 90-MINUTE LESSON PLAN

Practice Options

- *Lab Book*, pp. 25–26 ▲ ● ■
- ***Cuaderno de vocabulario y gramática***, pp. 52–54 ▲ ◆ ●
- *Activities for Communication*, pp. 17–18, 63–64 ▲ ■
- ***Cuaderno de actividades***, pp. 41–43 ■
- *Teaching Transparencies:* Bell Work, 5.3; ***Vocabulario y gramática*** Answers, pp. 52–54 ▲ ● ■
- *Video Guide*, pp. 44–45 ▲ ● ■
- *Grammar Tutor for Students of Spanish*, pp. 27–28, 172–173 ◆ ●
- *Interactive Tutor* (Disc 1) or *DVD Tutor* (Disc 1) ▲ ● ■
- Online practice, Chapter 5 (go.hrw.com, Keyword: EXP1A CH5) ▲ ● ■

▲ = Advanced Learners   ◆ = Slower Pace Learners   ● = Special Learning Needs   ■ = Heritage Speakers

(271)

En casa con la familia

BLOCK 5 90-MINUTE LESSON PLAN

NATIONAL STANDARDS

Gramática en acción 1

Communication 1.1: Student engages in oral and written exchanges of learned material to socialize and to provide and obtain information.

Communication 1.2: Student demonstrates understanding of simple, clearly spoken, and written language such as simple stories, high-frequency commands, and brief instructions when dealing with familiar topics.

Communication 1.3: Student presents information using familiar words, phrases, and sentences to listeners and readers.

CORE INSTRUCTION

Warm Up

- (5 min.) Present Common Error Alert, p. 197.

Gramática en acción 1

- (5 min.) Have students do Bell Work 5.4, p. 196.
- (10 min.) Show **GramaVisión** (*stem–changing verbs:* **e→ie**), *Video Program* (Videocassette 3) or *DVD Tutor* (Disc 1).
- (15 min.) Present **Gramática:** *Stem–changing verbs:* **e→ie,** using Teaching **Gramática,** p. 196.
- (35 min.) Have students do Activities 18–20, pp. 196–197.
- (15 min.) Review **Gramática 1,** pp. 192–197.

Wrap-Up

- (5 min.) Review the present-tense conjugation of **merendar.** Remind students to study for **Prueba: Gramática 1.**

OPTIONAL RESOURCES

- (5 min.) See Slower Pace Learners, p. 197. ◆
- (10 min.) See Multiple Intelligences, p. 197. ●
- (25 min.) See **Comunicación** (TE), p. 197.

▲ = Advanced Learners   ◆ = Slower Pace Learners   ● = Special Learning Needs   ■ = Heritage Speakers

BLOCK 5 90-MINUTE LESSON PLAN

Practice Options

- *Lab Book*, pp. 25–26 ▲ ● ■
- ***Cuaderno de vocabulario y gramática***, pp. 52–54 ▲ ◆ ●
- ***Cuaderno de actividades***, pp. 41–43
- *Activities for Communication*, pp. 17–18, 63–64 ▲ ■
- *Teaching Transparencies:* Bell Work, 5.4; ***Vocabulario y gramática***
  Answers, pp. 52–54 ▲ ● ■
- *Grammar Tutor for Students of Spanish*, pp. 27–28, 172–173 ◆ ●
- *Video Guide*, pp. 44–45 ▲ ● ■
- *Interactive Tutor* (Disc 1) or *DVD Tutor* (Disc 1) ▲ ● ■
- Online practice, Chapter 5 (go.hrw.com, Keyword: EXP1A CH5) ▲ ● ■

▲ = Advanced Learners   ◆ = Slower Pace Learners   ● = Special Learning Needs   ■ = Heritage Speakers

CAPÍTULO

5

En casa con la familia

BLOCK 6 90-MINUTE LESSON PLAN

NATIONAL STANDARDS

Gramática en acción

Communication 1.1: Student engages in oral and written exchanges of learned material to socialize and to provide and obtain information.

Communication 1.2: Student demonstrates understanding of simple, clearly spoken, and written language such as simple stories, high-frequency commands, and brief instructions when dealing with familiar topics.

Cultura

Communication 1.2: Student demonstrates understanding of simple, clearly spoken, and written language such as simple stories, high-frequency commands, and brief instructions when dealing with familiar topics.

Cultures 2.1: Student demonstrates an understanding of the practices (what people do) and how they are related to the perspectives (how people perceive things) of the cultures studied.

Connections 3.2: Student uses resources (that may include technology) in the language and cultures being studied to gain access to information.

Connections 3.1: Student uses the language to obtain, reinforce, or expand knowledge of other subject areas.

Comparisons 4.2: Student demonstrates an understanding of the concept of culture through comparisons of the student's own culture and the cultures studied.

Vocabulario en acción 2

Communication 1.2: Student demonstrates understanding of simple, clearly spoken, and written language such as simple stories, high-frequency commands, and brief instructions when dealing with familiar topics.

CORE INSTRUCTION

Warm-Up
- (5 min.) Ask students **¿A qué hora empieza la clase de español?** and **¿A qué hora empiezas a hacer tu tarea?**

Gramática en acción 1
- (5 min.) Review **Gramática 1,** pp. 192–197.

Assessment
- (20 min.) Give **Prueba: Gramática 1.**

Cultura
- (25 min.) Present **Cultura,** pp. 198–199, using Teaching **Cultura,** p. 198.
- (5 min.) Discuss and assign **Comunidad,** p. 199.

Vocabulario en acción 2
- (25 min.) Present **Vocabulario,** pp. 200–201, using Teaching **Vocabulario,** p. 200.

Wrap-Up
- (5 min.) See Map Activities, p. 198.

OPTIONAL RESOURCES
- (5 min.) See Interdisciplinary Link, p. 199.
- (15 min.) See Advanced Learners, p. 199. ▲
- (5 min.) See Multiple Intelligences, p. 199. ●
- You can find alternative quizzes in the Assessment Options on the next page.

▲ = Advanced Learners   ◆ = Slower Pace Learners   ● = Special Learning Needs   ■ = Heritage Speakers

BLOCK 6 90-MINUTE LESSON PLAN

Practice Options
- *Lab Book*, p. 57 ▲ ● ■
- ***Cuaderno de actividades***, p. 44 ▲ ● ■
- ***Cuaderno de vocabulario y gramática***, pp. 55–57 ▲ ◆ ●
- ***Cuaderno para hispanohablantes***, pp. 55–56 ■
- *Video Guide*, pp. 44–45, 47 ▲ ● ■
- *Teaching Transparencies:* **Vocabulario** 5.3; ***Cuaderno de Vocabulario y gramática*** pp. 55–57 ▲ ● ■
- *Interactive Tutor* (Disc 1) or *DVD Tutor* (Disc 1) ▲ ● ■
- Online practice, Chapter 5 (go.hrw.com, Keyword: EXP1A CH5) ▲ ● ■

Assessment Options
- *Assessment Program*: **Prueba: Gramática 1**, pp. 83–84 ▲ ● ■
- *Assessment Program*: **Prueba: Aplicación 1**, pp. 85–86 ▲ ● ■
- Audio CD 5, Tr. 15 ▲ ●
- Test Generator ▲ ● ■

▲ = Advanced Learners   ◆ = Slower Pace Learners   ● = Special Learning Needs   ■ = Heritage Speakers

En casa con la familia

NATIONAL STANDARDS

Vocabulario en acción 2

Communication 1.1: Student engages in oral and written exchanges of learned material to socialize and to provide and obtain information.

Communication 1.2: Student demonstrates understanding of simple, clearly spoken, and written language such as simple stories, high-frequency commands, and brief instructions when dealing with familiar topics.

Communication 1.3: Student presents information using familiar words, phrases, and sentences to listeners and readers.

CORE INSTRUCTION

Warm-Up

- (5 min.) Present **También se puede decir...**, p. 201.

Vocabulario en acción 2

- (10 min.) Show **ExpresaVisión,** Ch. 5.
- (5 min.) Review **Vocabulario 2,** pp. 200–205.
- (10 min.) Present **¡Exprésate!** expressions, p. 201.
- (15 min.) Have students do Activities 21–22, p. 202.
- (10 min.) Present **Más vocabulario,** p. 202.
- (15 min.) Have students do Activity 23, p. 203.
- (15 min.) Present **¡Exprésate!,** p. 204, using Teaching **¡Exprésate!,** p. 204.

Wrap-Up

- (5 min.) Ask students to tell a partner in Spanish whether they like or dislike the chores listed in **Más vocabulario,** p. 202.

OPTIONAL RESOURCES

- (25 min.) See TPR, p. 201. ●
- (10 min.) See Slower Pace Learners, p. 201. ◆
- (15 min.) See Comparisons, p. 202.
- (25 min.) See Game, p. 202. ●
- (15 min.) See Slower Pace Learners, p. 203. ◆
- (5 min.) See Practices and Perspectives, p. 203.
- (10 min.) See **Comunicación** (TE), p. 203.
- (30 min.) See Multiple Intelligences, p. 203. ●

▲ = Advanced Learners   ◆ = Slower Pace Learners   ● = Special Learning Needs   ■ = Heritage Speakers

BLOCK 7 90-MINUTE LESSON PLAN

Practice Options
- *Lab Book*, pp. 27–28, 58 ▲ ● ■
- **Cuaderno de vocabulario y gramática**, pp. 55–57 ▲ ◆ ●
- *Teaching Transparencies:* **Vocabulario** 5.3, 5.4; **Vocabulario y gramática**
  Answers, pp. 55–57 ▲ ● ■
- *Video Guide*, pp. 44–45, 48 ▲ ● ■
- *Interactive Tutor* (Disc 1) or *DVD Tutor* (Disc 1) ▲ ● ■
- Online practice, Chapter 5 (go.hrw.com, Keyword: EXP1A CH5) ▲ ● ■

▲ = Advanced Learners   ◆ = Slower Pace Learners   ● = Special Learning Needs   ■ = Heritage Speakers

277

CAPÍTULO

5

En casa con la familia

BLOCK 8 90-MINUTE LESSON PLAN

NATIONAL STANDARDS

Vocabulario en acción 2

Communication 1.1: Student engages in oral and written exchanges of learned material to socialize and to provide and obtain information.

Communication 1.2: Student demonstrates understanding of simple, clearly spoken, and written language such as simple stories, high-frequency commands, and brief instructions when dealing with familiar topics.

Communication 1.3: Student presents information using familiar words, phrases, and sentences to listeners and readers.

Gramática en acción 2

Communication 1.2: Student demonstrates understanding of simple, clearly spoken, and written language such as simple stories, high-frequency commands, and brief instructions when dealing with familiar topics.

Cultures 2.2: Student demonstrates an understanding of the products (what people create) and how they are related to the perspectives (how people perceive things) of the cultures studied.

Comparisons 4.2: Student demonstrates an understanding of the concept of culture through comparisons of the student's own culture and the cultures studied.

CORE INSTRUCTION

Warm-Up

- (5 min.) Present Practices and Perspectives, p. 205.

Vocabulario en acción 2

- (10 min.) Review **Más vocabulario** and **¡Exprésate!,** pp. 202, 204.
- (10 min.) Play Audio CD 5, Tr. 6, for Activity 24, p. 204. ●
- (35 min.) Have students do Activities 25–28, p. 204–205.

Gramática en acción 2

- (15 min.) Present **Gramática: Estar** with prepositions, p. 206, using Teaching **Gramática,** p. 206.
- (10 min.) Present **Nota cultural,** p. 206.

Wrap-Up

- (5 min.) Have students do the activity described in **Más práctica,** p. 207.
- Remind the class to study for **Prueba: Vocabulario 2.**

OPTIONAL RESOURCES

- (15 min.) See **Comunicación** (TE), p. 205.
- (10 min.) See Advanced Learners, p. 205. ▲
- (25 min.) See Multiple Intelligences, p. 205. ●

▲ = Advanced Learners   ◆ = Slower Pace Learners   ● = Special Learning Needs   ■ = Heritage Speakers

BLOCK 8 90-MINUTE LESSON PLAN

Practice Options

- *Lab Book*, pp. 27–28, 58 ▲ ● ■
- ***Cuaderno de vocabulario y gramática***, pp. 55–57, 58–60 ▲ ◆ ●
- *Activities for Communication*, pp. 19–20, 63–64 ▲ ■
- *Teaching Transparencies:* Bell Work, 5.6; **Vocabulario** 5.3, 5.4; ***Vocabulario y gramática*** Answers, pp. 55–57, 58–60 ▲ ● ■
- *Video Guide*, pp. 44–45, 48 ▲ ● ■
- *TPR Storytelling Book*, pp. 26–27 ▲ ●
- *Interactive Tutor* (Disc 1) or *DVD Tutor* (Disc 1) ▲ ● ■
- Online practice, Chapter 5 (go.hrw.com, Keyword: EXP1A CH5) ▲ ● ■

▲ = Advanced Learners   ◆ = Slower Pace Learners   ● = Special Learning Needs   ■ = Heritage Speakers

Holt Spanish 1A

Lesson Planner

CAPÍTULO
5

En casa con la familia

NATIONAL STANDARDS

Vocabulario en acción 2

Communication 1.1: Student engages in oral and written exchanges of learned material to socialize and to provide and obtain information.

Communication 1.2: Student demonstrates understanding of simple, clearly spoken, and written language such as simple stories, high-frequency commands, and brief instructions when dealing with familiar topics.

Communication 1.3: Student presents information using familiar words, phrases, and sentences to listeners and readers.

Gramática en acción 2

Communication 1.1: Student engages in oral and written exchanges of learned material to socialize and to provide and obtain information.

Communication 1.2: Student demonstrates understanding of simple, clearly spoken, and written language such as simple stories, high-frequency commands, and brief instructions when dealing with familiar topics.

Communication 1.3: Student presents information using familiar words, phrases, and sentences to listeners and readers.

CORE INSTRUCTION

Warm-Up

- (5 min.) Ask students the following questions: **¿Qué te parece tener que ayudar en casa? / ¿Qué te toca hacer a tí para ayudar en casa?**

Vocabulario en acción 2

- (5 min.) Review **Vocabulario 2,** pp. 200–205.

Assessment

- (20 min.) Give **Prueba: Vocabulario 2.**

Gramática en acción 2

- (5 min.) Review **estar** with prepositions, p. 206.
- (25 min.) Have students do Activities 29–32, pp. 206–207.
- (25 min.) Present **Gramática:** *Negation with* **nunca, tampoco, nadie,** *and* **nada**, p. 208, using Teaching **Gramática,** p. 208.

Wrap-Up

- (5 min.) Have students do Bell Work 5.7, p. 208.

OPTIONAL RESOURCES

- (10 min.) See **GramaVisión** (**estar** *with prepositions*), *Video Program* (Videocassette 3) or *DVD Tutor* (Disc 1).
- (20 min.) See **Comunicación** (TE), p. 207.
- (5 min.) See Slower Pace Learners, p. 207. ◆
- (5 min.) See Special Learning Needs, p. 207. ●
- You can find alternative quizzes in the Assessment Options on the next page.

▲ = Advanced Learners   ◆ = Slower Pace Learners   ● = Special Learning Needs   ■ = Heritage Speakers

BLOCK 9 90-MINUTE LESSON PLAN

Practice Options
- *Lab Book*, pp. 27–28, 58 ▲ ● ■
- ***Cuaderno de vocabulario y gramática***, pp. 58–60 ▲ ◆ ●
- ***Cuaderno de actividades***, pp. 45–47
- *Activities for Communication*, pp. 19–20, 63–64 ▲ ■
- *Teaching Transparencies:* ***Vocabulario y gramática*** Answers, pp. 58–60 ▲ ● ■
- *Video Guide*, pp. 44–45 ▲ ● ■
- *Grammar Tutor for Students of Spanish*, pp. 29–32, 172–173 ◆ ●
- *Interactive Tutor* (Disc 1) or *DVD Tutor* (Disc 1) ▲ ● ■
- Online practice, Chapter 5 (go.hrw.com, Keyword: EXP1A CH5) ▲ ● ■

Assessment Options
- *Assessment Program:* **Prueba: Vocabulario 2**, pp. 87–88 ▲ ● ■
- Test Generator ▲ ● ■

▲ = Advanced Learners   ◆ = Slower Pace Learners   ● = Special Learning Needs   ■ = Heritage Speakers

281

CAPÍTULO
5

En casa con la familia

NATIONAL STANDARDS

Gramática en acción 2

Communication 1.1: Student engages in oral and written exchanges of learned material to socialize and to provide and obtain information.

Communication 1.2: Student demonstrates understanding of simple, clearly spoken, and written language such as simple stories, high-frequency commands, and brief instructions when dealing with familiar topics.

Communication 1.3: Student presents information using familiar words, phrases, and sentences to listeners and readers.

CORE INSTRUCTION

Warm-Up

- (5 min.) Have students do Bell Work 5.8, p. 210.

Gramática en acción 2

- (10 min.) Show **GramaVisión** (*negation with* **nunca, tampoco, nadie,** *and* **nada**), *Video Program* (Videocassette 2) or *DVD Tutor* (Disc 1).
- (5 min.) Review negation with **nunca, tampoco, nadie,** and **nada.**
- (10 min.) Play Audio CD 5, Tr. 7, for Activity 33, p. 208.
- (15 min.) Have students to Activities 34–36, p. 209.
- (15 min.) Present **Gramática: tocar** and **parecer,** p. 210, using Teaching **Gramática,** p. 210.
- (10 min.) Play Audio CD 5, Tr. 8, for Activity 37, p. 210. ●
- (10 min.) Have students do Activity 38, p. 211.

Wrap-Up

- (10 min.) Have students do the activity described in **Más práctica,** p. 209.
- Remind the class to study for **Prueba: Gramática 2.**

OPTIONAL RESOURCES

- (10 min.) See **GramaVisión** (**tocar** *and* **parecer**), *Video Program* (Videocassette 3) or *DVD Tutor* (Disc 1).
- (15 min.) See **Comunicación** (TE), p. 211.
- (5 min.) See Special Learning Needs, p. 211. ●
- (25 min.) See Special Learning Needs, p. 213. ●

▲ = Advanced Learners   ◆ = Slower Pace Learners   ● = Special Learning Needs   ■ = Heritage Speakers

BLOCK 10 90-MINUTE LESSON PLAN

Practice Options

- *Lab Book*, pp. 27–28 ▲ ● ■
- ***Cuaderno de vocabulario y gramática***, pp. 58–60 ▲ ◆ ●
- ***Cuaderno de actividades***, pp. 44–47 ▲ ●
- *Activities for Communication*, pp. 19–20, 63–64 ▲ ■
- *Teaching Transparencies:* Bell Work, 5.8; ***Vocabulario y gramática*** Answers, pp. 58–60 ▲ ● ■
- *Video Guide*, pp. 44–45 ▲ ● ■
- *Grammar Tutor for Students of Spanish*, pp. 29–32, 172–173 ◆ ●
- *Interactive Tutor* (Disc 1) or *DVD Tutor* (Disc 1) ▲ ● ■
- Online practice, Chapter 5 (go.hrw.com, Keyword: EXP1A CH5) ▲ ● ■

▲ = Advanced Learners   ◆ = Slower Pace Learners   ● = Special Learning Needs   ■ = Heritage Speakers

(283)

En casa con la familia

BLOCK 11 90-MINUTE LESSON PLAN

Gramática en acción 2

Communication 1.1: Student engages in oral and written exchanges of learned material to socialize and to provide and obtain information.

Communication 1.2: Student demonstrates understanding of simple, clearly spoken, and written language such as simple stories, high-frequency commands, and brief instructions when dealing with familiar topics.

Communication 1.3: Student presents information using familiar words, phrases, and sentences to listeners and readers.

Cultures 2.2: Student demonstrates an understanding of the products (what people create) and how they are related to the perspectives (how people perceive things) of the cultures studied.

Comparisons 4.2: Student demonstrates an understanding of the concept of culture through comparisons of the student's own culture and the cultures studied.

Conexiones Culturales

Communication 1.3: Student presents information using familiar words, phrases, and sentences to listeners and readers.

Cultures 2.2: Student demonstrates an understanding of the products (what people create) and how they are related to the perspectives (how people perceive things) of the cultures studied.

Comparisons 4.2: Student demonstrates an understanding of the concept of culture through comparisons of the student's own culture and the cultures studied.

CORE INSTRUCTION

Warm-Up
- (5 min.) Review the answers for Activity 38, p. 211.

Gramática en acción 2
- (15 min.) Have students do Activities 39–40, p. 211.
- (15 min.) Review **Gramática 2,** pp. 206–211.

Assessment
- (20 min.) Give **Prueba: Gramática 2.**

Conexiones culturales
- (30 min.) Present **Conexiones culturales,** p. 212, using Teaching **Conexiones culturales,** #s 1–6, p. 212.

Wrap-Up
- (5 min.) Assign **Más práctica,** p. 212, as homework.

OPTIONAL RESOURCES
- (5 min.) See Special Learning Needs, p. 211. ●
- (20 min.) See **Comunicación** (TE), p. 213.
- You can find alternative quizzes in the Assessment Options on the next page.

▲ = Advanced Learners ◆ = Slower Pace Learners ● = Special Learning Needs ■ = Heritage Speakers

BLOCK 11 90-MINUTE LESSON PLAN

Practice Options
- Online practice, Chapter 5 (go.hrw.com, Keyword: EXP1A CH5) ▲ ● ■

Assessment Options
- *Assessment Program:* **Prueba: Gramática 2,** pp. 89–90 ▲ ● ■
- *Assessment Program:* **Prueba: Aplicación 2,** pp. 91–92 ▲ ● ■
- Audio CD 5, Tr. 16 ▲ ●
- Test Generator ▲ ● ■

▲ = Advanced Learners ◆ = Slower Pace Learners ● = Special Learning Needs ■ = Heritage Speakers

CAPÍTULO

5

En casa con la familia

BLOCK 12 90-MINUTE LESSON PLAN

NATIONAL STANDARDS

Conexiones culturales

Cultures 2.1: Student demonstrates an understanding of the practices (what people do) and how they are related to the perspectives (how people perceive things) of the cultures studied.

Cultures 2.2: Student demonstrates an understanding of the products (what people create) and how they are related to the perspectives (how people perceive things) of the cultures studied.

Comparisons 4.1: Student demonstrates an understanding of the nature of language through comparisons of the student's own language and the language studied.

Comparisons 4.2: Student demonstrates an understanding of the concept of culture through comparisons of the student's own culture and the cultures studied.

Novela en video

Communication 1.2: Student demonstrates understanding of simple, clearly spoken, and written language such as simple stories, high-frequency commands, and brief instructions when dealing with familiar topics.

Connections 3.2: Student uses resources (that may include technology) in the language and cultures being studied to gain access to information.

Leamos y escribamos

Communication 1.2: Student demonstrates understanding of simple, clearly spoken, and written language such as simple stories, high-frequency commands, and brief instructions when dealing with familiar topics.

Communication 1.3: Student presents information using familiar words, phrases, and sentences to listeners and readers.

Connections 3.2: Student uses resources (that may include technology) in the language and cultures being studied to gain access to information.

CORE INSTRUCTION

Warm-Up
- (5 min.) Present Practices and Perspectives: Names, p. 213.

Conexiones culturales
- (15 min.) Present **Conexiones culturales,** p. 213, using Teaching **Conexiones culturales,** #s 7–8, p. 212.

Novela en video
- (30 min.) Present **Novela en video,** pp. 214–215. See Teaching **Novela en video,** #1, p. 214.

Leamos y escribamos
- (30 min.) Begin presenting **Leamos,** using Teaching **Leamos,** p. 214.

Wrap-Up
- (10 min.) Have students do the activity described in Connections, p. 214.

OPTIONAL RESOURCES
- (15 min.) See Variation, p. 213.
- (15 min.) See Advanced Learners, p. 213. ▲
- (5 min.) See Gestures, p. 216.
- (5 min.) See Career Path, p. 216.
- (20 min.) See **Comunicación** (TE), p. 217.
- (35 min.) See Advanced Learners, p. 217. ▲
- (20 min.) See Multiple Intelligences, p. 217. ●
- (20 min.) See Advanced Learners, p. 219. ▲
- (5 min.) See Special Learning Needs, p. 219. ●

▲ = Advanced Learners ◆ = Slower Pace Learners ● = Special Learning Needs ■ = Heritage Speakers

BLOCK 12 90-MINUTE LESSON PLAN

Practice Options
- *Lab Book*, p. 59 ▲ ● ■
- ***Cuaderno de actividades***, p. 48 ▲ ●
- *Student Edition*, **Literatura y variedades,** pp. 236–237 ▲ ● ■
- *Reading Strategies and Skills Handbook,* pp. 70, 2–5 ▲ ● ■
- *¡Lee conmigo!* Level 1 Reader
- *Video Guide*, pp. 44–45, 49 ▲ ● ■
- *Interactive Tutor* (Disc 1) or *DVD Tutor* (Disc 1) ▲ ● ■
- Online practice, Chapter 5 (go.hrw.com, Keyword: EXP1A CH5) ▲ ● ■

▲ = Advanced Learners ◆ = Slower Pace Learners ● = Special Learning Needs ■ = Heritage Speakers

(287)

CAPÍTULO
5

En casa con la familia

BLOCK 13 90-MINUTE LESSON PLAN

NATIONAL STANDARDS

Leamos y escribamos

Communication 1.2: Student demonstrates understanding of simple, clearly spoken, and written language such as simple stories, high-frequency commands, and brief instructions when dealing with familiar topics.

Communication 1.3: Student presents information using familiar words, phrases, and sentences to listeners and readers.

Repaso

Communication 1.2: Student demonstrates understanding of simple, clearly spoken, and written language such as simple stories, high-frequency commands, and brief instructions when dealing with familiar topics.

Communication 1.3: Student presents information using familiar words, phrases, and sentences to listeners and readers.

Cultures 2.1: Student demonstrates an understanding of the practices (what people do) and how they are related to the perspectives (how people perceive things) of the cultures studied.

Cultures 2.2: Student demonstrates an understanding of the products (what people create) and how they are related to the perspectives (how people perceive things) of the cultures studied.

CORE INSTRUCTION

Warm-Up

- (10 min.) Ask students to work with a partner to write a new listing for a house to appear in the **Casas y apartamentos** catalog, p. 218.

Leamos y escribamos

- (20 min.) Present **Taller del escritor,** p. 219, using Teaching **Escribamos,** p. 218.

Review

- (25 min.) Have students do Activities 1–5, p. 220–221.
- (10 min.) Play Audio CD 5, Tr. 11, for Activity 6, p. 221.
- (10 min.) Have students do Activity 7, p. 221.
- (10 min.) Play Audio CD 5, Tr. 12, 13, 14, for **Letra y sonido,** p. 222. ●

Wrap-Up

- (5 min.) Present the Fold-N-Learn activity suggestion on p. 220. Suggest that students use the activity as part of their review for the Chapter Test. ●

OPTIONAL RESOURCES

- (25 min.) See Process Writing, p. 219.
- (35 min.) See Teacher to Teacher, p. 220.
- (10 min.) See AP Language Examination, p. 221.
- (20 min.) See Reteaching, p. 222.
- (15 min.) See Game, p. 223.

▲ = Advanced Learners ◆ = Slower Pace Learners ● = Special Learning Needs ■ = Heritage Speakers

Holt Spanish 1A   Lesson Planner

BLOCK 13 90-MINUTE LESSON PLAN

Practice Options

- *Cuaderno de actividades*, p. 48 ▲ ■
- *Student Edition*, **Literatura y variedades,** pp. 236–237 ▲ ● ■
- *Reading Strategies and Skills Handbook,* pp. 70, 2–5 ▲ ● ■
- *¡Lee conmigo!* Level 1 Reader ▲ ■
- *Lab Book*, pp. 27–28, 60 ▲ ● ■
- *Activities for Communication*, pp. 47, 63–64 ▲ ■
- *Teaching Transparencies:* Situation; Picture Sequences ▲ ● ■
- *Video Guide*, pp. 44–45, 50 ▲ ● ■
- *Interactive Tutor* (Disc 1) or *DVD Tutor* (Disc 1) ▲ ● ■
- Online practice, Chapter 5 (go.hrw.com, Keyword: EXP1A CH5) ▲ ● ■

▲ = Advanced Learners   ◆ = Slower Pace Learners   ● = Special Learning Needs   ■ = Heritage Speakers

Holt Spanish 1A

Lesson Planner

CAPÍTULO
5

En casa con la familia

BLOCK 14 90-MINUTE LESSON PLAN

NATIONAL STANDARDS

Integración

Communication 1.2: Student demonstrates understanding of simple, clearly spoken, and written language such as simple stories, high-frequency commands, and brief instructions when dealing with familiar topics.

Communication 1.3: Student presents information using familiar words, phrases, and sentences to listeners and readers.

CORE INSTRUCTION

Assessment

- (50 min.) Give the Chapter 5 Test.

Integración

- (10 min.) Play Audio CD 5, Tr. 15, for Activity 1, p. 224. ●
- (30 min.) Have students do Activities 2–4, pp. 224–225.

OPTIONAL RESOURCES

- (25 min.) See Culture Project, p. 224.
- (35 min.) See Fine Art Connection, p. 224.
- You may also choose from the other modes of assessment listed in the Assessment Options box on the next page.

▲ = Advanced Learners　◆ = Slower Pace Learners　● = Special Learning Needs　■ = Heritage Speakers

CAPÍTULO

5

BLOCK 14 90-MINUTE LESSON PLAN

Practice Options
- *Cuaderno de actividades*, pp. 49–50 ▲ ●
- *Teaching Transparencies:* Fine Art, Chapter 5 ▲ ● ■
- *Lab Book*, pp. 27–28, 60 ▲ ● ■
- *Interactive Tutor* (Disc 1) or *DVD Tutor* (Disc 1) ▲ ● ■
- Online practice, Chapter 5 (go.hrw.com, Keyword: EXP1A CH5) ▲ ● ■

Assessment Options
- *Assessment Program:* **Prueba: Lectura,** pp. 93, 99 ▲ ● ■
- *Assessment Program:* **Prueba: Escritura,** pp. 94, 99 ▲ ● ■
- *Assessment Program:* **Examen: Capítulo 5,** pp. 169–179 ▲ ● ■
- *Assessment Program:* **Examen oral: Capítulo 5,** p. 180 ▲ ● ■
- *Assessment Program:* Alternative Assessment, pp. 216, 222, 229 ▲ ● ■
- Audio CD 5, Tr. 17–18, 19–20 ●
- **Examen final: Capítulos 1–5,** pp. 181–191 ▲ ● ■
- Test Generator ▲ ● ■

▲ = Advanced Learners   ◆ = Slower Pace Learners   ● = Special Learning Needs   ■ = Heritage Speakers

Substitute Teacher Lesson Plans

These lesson plans have been designed with the goal of making class time productive on the days when a substitute teacher conducts class. They provide instructive activities that can be administered by a substitute who does not speak Spanish. Each chapter has several days' worth of suggestions for activities.

Most activities require little preparation. Those activities that do require more preparation are signaled by a clock icon and a box containing the instructions the teacher will need to set up the activity before class starts.

These plans have been organized into three sections: suggestions for the **Geocultura,** suggestions for the Chapter, and suggestions for the **Repaso** and **Integración.** Use the suggestions for the **Geocultura** and suggestions for the Chapter at any point in the chapter. To summarize a chapter or review for a test, use the suggestions for **Repaso** and **Integración**

In the Substitute Teacher Lesson Plans, you will find suggestions for creative and fun activities for each chapter. If you prefer to have a study hall, consider having students practice the grammar and vocabulary presented in the chapter with the following components of our series:

- *Cuaderno de vocabulario y gramática*
- *Cuaderno de actividades*
- *Interactive Tutor* or *DVD Tutor*
- the Web pages at *http://go.hrw.com.* You can find the keyword to enter throughout the pages of each chapter or **Geocultura** of the *Student Edition*.

¡Empecemos!

Geocultura—España
Map Project

🕐 **Preparation:** You will need tracing or unlined paper, pencils, colored pencils and/or felt tip pens.

Have students trace the map of Spain on page R2 of the *Student Edition*, using a pencil. Next, have them label the countries and bodies of water bordering Spain, and color each of the 15 provinces. Finally, have them mark and label the capital city and at least one city in each province.

Chapter 1
Video/Writing Activity

Show students the captioned **VideoNovela**, **Episodio** 1 on Videocassette or DVD. Then have each student write five true or false statements (in English) about the people and/or actions in the video. They should leave space between the statements. Have them exchange their papers with a classmate and mark the statements either T or F. If a statement is false, have them rewrite it in the space provided to make it read true. If time allows, let them check their answers by reading the statements aloud with a different partner.

Craft/Speaking Activity

🕐 **Preparation:** You will need old magazines or catalogs, scissors, unlined paper, tape and/or glue.

Have students create a fictitious friend to introduce to a classmate. They should cut out a picture of a person from a magazine and glue or tape it to a sheet of blank paper. Then have them write information on the page about this person, including: Spanish name, country of origin, birth date, phone number and e-mail address. They should then introduce this friend to a classmate, giving all the information, and the classmate should greet this person in an appropriate manner.

Game

🕐 **Preparation:** You will need index cards, pens or markers.

Give each student four index cards. They should draw a clock face on two of the cards, and then write the corresponding times in Spanish on the other two cards. Divide the students into groups of four. Have one student combine and shuffle all the cards together and lay them out in a grid on the desk, blank side up. Players take turns turning over two cards each. If they match, the player takes them. If they don't, they are returned, face down, to their original place. Play continues until all the cards are paired. The player with the most matches wins.

Repaso/Integración
Review Activity

Have students write e-mails introducing themselves to a Spanish-speaking e-pal. (Refer them to *Student Edition*, page 27 for model.) They should include their name, age, birthday, where they are from, the name of their Spanish teacher, their phone number and e-mail address. (These can be fictitious if they prefer.) Then they should ask at least three questions they would like their e-pal to answer.

A conocernos

Geocultura—Puerto Rico

Research Activity

🕐 **Preparation:** You will need access to the Internet or books about Puerto Rican foods/cooking, magazines with pictures of food, scissors, and glue.

Have students work in pairs to research Puerto Rican foods and recipes on the Internet. They should use "Puerto Rican Foods" as their search words. Have them write the name of the food, a description and/or the recipe on a sheet of paper. Then have them illustrate the information with drawings or cutouts of appropriate ingredients. They can then share the information with the rest of the class.

Chapter 2

Speaking/Writing Activity

Have students review the article **¿De qué color eres?** on page 80 of the *Student Edition*. Then have students write down their favorite color, followed by four adjectives that best describe themselves. Write color names on the board, leaving space under each one. Have student volunteers write adjectives under the color names as each student tells his or her favorite color and the adjectives that best describe him or her. When all students have spoken, tally the adjectives under each color and have students write a summary that tells the four most common adjectives for each favorite color. They can use the article on page 80 as a model for writing the summaries.

Game

🙂 **Preparation:** You will need construction paper or index cards, scissors and pens or markers.

Have students cut the construction paper or index cards into 2-inch squares, and write a word from **Vocabulario**, one letter on each square. Have them shuffle the squares and exchange with a partner. They should try to unscramble the squares to form the correct word. They can continue exchanging squares with partners as they practice a variety of words.

Culture/Writing Activity

Show **VideoCultura** for Chapter 2. Then have students copy the questions from the interview with Andrea on page 61 of the *Student Edition* onto a blank piece of paper, leaving room for answers after each question. Ask each student to write answers to the questions and give information about themselves and their best friend.

Repaso/Integración

Review Activity

🕐 **Preparation:** You will need colored pens or markers and construction paper.

Have students write a poem about themselves, using this format and following the model. They can rewrite the poem on construction paper using colorful markers and add illustrations and/or border decoration, then display the poems on the bulletin board.

Model:

Line 1: First Name	Juanita
Line 2: Two adjectives	Divertida, Bonita
Line 3: Me gusta(n)…	Me gustan los libros.
Line 4: No me gusta(n)…	No me gustan las verduras.
Line 5: Last Name	García

¿Qué te gusta hacer?

SUBSTITUTE TEACHER LESSON PLANS

Geocultura—Texas

Craft Activity

🕐 **Preparation:** You will need blank paper, markers and/or colored pencils.

Have students study the art work by Carmen Lomas García on page 90 of the *Student Edition*. Ask them to think about their own family's activities or traditions. Have them draw and color a traditional scene from their own family, and label the people in the pictures. Then they should write a few sentences to tell what the occasion is and what each person is doing. They may share their pictures with a classmate and talk about the family tradition they drew.

Chapter 3

Vocabulary/Writing Activity

On the board or overhead transparency make a list of ten cities in Spain. Next to each city's name write, in English, one or more of the weather conditions listed on page 118 of the *Student Edition*. Have students write a sentence in Spanish about each city that tells what the weather is like, and what activity they like to do in the weather conditions given.

Video/Writing Activity

Have students make three columns on a sheet of paper, and title the columns WORDS, PHRASES, and MAIN IDEAS. Play the **Variedades** feature on the video program for Chapter 3. Play it once all the way through while students just watch. Play it a second time, this time pausing every 30–35 seconds for students to write notes in their three columns. Play the video a final time all the way through, and encourage students to add to their notes. Then have students work in pairs to compare notes and write a summary of the video content.

Game

🕐 **Preparation:** You will need blank paper, colored markers, pencils or pens, and scissors.

Have students make puzzles to practice vocabulary. They will fold a blank piece of paper four times each way to create a grid of 16 squares. Have them draw a line with a marker around the outer edge of the paper to mark the outer edges of the puzzle. Then have them write a vocabulary word on one side of a fold, with the corresponding English word on the other side of the fold. Tell them to write near, but not on, the folds! Continue until there are words along all the folds, then cut the squares apart on the fold lines. They can then mix up the pieces, trade with another person, and put the puzzle together.

Repaso/Integración

Review Activity

Have students work in pairs to write a story for the four pictures on page 129 of the *Student Edition*. Then have them copy the story neatly onto another sheet of paper, this time inserting a blank line in place of every fifth or sixth word. They can then trade stories with another pair, and try to fill in all the blanks with words that make sense for the story. Have them read the stories aloud if time permits.

La vida escolar

SUBSTITUTE TEACHER LESSON PLANS

Geocultura—Costa Rica
Video/Craft Activity

🕐 **Preparation:** You will need large index cards, felt-tip pens and/or colored pencils.

Show **GeoVisión** video for Chapter 4. Then have students create postcards for the things or places of interest shown in the *Student Edition*, pages 134–137. On the back of the postcards have students write a note to a friend describing the illustration on the front. Include information on things to see and places to visit in Costa Rica.

Chapter 4
Craft/Writing Activity

🕐 **Preparation:** You will need index cards or construction paper, scissors and colored pens or markers in red and blue.

Divide students into groups of three, and have each group cut index cards or paper into 2-inch x 2-inch squares. Each student will use five cards to write the subject pronouns: **yo, tú, él/ella/usted, nosotros, ellos/ellas,ustedes**, and put a red mark on the reverse side. Then each student will write each conjugation of two of the verbs **Gramática** on page 164 of the *Student Edition*, and put a blue mark on the reverse side. Have students shuffle all their cards together and lay them in a grid, color side up on the desk. Students alternate turning over two cards at a time until they find a subject/verb match.

Vocabulary Activity/Game

🕐 **Preparation:** You will need blank or graph paper, pencils and rulers. Have students create word-find puzzles using the vocabulary listed on page 177 of the *Student Edition*. Emphasize neatness and legibility, and make sure students create an answer key for their game. If computers are available, student should create the game on the computer. If there is time and access to a photocopier, copy the games and pass them out for students to complete.

Writing/Drawing Activity

Have students open the *Student Edition* to page 145. On a blank sheet of paper, have each student draw pictures that represent each of their classes, leaving some blank space underneath each picture. They can trace pictures from the book or create their own. Under each picture they should write: the name of the class, at what time it begins, name of the teacher, and supplies needed for the class. Then have students write one or two sentences that tell what they have to/like to/need to do in that class.

Repaso/Integración
Review Activity

Show **Novela en video**, Chapter 4. Also have students refer to pages 168–171 in the *Student Edition*. After the video, have students write six true or false statements about people and actions in the video. Make sure they include a space to write answers and to correct false statements. Have students exchange papers and mark the statements T or F and write a correction for each statement that is false.

En casa con la familia

Geocultura—Chile
Research/Craft Activity

🕐 **Preparation:** You will need large index cards, felt-tip pens and/or colored pencils.

Review with the class the text on pages 180–183 of the *Student Edition*. Next, tell students to imagine that they are on vacation in Chile and would like to send a postcard home to a friend. Have students design a postcard featuring one of the regions of Chile or some aspect of Chilean culture. On the other side of their postcard, have them write home telling about what they've seen and learned on their trip. Students should include in their note at least three facts they learned about Chile.

Chapter 5
Craft/Writing Activity

🕐 **Preparation:** You will need old magazines and catalogs, scissors, tag board, felt-tip pens or colored pencils, and tape or glue.

Have students review the vocabulary on pages 186–187. Students then work individually to create a fictitious family tree of three generations. For each person, they should label the person with his or her role in the family. (**abuelo, padre, hijo**) After the family tree is created, the students write a description of each person in the family and state one thing he or she does. (**El hermano tiene los ojos azules. Él duerme mucho.**)

Video/Writing Activity

Have students open their books to page 214. Show the captioned version of the **Novela en video, Episodio 5** on Videocassette or DVD, having students follow along in their book if desired. Draw a vertical line on the board and write Sofía on one side and Nicolás on the other. Have the class list in the two columns the descriptions Sofía and Nicolás give on the video about their family's expectations

for participating in chores. Then have students work individually to write a short essay to turn in, comparing and contrasting the chores they have to do at home with those of the characters in the **Novela**.

Writing Activity

🕐 **Preparation:** You will need Spanish-English dictionaries, old magazines and catalogs, scissors, unlined paper, and tape or glue.

Have students work with a partner and scan the real estate ads on page 218. Each pair should then find an image from a magazine or catalog for which they will write their own real estate ad, clip it, and attach to a sheet of paper. Below the image students write a description of the home, how many and what kinds of rooms it has, and a feature that makes it unique.

Repaso/Integración
Review Activity

Have students fold a sheet of paper, making two columns. At the top of the first column, have them write "Talking about family," and at the top of the second column, "Where someone lives." Next, have students look through the chapter for expressions that describe family relationships and home descriptions and write them under the appropriate heading. (pages 187 and 201, in particular) Then have students work with a partner to write a conversation using these expressions. They should be prepared to present their conversation to the class the next class period.